Right-Time Experiences

Right-Time Experiences

DRIVING REVENUE WITH MOBILE AND BIG DATA

Maribel Lopez

Library of Congress Cataloging-in-Publication Data:

Lopez, Maribel, 1968-
  Right-time experiences : driving revenue with mobile and big data / Maribel Lopez.
    pages cm
  Includes index.
  ISBN 978-1-118-84735-0 (cloth); 978-1-118-94288-8 (ebk); 978-1-118-94289-5 (ebk)
  1. Information technology–Management. 2. Technological innovations–Management.
  3. Big data–Economic aspects. 4. Strategic planning. I. Title.
  HD30.2.L667 2014
  658.4'038–dc23
                                                                    2014018630

To my dearest Marco.

Contents

Preface

Mobile, cloud computing, and big data are changing the world as we speak. While we've had mobile technology for years, the combination of powerful devices, near-ubiquitous wireless networks, and widespread enthusiastic consumer adoption of mobile has changed the way we live, play, and work. Consumers now hold access to information, games, and services in the palm of their hand. Businesses have the opportunity to offer workflows and business processes to employees wherever they are and on the go. As a result, visionary managers are creating contextual services, in which products, services, and communications adapt to the user (consumers, prospects, and employees) and the situation on the fly, via technology. I show in the pages ahead exactly what this means and how it works.

The move to contextual services—being in the right place at the right time with the right experience—requires more than mobile. It requires breaking down information silos to modify business processes and coordinating IT and business strategies that employ mobile, cloud computing, big data, and the analytics necessary to turn data into information. With these four technologies, businesses are able to do things now that were either immensely difficult or exorbitantly expensive in the past, if they could be done at all.

In this brave new world, the most effective, successful companies will collect and integrate data points, such as location and previous transactions, to generate insights into the needs of employees, prospects, and customers. This integration will lead to better products, services, and business processes. A few organizations today are using some or all of these technologies to deliver economic value and competitive advantage.

Instead of calling these contextual services, real-time services, or personalized services, I believe they are *right-time experiences* (RTEs) because they occur at the time customers, employees, or partners need them most. While people may not know what a right-time experience is exactly (or how to have it), they understand the value of having the right information or experience at the proper moment. In some cases, RTEs may anticipate a need or desire before it materializes. RTEs don't have to be in real time—for example, an HVAC can alert a business when it's time to order new air filters—but these experiences are the most compelling.

While the concept of contextual services is not new, we are now on the brink of having all of the technology necessary to make an experience's context—its time, place, frequency, and more—available in our applications and services. Executives legitimately worry about issues of privacy and transparency, cost, and control—while more far-sighted competitors take away their business. What most firms are missing is a strategy to turn context into something that improves profits, increases stakeholder engagement, and minimizes user dissatisfaction. Technology is the foundation for enabling the best experience possible.

Right-time experiences are for senior executives, marketers, and IT leaders at established companies. The concept is designed to help leaders of established businesses understand and plan for the massive market transitions that are in the offing. It will also help entrepreneurs, because in many cases they have the ability to build right-time experiences from the beginning and can more easily adjust business models as circumstances change.

This book has three parts. Part I lays out the opportunities and problems, describing technology, market models, and shifts that are right now demanding business leaders to create new strategies or risk extinction.

Part II discusses a new way to think about designing business processes, building products, and creating compelling right-time experiences. It also provides practical, real-world examples of how businesses are building strategies to deal with these changes and deliver RTEs.

Part III provides a framework for an effective action plan for implementing RTEs. Every organization will be different, but the framework's basic elements span different-size companies and various industries. Part III basically answers the question, How do you get started? As a business, you need to figure out a technology, people, and processes strategy. What are the business processes that you might need to change? How do you create these right-time experiences?

This book will illustrate the challenges you'll face and provide guidelines for overcoming these obstacles. At a high level, it will highlight what technologies will be important for your business. It will describe the process changes you need to think about. Once you understand this, you may want to know more about the detailed technical aspects of big data, analytics, and cloud computing. For these technical implementation details, you'll go to another book. This book will provide an understanding of the landscape and what your business needs to plan for.

By the end of the book, leaders will be better prepared to capitalize on the changes in mobile, big data, and cloud computing. Just as important, this book will inspire organizations to provide right-time experiences to customers, prospects, and employees. The results—as I demonstrate in the pages ahead—can be improved margins, higher profits, and enhanced engagement with key stakeholders.

Part I: Adapt or Fail

Mobile, big data, and cloud computing are disrupting traditional business models and giving start-ups and tech-savvy organizations opportunities to give consumers and employees right-time experiences.

Chapter 1: The Future Is Here

Today, technology enables changes in behavior and business processes that were never possible in the past. This confluence of technology and new possibilities is disrupting existing business models. Start-ups across a wide range of industries have challenged established business practices and created new market dynamics. This chapter describes just a few of the possibilities to offer right-time experiences and shows how these benefit the organization and damage the competition.

Chapter 2: Marching Backwards into the Future

Industry leaders recognize that many of today's products and services do not meet current customer expectations, but they don't know what to do about it. In many cases, a substantial change is required, which is always difficult, and rapid change with an unknown outcome is even harder. New market models, however, offer opportunities and threats for established businesses. This chapter discusses the reasons senior executives give for not taking action and how this indecision will impact their companies. It also provides several recommendations for overcoming roadblocks.

Part II: Why Right-Time Experiences Are Key

Chapter 3: New Realities Demand Right-Time Experiences

If existing business practices are about to be outdated, what does a company need to be successful? Businesses need to leverage these new market forces to create RTEs. Mobile, social, sensor, and transaction data provide multiple information sources. Organizations will use new storage and analytics to turn context into actionable insight. New insights from ever-increasing data sources enable businesses to transform generic, rigid products and processes into adaptive and satisfying RTEs. While the number of RTEs possible are limited only by imagination, companies should create at least three that improve the experience: care, commerce, and communications.

Chapter 4: Communications in a Right-Time Experience

Using context such as presence, social network status, and location, a business can transform when, how, and what it communicates to its employees and customers. In the future, software such as augmented reality browsers will be used to overlay digital data on the physical view of an object from a device's camera. For consumers, businesses will link location, product information, and employee availability to build concierge apps that customize services based on a customer's immediate needs. Communications is an integral part of every right-time experience, but in many cases, it is the entirety of a right-time experience.

Chapter 5: Care in a Right-Time Experience

Companies will reshape their business models, increase collaboration, and improve customer relationships with right-time experiences. Enterprises that excel at customer experience understand aspects of customer care exist in every part of a transaction, from presales through postsale service. Technology now enables organizations to deliver service that wasn't possible in the past. If a business is listening, it can learn about problems and potential product opportunities on social media faster than it would through existing customer care channels. In addition, mobile provides a channel for companies to create one-to-one relationships and tap into contextual data from mobile devices. This chapter also discusses how care can be also applied to a company's employees.

Chapter 6: Commerce in a Right-Time Experience

Today, consumers are using smartphones in the store to check pricing, inventory availability, and product reviews. Retailers have to contend with "showrooming"—the phenomenon of a customer viewing merchandise and checking prices in a physical store only to then purchase online or from another retailer. While showrooming has created challenges, mobile also provides an opportunity to reach consumers wherever they are—and frequently at the point of decision. The challenge is to build an information technology and customer-facing strategy that capitalizes upon mobile attributes such as location, activity, and image capture. Additionally, businesses are using mobile and big data to improve business-to-business (B2B) commerce with data capture, analytics, and service at the point of need.

Part III: How to Prepare for Change

Part I set the context of the tectonic shift we are experiencing in technology, society, and business models. Part II demonstrated the value of right-time experiences. Part III describes what organization managers can do to capitalize on this brave new world.

Chapter 7: Evolve to Right-Time Experiences in Three Phases

Business leaders must keep their organizational strategies updated in the face of continually evolving technologies, ensure that their organizations continue to look ahead, and use technologies to improve internal performance. These include extending business processes, improving processes, and transforming the business with new processes. In the first phase, companies will seek efficiencies by moving to cloud computing, shifting business applications to mobile devices, and delivering new collaboration tools. In the second phase, companies push beyond efficiencies and seek ways to improve a business process through mobile enablement and introducing big data and analytics. The third phase transforms the business when a company uses connected devices to deliver new workflows and products it could not create in the past.

Chapter 7 also discusses the need to build a new strategic plan for businesses that combines changes to how we build our processes and technology as well as how we manage our people. The following three chapters will discuss the game plan for each of these in more detail.

Chapter 8: Understanding the Components of the Technical Plan: Mobility

The technical plan has three separate areas: a mobile-enablement strategy, big data, and analytics. As more employees bring their own devices into the workplace, CIOs need a mobile-enablement strategy to distribute, manage, and secure information—a strategy to reduce costs, minimize risk, and provide a path for technological change. Right-time experiences require a business to collect and store more data than it has in the past. Fortunately, big data tools allow IT and business leaders to test numerous hypotheses rapidly. This chapter discusses the tools and options available to executives for mobile enablement.

Chapter 9: Understanding the Components of the Technical Plan: Big Data

This chapter continues on the theme of understanding the technical plan but is specifically related to big data. It defines big data and its challenges. It also provides suggestions for overcoming the challenges of a fragmented and evolving technology landscape as well as a skills shortage of data scientists.

Chapter 10: Engage and Empower Employees

Organizations that find and keep top talent are able to gain competitive advantage, improve customer satisfaction, and dramatically impact the bottom line. This chapter describes how businesses may need to build new roles or groups to deal with technology change. It discusses changes in recruiting and building a training plan to maximize your existing talent. Gamification (a clunky word for an important concept) improves consumer and employee engagement. It drives certain desired behaviors by tapping into an individual's desire for status, achievement, competition, and self-expression. This chapter describes gamification and provides examples to show how the idea can help an organization achieve its goals.

Chapter 11: Closing Thoughts

This final, brief chapter sums up the ideas of right-time experiences. It encourages readers to take advantage of the possibilities that we've only just begun to explore.

Acknowledgments

First and foremost, I'd like to thank my husband, Mark, for his support over the past year and encouragement during the process. A special thanks to Wally Wood, whose support helped me understand that a business book should have more prose and feel less like a boring market research report. To my friends and family, who listened to me whine over the past year. You know who you are, but a sincere thankyou to Amisha Gandi, Nicole Hall, Jo Ann McManamy, and Ricarda Rodatus. To my dear industry friends—Neil Cohen, David Gutleius, Brian Katz, Ray Potter, Benjamin Robbins, Evan Quinn, and Joe Weinman. These people lent their technical knowledge to the task through interviews and reviews. Finally, I'd like to thank all of the companies and interviewees mentioned in the book who've made great strides in building what I call right-time experiences.

PART

I

ADAPT OR FAIL

Do you remember your first mobile phone? I thought you would. I purchased mine in 1993 when I worked for Motorola. Buying my first mobile phone was as liberating as learning to drive. Mobility had changed my world, and I knew it would change the world in general. I just had no idea that it would take the next two decades to hit mainstream adoption.

We've experienced massive changes in the telecommunications industry. We've seen the rise of the Internet, the e-commerce evolution, and the emergence of nearly ubiquitous broadband wired and wireless networks. I experienced firsthand the impact Nokia's first smartphones had on Motorola's business and how business executives were drawn to the power of communicating with RIM's BlackBerry devices. By the mid-2000s, I was convinced mobility would be the next big thing, and I founded Lopez Research in 2008 to help companies understand the impact mobile technologies would have on their business.

After all my years of writing about the mobile revolution, it was finally here. By 2013, consumers around the globe were using smartphones and other connected devices like digital fitness bands. Employees had begun to bring their personal devices into the workplace, and CIOs around the globe were wrestling with strategies to support this trend while keeping corporate data secure. My clients began to ask questions about building mobile applications and mobile-enabling business processes.

There were still debates over how many mobile operating systems a business should support, but most companies agreed it would be more than one. I realized we had hit the beginning of the mobile maturity curve. It was thrilling and terrifying. Everyone has recognized the importance of mobility and wants to learn more about it. As a business owner, I began to wonder what my business, or any business, would look like in the next five years. I believed the future of mobility was about more than devices and networks. It was also about more than extending existing PC-based business processes to mobile devices.

In 2011, I wrote and presented on what I called contextual communications. I wasn't the only person discussing contextual services, but I found the term didn't resonate with the market at the time. It was difficult to explain contextual services when most people were still using basic mobile phones with limited web browsing. There wasn't a 30-second elevator pitch to describe context-based services. I attempted to define them as personalized and targeted experiences based on knowledge of your previous transactions and current context. Many people equated this with targeted advertising. After years of irrelevant communications and failed promises, people didn't believe compelling and customized business-to-employee (B2E) and business-to-consumer (B2C) communications were possible.

Once mobile becomes an embedded part of a company's technology fabric, how does the future of business products and services change? Will mobile be as transformative as the Internet? What's the future of mobile? This was the shift I set out to understand in 2012. I'm not a futurist, but understanding this transition was critical for my business. We are in the midst of a technology and market transition that is similar to others we've experienced in the recent past but different in subtle ways. Businesses have seen rapid technology change in the past few decades. However, today's environment differs in the pace of change, the economic impact of these changes, and the number of areas that are changing simultaneously. The move to mobile will provide as great of a change as the move from mainframes to PCs.

What I rapidly discovered is the future of mobile isn't about devices and networks. While these items are important, mobility is just the beginning of what a business needs to consider. Mobile's future is in creating contextual services, which are products, services, and communications that adapt to the user and the situation in near-real time. The move to contextual services requires more than just mobile technology. It requires harvesting and combining the benefits of several technology trends simultaneously. It requires breaking down information silos to change a company's existing business processes. It requires building coordinated IT and business strategies that leverage mobile, cloud computing, big data, and analytics.

Leading companies will collect and integrate contextual data points, such as location and previous transactions, to generate new insights into the needs and desires of employees, prospects, and customers. This insight will help businesses create better products, services, and business processes. Businesses are using some or all of these technologies today, but few have combined them in a way that delivers substantial economic value and competitive advantage.

Ultimately, instead of calling these contextual, real-time, or personalized services, I choose to call them right-time experiences (RTEs). While a person might not know what a right-time experience is specifically, he intuitively understands the value of having the right information or experience at the proper moment. Right-time experiences deliver value at the point of need or desire to a company's employees, customers, and partners. In some cases, these experiences may even anticipate a need or desire before it materializes. Right-time experiences don't have to be real time, but those are frequently the most compelling experiences for the recipient.

While the concept of contextual services has been dabbled in before, we are now on the brink of having all of the basic technology to make the contextual information available in our applications and services. What most businesses are missing is a strategy to turn that context into something that improves profits, increases engagement, and minimizes customer dissatisfaction. Right-time experiences aren't about technology. However, technology is the foundation for enabling the best experience possible.

This book is for business and senior IT leaders at established companies. While start-ups may gain insights for future products and services, this book is designed to help leaders of established businesses understand and plan for massive market transitions. In many cases, start-ups are already building right-time experiences and can more easily adjust business models in the face of change.

This book is broken into three parts. The first part discusses technology, market models, and societal shifts that will require business leaders to create new strategies or risk extinction. Part II discusses a new way to think about designing business processes, building products, and creating compelling experiences. It will also provide practical, real-world examples of how businesses are building strategies to deal with these changes. Part III discusses what you'll need to know about the technical components of delivering a right-time experience—particularly mobile and big data.

Each organization will be different, but the basic elements for the framework should span different company sizes and various industries. At the end of the book, I hope you'll feel better prepared for the coming changes and inspired to participate in the new contextual right-time experience economy.

CHAPTER 1

The Future Is Here

Films frequently combine imagination, inspiration, and aspiration. Many films depict life as we wish it to be. The cinema can portray new worlds and new possibilities. Over the years, science fiction has portrayed a world with self-driving cars, robots that clean your house, and smartwatches that can be used as communications devices. In the 2002 science fiction movie *Minority Report*, a person could walk into a store and be recognized. There were multitouch interfaces for screens, retina scanning, personalized advertising, and electronic readers. There were smart homes that could sense when you walked into the room and adjust the lights and music to suit your mood. Crime prevention was also automated with computers.

Fast-forward to the present. Today, you can see the prototypes of self-driving cars on the roads in many cities around the world. At the 2014 Consumer Electronics show, BMW revealed a modified version of the M235i Coupe that can brake, steer, and accelerate without driver intervention. The iRobot Roomba vacuums your floor, and the company offers a higher-end autonomous robot that can be controlled by a person and used to deliver aspects of healthcare in hospitals and remote inspections in manufacturing plants.

Qualcomm, Samsung, and others announced smartwatches that act as minicomputers and extensions of your phone by receiving text messages, placing phone calls, and sending calendar reminders. Meanwhile, tablets and electronic readers are offering a second wave of change in the publishing industry that includes interactive content and social interaction with content, such as through sharing and commenting.

While public safety departments aren't quite predicting who will commit a crime before it happens, they are using video, mobile, and analytics to fight crime and keep people safe. In the world of film, we have seen gadgets that know who you are, sense things about you, and offer services or guidance based on this knowledge. These imagined services would talk to us and be an extension of who we are. Today, we live in that world. What we once considered fiction is now reality.

With sensors in smartphones and throughout a physical location, a retailer can know if you've entered a store. If you've downloaded their mobile app, they'll know who you are and if you're a frequent shopper. Ads can be personalized based on context, such as where you are standing, what you've bought in the past, and the time of day or the weather.

We have clothing and wristbands that can sense how hard our workout has been. We can swallow sensors to help us track our vital statistics. For example, the Proteus "smart pill" system consists of a pinhead-sized sensor embedded in a pill and a battery-powered patch that monitors various health indicators, such as sleep, activity, respiration, and heart rate. MC10 offers what it calls a Biostamp. This is a patch that looks like a Band-Aid but is actually a stretchable sensing device that measures a variety of physiological functions, providing data on the brain, muscles, heart, body temperature, and even hydration levels. Reebok is using it in sports helmets for athletes. Google, picking up on work Microsoft started several years ago, announced the company is working on a contact lens that could track blood glucose. Imagine the life-changing impact these technologies can provide for diabetics, athletes, and the populace at large.

The smart home from *Minority Report* is here, and the smartphone is its controller. You can open your front door, turn on your lights, and control your thermostat all with the tap of a finger.

Over the holidays, I sat with a friend who was wearing Google Glass. He could speak to his glasses and they would record his kid playing or anything else he could see. He could use them to read his email without touching a keyboard. He was wearing a voice-activated computer, just as we'd seen in the *Star Trek* TV series. While we haven't cracked space travel yet, Richard Branson, CEO of Virgin, and Elon Musk, CEO of Tesla Motors, are both working on it.

The future is here, and the convergence of four major technology trends—mobile, cloud computing, social, and big data—is making what we loved in the movies a reality (see Figure 1.1). The

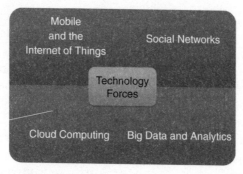

Figure 1.1   Four Trends Changing the World
Source: Lopez Research.

combination of these technologies has irreversibly changed both societal behaviors and market models.

In this chapter, I discuss how these four technologies continue to transform how we live, work, and play.

We Are Living in a Connected World

Mobile and the so-called Internet of Things (IoT) are creating a new connected and sensory world. It's been over four decades since Motorola employee Martin Cooper, "the father of the cell phone," placed the first mobile telephone call. It was a call that changed the world. But for many years, mobile devices were expensive and clunky and placed only telephone calls. The first mobile phones weighed two and a half pounds (1.15 kg), were 10 inches long, and could be used for just 20 minutes before the battery died. The first commercial portable cell phone cost $4,000 in 1984.[1] It was hardly affordable, and mobile adoption was slow.

Today, mobile phones are a completely different product. Yes, you can still place a call with one, but this is where the similarities begin and end. Mobile devices are sleek. They fit in your pocket and on your wrist. They are powerful computing tools. In 2012, a smartphone had more computing power than the first space shuttle that landed on the moon. Today they are also relatively cheap, with smartphones ranging from $150 to $700.

The International Telecommunications Union reported there would be over 6.8 billion mobile subscriptions by the end of 2013.[2] While a person may have two or more mobile subscriptions, this still means over 50 percent of the world's population has a mobile phone.

According to the source you check, there were more than 1.9 billion smartphones in use at the end of 2013, and that number could grow to more than 5.6 billion by 2019.

Imagine: Almost 80 percent of the population could be using a smartphone by 2019. For the first time in history, we can see a path by which computing becomes accessible to the masses. In September 2013, there were 143.2 million Internet users in India, of which roughly 16 percent (23.8 million) were mobile-only data users.[3] Globally, many individuals may use a mobile device as their primary Internet access method going forward. Consumers are obviously using these phones for much more than making a phone call. They are embracing new options and participating in new experiences. Today's smartphones act as your navigation system, your gaming console, your personal concierge, and your camera.

In 2014, many individuals are carrying more than one connected device, as mobile options have expanded to include tablets, e-readers, and fitness devices. Smartphone and tablet sales had passed traditional desktop and personal computer sales by the end of 2010. The pace of mobile device adoption also continues to accelerate. It took notebook computers over a decade to reach 50 million units in annual sales. It took only three years for tablets to reach the same unit sales volume.

The combination of powerful devices, near-ubiquitous wireless networks, and widespread consumer adoption has changed how organizations are able to connect and communicate information. However, many companies have yet to take maximum advantage of the possibilities mobility affords. The big transformation is in what we connect, how we connect, and how we engage and transact once connected.

A Computer in Every Pocket

In the 1990s, Bill Gates from Microsoft said, the company was founded with a vision of "a computer on every desk, and in every home."[4] PCs were the third wave of computing, after mainframes and minicomputers. Their rise brought computing to a person's desk and made it individual. In the 2000s, the laptop made computing smaller, lighter, and more portable. But for the most part, users weren't stuffing a laptop into a pocket or a purse. Limited connectivity and unwieldy size meant that computing couldn't be done everywhere. Today, we are living in a world where computing and wireless connectivity surround us. They're everywhere we go, and we carry them with us. Wireless connectivity, increasingly small computing chips, and sensors have moved computing beyond the domain of the PC.

Internet portability was one of the first changes that mobile computing provided. People could take their laptop with them anywhere, but if there wasn't a Wi-Fi signal or an Ethernet connection, they probably weren't linked to the Internet or the office. Today, mobile devices have multiple types of connectivity, which means they can be used almost anywhere. You can call or email someone from a ski slope in Switzerland or in a subway station in Boston. Within 10 years, there'll be a computer in almost every pocket.

Smartphones: The Twenty-First-Century Swiss Army Knife

Computing capabilities have also changed. For the most part, PCs didn't have touch screens, voice recognition, and GPS location. A laptop may have had a camera, but few users were doing much with it. Desktop videoconferencing wasn't widespread, and no one thought a laptop's camera would replace a handheld video camera. Today's smartphones and tablets contain still and video cameras. Over time, PCs grew to be multifunction machines that allowed you to work, shop, and play. But in general, PCs did not replace special-purpose devices such as your camera, your gaming console, and your GPS.

Now people use smartphone and tablet cameras to capture life's fleeting moments, such as a baby's first steps, the final touchdown of a football game, or a favorite song at a rock concert. The move to digital photography destroyed Kodak, Polaroid, and countless others who couldn't adapt quickly enough. Smartphones and tablets are eliminating the need for point-and-shoot cameras. According to Christopher Chute, IDC's research director of worldwide digital imaging, the rate of decline in digital camera sales, which began in early 2013, is accelerating. By October 2013, Canon's camera sales were down 23 percent, Nikon's were down about 18 percent, and Sony and Fujifilm were down about 35 percent each.[5] Video calls and video chats are now commonplace. There's a famous set of images that presenters use to highlight the change in behavior within five years. In 2007, a photograph shows people taking pictures at the Vatican with cameras. In 2012, a similar photograph shows a majority of the people capturing photographs and video with smartphones and tablet.

Today's smartphones are filled with sensors. The average smartphone has over 16 sensors that can track motion, orientation, humidity, and much more. For example, magnometers and accelerometers in mobile devices allow a smartphone to act as a compass and to play elaborate driving games that require motion sensing to control a car racing on a track. If your phone can double as your gaming console, is it even necessary to purchase portable gaming devices such as Nintendo DS and Sony PSP?

Perhaps even more useful are the location sensors and mapping applications that help a person find the address of the nearest café or the current position of the next bus. The rise of smartphones as the new personal navigation device has taken a toll on companies such as Garmin and TomTom. Makers of personal navigation devices now must find new revenue sources by selling software and services or face extinction.

A smartphone is not just a phone. It's a camera, a navigation system, a gaming console, a media player, a web browsing device, and even a flashlight. It can be the remote control for your lights, your garage, and your television. It's completely upended the consumer electronics industry—and this is just the beginning.

Smartphones and tablets have clearly changed how people connect with each other and with services. But the connected devices wave is just gaining momentum. Estimates from Cisco claim there will be over 50 billion connected devices by 2020.[6] These connected devices are what is frequently called the Internet of Things.

Talking Devices Make Businesses and Consumers Smarter

Wireless connectivity and sensors are changing the types of devices that are connected and the types of information they provide and are helping businesses automate tasks. Whereas the Internet was defined as a computer network providing email and information from computers to the general public, the Internet of Things is a network of devices that expands beyond computers. These physical objects have sensors and connectivity that allow them to communicate with computers, people, and other similar devices. IoT devices could be stationary equipment, such as an HVAC system, with fixed or wireless connections, or mobile with wireless connectivity, such as a car or a Polar heart rate monitor. These physical objects can also be connected sensors on living objects such as farm animals, plants, and even people.

A device that in the past either told you nothing—or very little—about its status will now tell you more and more. Simple example: For years, your car's fuel-gauge needle told you when you needed gas. Today, cars can tell you that the tire pressure is off or even be used to automatically park your car. Sensors have been built into vehicles for years, but automakers are increasingly making this data accessible to vehicle owners, service centers, and potentially other interested parties.

This became obvious in the case of a *New York Times* article about a Tesla Motors test drive. When Tesla Motors claimed the article didn't reflect the conditions of the test drive, it had the data to prove it. It turns out that sensors in the car can track everything from speed to how long you charged the vehicle. Your car is part of the Internet when it's connected to your smartphone, to the dealer, and to the manufacturer.

The Internet of Things, of course, involves much more than consumers and their devices. It can involve anything with a sensor and wireless or wired connectivity for communication. It can connect and share information from equipment with a company's operational systems, providing new insight and new opportunities to improve operations. Have you ever considered what might happen if wind turbines could talk to each other and to the utility company?

First Wind, a Boston-based operator of 16 wind farms in the United States, has been adding more sensors, controls, and optimization software to its wind turbines. The new sensors measure temperature, wind speeds, location, and blade pitch. In very high winds, for example, First Wind has had to routinely shut down an entire farm by changing the blade pitch to prevent turbine damage from the blades rotating too fast. The new sensors mean that First Wind is able to shut down only the affected portion of the turbines rather than an entire farm. In the winter, the sensors can detect when the blades are icing up and speed up or change pitch to knock off the ice.

The new sensors collect three to five times as much data as the sensors on turbines of just a few years ago, says Paul Gaynor, chief executive of First Wind. This is an example of the fourth trend I discuss later in this chapter, the rise of new information and the tools to process big data.

First Wind uses General Electric software to collect and analyze wind turbine data. The utility uses this new insight to refine the operation of each turbine for the greatest efficiency. According to the company, upgrades on 123 turbines on two wind farms have delivered a 3 percent increase in energy output, or about 120 megawatt hours per turbine in the first year. This translates to $1.2 million in additional revenue a year from those two farms, said Gaynor. "It's not earthshaking, but it is meaningful. These are real commercial investments for us that make economic sense now."[7]

In the past, machine diagnostic measurements were fairly crude. You could have, for example, a piece of equipment that runs optimally at a temperature of 75 degrees. Meters would alert the operator when the temperature fell below 50 degrees or rose above 100 degrees. But what happened if the machine began to run at 85 degrees? No warning bells would go off. You'd only know there was a problem when the equipment broke down after running hot for three weeks. Today, the sensors and software within the device will tell you the equipment is running at 85 degrees and as a result will probably fail in three weeks. This is what's known as using IoT data to make more informed decisions. The device—an electric turbine, an aircraft engine, a locomotive, a farm combine, a manufacturing robot—communicates its health at a point in time and gives the organization an opportunity to perform preventive maintenance and extend the equipment's health.

This is just one example of the power of the Internet of Things. It allows us to understand what is going on with the equipment around us, to control it, to maintain it, and to save money as a result.

These devices are not computers per se (although they may share computer-like characteristics), but they provide data to our software information systems that was difficult or even impossible to obtain in the past. The shifts in the availability and cost of sensors and wireless connectivity chips have also made it less expensive to collect this data than it was in the past. The business software, which may be on several linked machines, can turn the data into information a human being can use to make an informed decision. It can provide alerts such as "Inspect the turbine's bushings, which are running hot," "Check the left rear tire," or "It costs twice as much to run the electric dryer in the middle of the afternoon."

Effectively, mobile devices and connected sensors will forever change the number of devices we connect and the data we can gather from these devices. Mobile and the IoT haven't just changed the device landscape. They are also changing the software landscape.

Is There an App for That?

Mobile and cloud computing technologies, which I'll describe in a moment, have created chaos and opportunity in both the consumer and enterprise software market. When Apple introduced the iPhone in 2007, no one expected the radical impact it would have on the software industry. Many applications, websites, and services that we use today were designed for PCs, not mobile devices such as smartphones and tablets. However, this is changing rapidly.

By October 2013, Apple announced that over a million applications had been designed for Apple's iOS within the past five years.[8] Several months later, Google's Android operating system had reached over 1 million apps.[9] In fact, mobile applications are a real industry, one in which developers can make good money. In 2013 alone, consumers spent $10 billion in Apple's app store.[10] Many of these applications were designed as simple consumer applications, but even that is changing. The opportunity for mobile applications within the business environment is a huge and largely untapped market for the software industry.

By 2013, employees were bringing their personal devices into the workplace. Over the past several years, the IT divisions of companies around the world have responded to this demand by creating a bring-your-own-device (BYOD) program. In a world where almost everyone is connected, employees expect real-time, on-demand access to business applications, regardless of who owns the device being used.

Over two-thirds of the companies Lopez Research surveyed at the end of 2013 were allowing employees to use their personal devices—largely smartphones and tablets—to access corporate data and applications. While a majority of the companies were offering only email and calendar access, it's clear this is the beginning of a larger trend. As in the consumer landscape, this trend is forcing companies to reimagine how the business should deliver applications and services.

Cloud Computing Enables New Entrants and Business Models

While mobile devices impacted the masses, the arrival of cloud computing and virtualization created shifts in business IT, the applications market, and prevailing market models. Step back in time for a moment. Not too long ago, companies built data centers and IT bought servers and storage for these data centers. The systems that ran this hardware were inefficient. Most of the processing within these data centers was normally utilized at roughly 30 to 40 percent of capacity.

Then, VMware and others built what was called the virtualization market. This technology helped companies get better performance out of underutilized hardware like servers and storage. In some cases, it increased the hardware's utilization to up to 80 or 90 percent, a huge improvement. With virtualization, the IT department could purchase less hardware or even forgo building data centers to support increases in computing demands.

Service providers such as Amazon and Rackspace kicked off a second wave of virtualization and a new generation of cloud-based computing services. Rather than spending millions on data center technology, enterprises and start-ups could buy computing power on demand and scale it as needed. Cloud computing services allowed an organization to buy capacity by the minute, by the hour, and by the day. Businesses could purchase just what they needed, exactly when they needed it.

The availability of cloud services meant companies didn't have to buy computing resources to meet peak demand. Cloud computing allowed established companies to use resources more wisely and respond to market changes. A company that owns its data centers may need more capacity at certain times of the year; with cloud computing, it can easily scale its IT services to meet fluctuations in demand. For example, a retailer knows it will have a high transaction volume at Christmas and needs more computing power during this time. Should the company build a data center large enough to support demand during the two months a year it needs the resource? Or should it build for the 10-month average and use the cloud provider for the peak-time demand? This gave companies an option that didn't exist before. In some cases, government regulations or security concerns stalled adoption back when cloud computing was an evolving set of technologies and services. Today many of these concerns have been alleviated as cloud providers have improved the technology, business processes, and product options for securing and managing data.

Today, there are different types of clouds and usage models for them that address different business requirements. Of course, the more you want a model to look like your existing infrastructure, the more it has the economics of your existing infrastructure as well. One organization may not care, for example, where its expense data resides as long as the company selling the service has built in strong security to protect it.

In his book, *Cloudonomics: The Business Value of Cloud Computing,* Joe Weinman addresses a variety of cloud scenarios, together with the economics behind them.[11] For example, a company might keep its core applications in its own data but use the cloud to distribute content closer to the end users, thus making the user experience richer and more interactive. Another company might use the cloud for business continuity and disaster recovery. In the same way that you might stay in a hotel if your house burned down, a company can recover applications in the cloud if its data center is damaged.

There are also more complex scenarios. For example, Sony normally servers all visitors to its online music store out of its own data center. However, during demand peaks, such as upon the death of a celebrity, information seekers are served out of the cloud, whereas actual purchases are still completed within Sony's data center. Weinman says that cloud computing is clearly having a huge impact on both consumers and enterprises. While few large companies have gone "all in" and committed to migrate all of their data to the cloud, as Netflix has, cloud computing will be a significant component of virtually all industries due to benefits such as reduced cost and risk, increased revenues, and business agility. Weinman also notes that cloud computing can provide enhanced computing performance and user experiences.

Cloud Computing Lowers Market Barriers

In the past, most start-ups needed millions of dollars to get started. They had to purchase and install expensive computing infrastructure just to start the business. Today, they can use cloud computing to launch with minimal capital investment while having a platform that can scale to accommodate millions of users on day one. These on-demand and highly scalable services also allow existing businesses of all sizes to have a more flexible and agile computing infrastructure that shifts to meet changes in demand. Cloud computing dramatically reduced the capital investment barrier.

With lower capital requirements, the number of start-ups has grown exponentially as cloud computing has made massive amounts of computing power available to anyone with a credit card. It's also changed the strategies for venture funding. Instead of placing big bets on one or two start-ups, a venture capitalist can fund dozens of companies for the same amount it would've taken to fund one hardware-oriented company in the early days of the Internet.

Technology and societal changes have also enabled consumers and wealthier "angel" investors to find and fund start-ups. Social networks, which I'll discuss in more detail shortly, have changed societal behaviors. People are using these networks to connect with people they know as well as share interests and find new products and services. Websites such as Kickstarter and Crowdfunder provide a destination for people to learn about and donate money to fund new projects. In 2013, 3 million people from 214 countries pledged $480 million to Kickstarter projects.[12] This works out to over $1.3 million in funding per day. Without these sites, many of these companies wouldn't have been funded since they didn't fit the traditional funding model for banks and venture capitalists. Hence, cloud computing and social networking have enabled an influx of start-ups and have created a very Darwinian environment.

New Pricing, Marketing, and Distribution Models Emerge

I have discussed how cloud computing changed the pricing and deployment models for hardware, but it also created tremendous shifts in the software landscape. Today a wide range of cloud applications and services are available. Many of these solutions are referred to as *software as a service* (SaaS). SaaS is a software delivery model in which an application and its associated data are hosted in the cloud. Other types of services could be cloud-based storage, which is what Box.com, Dropbox, and others offer. Social networks such as Facebook, Pinterest, and Twitter also use cloud computing to host and deliver their services. As you can see, cloud computing has opened up a new world of innovation.

The distribution of services and software happens in the cloud, which means anyone with Internet access can find and use a company's products and services. A vendor doesn't need physical stores or even channel partners. With low infrastructure and distribution costs, these start-ups could try new distribution and pricing models to win market acceptance. Some companies offer free applications and services but charge for premium features.

For example, a person can sign up for 2G of storage for free on Dropbox.com but would be charged for more storage. Zoho.com offers free customer relationship management (CRM) for up to three users, but if you want email integration, you'll need to purchase a premium service. Other businesses charge monthly or annual fees for a service. It's a radical change in the software industry that has eliminated many market-entry barriers. It also means a company can potentially deliver services globally, assuming there are minimal language and regulatory constraints.

Payment-processing companies like Square are disrupting the credit card processing market by making it easier and cheaper to collect payments. Now anyone with smartphone or tablet can collect payment using Square, a one-inch-square credit card reader that plugs into iPhones, iPads, and most Android devices. Businesses download the free Square Register application to link the reader to their bank accounts. Once a customer has used a credit card with Square, the merchant can enter the customer's phone number or email address and send a receipt for the purchase. The device is free, and retailers can pay either per swipe (2.75 percent for Visa, MasterCard, American Express, and Discover, the cards it reads) or $275 per month.

"A standard POS and credit card system would have set me back about $5,000–$10,000," says Adam Schneider, owner of Little Muenster, an artisanal grilled cheese shop in New York City. "But, like a lot of people, I already had an iPad." Schneider downloaded Square Register, bought a receipt printer, and was in business for a few hundred dollars. He says a major selling point was Square's portability and the swipe fee.[13]

In the beginning, most of the financial institutions thought Square wouldn't work. But it did work, and it worked in a big way. In 2012, Square received an investment from Starbucks and a majority of the Starbucks locations began using it as a method of accepting and clearing credit card payments. Square built a business by simply making an existing service easier to use, with better service. Businesses can understand the fees and the fees were frequently cheaper. It replaced expensive POS terminals and telecom lines with smartphones and tablets.

Competition from the established financial market players and other start-ups quickly ensued. Square continues to focus on finding inefficiencies in other parts of the financial market and providing better right-time experience solutions related to care and commerce. For example, most small merchants have difficulty creating websites that can accept payments. Square offers Square Market to solve this problem. It also offers a person-to-person payments market, competing with services like PayPal. Payment processing was a market that was ripe for disruption. In each case described, the real innovation delivered is simplicity and value, not necessarily the lowest prices.

SaaS Shakes Up the Business Applications Market

SaaS is an increasingly common delivery model for many consumer applications. Consumers have embraced a wide range of cloud-delivered solutions, from music services such as Pandora to storage services such as Box.com. But SaaS and cloud-resident services aren't only a consumer phenomenon. Salesforce.com, whose revenue exceeded $2 billion in 2013, is the poster child for building rich cloud-resident enterprise applications. Large companies such as Burberry, Toyota, and GE trust Salesforce.com (a cloud SaaS company) to deliver reliable and best-in-class CRM services.

While companies like Salesforce.com were early pioneers of SaaS, the market took off once a bunch of entrepreneurs had readily available access to cheap computing. A business can find a SaaS offering for almost any functions within its organization, from human resources management to help desk support to financial solutions.

Still, we shouldn't think of cloud services as solutions that are offered only by start-ups. Established companies, such as Intuit and Oracle, also provide cloud-resident services. For example, Intuit's successful accounting application, QuickBooks, is available both as a SaaS service and as a standalone software package.

The evolution of SaaS is a revolution for software buyers. Cloud computing and SaaS are a big deal to corporations that frequently spend millions to buy hardware and software and pay huge annual fees for maintenance contracts to support these purchases. A business can now rent access to applications, such as enterprise resource planning, human resources management, and accounting, on a monthly or annual basis. For example, a company may spend $5 million up front to purchase enterprise resource planning (ERP) software and 18 percent of that $5 million, or $900,000, every year in a maintenance contract. SaaS provides the opportunity for a company to buy software for a monthly fee, with updates included.

In some ways, SaaS even offers customers a better product experience because the company is always using the latest version. A company can always have the latest features without the customer using any of its internal resources to update and manage the application. You pay by the month, and while you are sleeping, somebody updates your software. You come in the next morning and you have all these new features you didn't have before. You didn't have to install them. You didn't have to do a six-month rollout of the new software package. You're always up to date. The only additional resources on your part might be to train your users on the new software.

The downside is that you can't change the application. If the corporation wants the software provider to change or customize the application, it's largely impossible for it to do so. If a company has already customized a packaged software application, it can't easily switch to the cloud version of this application. One of the reasons SaaS software is economical is because there is essentially one version of the software for everyone. There may be various tiers of the software application from basic to premium. It may offer minor customization, but that's it. If you want a specific feature, you need to request it and hope the SaaS provider will build it.

SaaS Helps Apps Go Mobile

I've talked about the profound changes mobile is delivering in the industry and how consumers are purchasing apps that were built specifically for mobile devices. In the business domain, a majority of enterprise applications and services must be redesigned as mobile-friendly applications or businesses will have to purchase mobile versions of these applications from their existing software suppliers.

Software as a service provides a third way for an organization to provide employees with mobile-friendly apps that work on all devices. SaaS gives businesses a quick way to mobile-enable applications because employees and consumers can access the software from any location and on any mobile device that can use a web browser.

Management doesn't have to understand if the operating system is Android, Apple, or Windows. It simply works. The company still has to deal with the fact that it may not be able to customize the system the way it wants, but then, it's not using resources to maintain or update the software. It can take those resources and use them for another project, which might be building a new product or providing a new service—basically redeploying resources to do something that differentiates the business from its competitors, as opposed to spending the time building software services.

Whether it needs equipment or software, a company can now rent a product or service by the hour, month, or bit. This fundamentally changes the economics for the vendors providing these services, and it changes the capital requirements for the companies consuming these services. There is also less risk involved for a customer to try a service. In the consumer world, this may translate into less stickiness, but in the enterprise world, you still have to invest in getting your data into or out of an SaaS solution. From an enterprise perspective, it's easy to try a service before you commit, the cost of the solution is easy to calculate, and it's easy to add new employees to the service.

Established companies competing with SaaS start-ups will experience a change in the amount of revenue they receive, the timing of revenue, and the margins associated with delivering a product. These companies may need to drop prices on existing products, design a new product line to compete with these cloud-based offerings, or both. Regardless of the approach, the new business models will affect both revenue and margins. Instead of using multimillion-dollar hardware or software deals with annual maintenance contracts, these companies will receive a smaller per-user, per-month fee with no additional revenue for maintenance. I'm not suggesting that the entire hardware and software market will vanish overnight. Far from it. Many companies—at least 35 percent of the firms Lopez Research interviewed at the end of 2013—have little or no interest in cloud service. But for the 65 percent that potentially open to purchasing cloud services, a business must be prepared to handle this disruption and opportunity.

Mobile and cloud computing have fundamentally disrupted hardware, software, and the consumer electronics industry. These technologies and pricing model changes have the potential to disrupt every industry and the structure of companies.

In addition to technology changes, there is another force at work that represents both a technological and a behavioral shift. This is social networks and the emergence of social businesses.

Mobile and Social Change Engagement

At the same time that mobile was on the rise, social networking sites, such as Facebook and Myspace, were using cloud computing to come online. In 2004 (which does not seem that long ago), Facebook was only getting started. YouTube did not exist, nor did Twitter. LinkedIn had just been launched. By 2008, social sites were experiencing a hockey stick–shaped adoption curve.

Today, Facebook has over 1 billion users. Twitter users send more than 500 million tweets per day. Over 100 hours of video are uploaded to YouTube every minute. Social networking changed how people communicate with each other and would go on to change how businesses communicate with customers and employees. It enabled a new culture of sharing and peer recommendations. It's fundamentally accelerated word-of-mouth marketing and created new channels for marketers to reach their target audience.

These social networks gave companies the opportunity to understand their customers in ways that weren't available in the past. Social provides access to a person's interests, acquaintances, and the emotional relevance of those connections. Social networks provide the raw data to feed sentiment analysis tools that help companies understand how their customers feel about a company's products and its competitor's offerings. After years of debating social networking merits and detriments, business leaders around the globe are using social to change the way their companies market and service customers.

Social and cloud computing fuel what Jeremiah Owang calls the collaborative economy. He defines this as an unstoppable trend "where brands will rent, lend, offer subscriptions to products and services to customers or, even further, allow their customers to lend, trade, or gift branded products or services to each other. Its specific features include relationships, online profiles, reputations, expressed needs and offerings, and ecommerce."[14] For example, EatWith is an app that allows people to connect and dine in homes around the world ("Meet interesting people, eat great food, and enjoy unforgettable experiences," says the site). What restaurateur saw that coming? I'll discuss other collaborative economy companies, such as Airbnb and Uber, that are leveraging mobile, social, and cloud computing to disrupt established businesses.

Consumer social networks also set off a new way of thinking about how employees can share data and collaborate in the business world. Collaboration was once thought of as email and document-storage solutions. Today, software companies are adding short messaging features that resemble Twitter into applications such as CRM solutions and collaboration tools. Companies such as Jive and Yammer built enterprise social networking software that offers the same ease of communications of consumer social networks with the security features companies demand. In fact, we now have a new term to describe enterprise software and processes that contain these functions. It's called social business.

Once mobile networks improved and people started buying smartphones, social networks got another boost in adoption, usage, and functionality. New social networks that could take advantage of mobile devices' new functions, such as cameras and location finding, hit the scene. Foursquare created a social network based on checking into a location such as a store, a restaurant, or an attraction. Instagram was founded to capture and share pictures while on the go. Pinterest is an online site for collecting and organizing items such as photographs and links to websites, but it is also available on the go with mobile.

Mobile access is now a major contributor to social networking traffic. In the Seeking Alpha transcript of Facebook's Q3 earnings call, CEO Mark Zuckerberg said, "Now 49 percent of our revenue comes from mobile and 48 percent of the people who use Facebook in any given day are only accessing it from mobile. That's almost half of the people only using Facebook from their phones, and it's a pretty incredible sign of how Facebook is evolved over the last year."[15]

It's clear that mobile, social, and cloud computing are transforming business in ways more profound than most people could have imagined even a decade ago. But I have yet to discuss big data and its role. Like cloud computing, it is a technology underpinning for understanding and utilizing the wide range of data that's now available.

Social, Mobile, and IoT Create Big Data

Mobile, IoT, and social media created even more data than we'd ever amassed. We thought we had large volumes of data before, but now we have a massive torrent. The data is a mixture of unstructured data, such as video, images, and short messages, and more structured data, such as spreadsheets, temperature readings, and text documents. It's data from every sensor on every piece of equipment that's connected. The sheer amount of information makes it difficult for businesses to process with existing tools.

These vast sources of data have a new term, which the industry has dubbed "big data." The combination of this new big data and the fact that much of it is contextual provides an opportunity for an organization to identify interesting trends. With the proper analytics and database foundation, a company can start to be predictive and prescriptive about what it does.

Organizations had analytical tools before, but they couldn't access all the data being generated. Big data storage and its analytical tools were not invented until the mid-2000s, and mainly Internet companies were using them until 2007. The problem has worsened for many organizations as we've added new sources of contextual data, such as location and social media updates. Without new tools to turn the data into useful information, an organization will have difficulty gaining new insight and designing new experiences based on the available data. Our established databases and analytics software aren't adequate for storing and analyzing vast amounts of data that varies in type. Fortunately, just as a tremendous amount of new data was being collected, big data platforms and analytic tools were being developed. I discuss what big data platforms are and how businesses can use them in Chapter 9. In the meantime, you should think of big data platforms as part of a tool kit that will help turn raw data created by mobile devices, social networks, and IoT sensors into new, actionable insights.

Delivering New Experiences

Technology transitions normally deliver cost savings and improved efficiencies. While mobile and cloud both offer the potential for efficiencies, when combined, these technologies offer much more. They present possibilities that simply did not exist in the past. For example, consider how companies such as Uber and Lyft are using cloud computing, social, and mobile technology to disrupt the taxi industry.[16]

It can be difficult to obtain a taxi in San Francisco. Cabs don't cruise the streets in far-flung areas of the city. Some trips don't seem worth the fare, so cab companies and drivers avoid them. This has sometimes meant the dispatcher promises a cab that never arrives. Enter Uber and Lyft.

Uber developed software that allows anyone with a smartphone to request a ride via mobile app, text message, or the web. The customer who has registered with Uber can choose a passenger car, limousine, or sport utility vehicle. Originally, Uber provided a way for limousine drivers to make additional money in between their existing appointments. Over a short period of time, Uber added the car option, which is people who are driving their personal vehicles and are not part of a limo company, and not necessarily even people who drive for a living. This is important because riders are now choosing average citizens over professionals because of cost *and* better service. Technology has made it possible for riders to find reliable drivers who are not licensed cabbies. It's a social and technological change that provides the right experience at the right place and right time. This is the essence of how technology will change our businesses and what we have to prepare for.

What makes this service better is that it offers both cost savings and additional value. Riders can track the vehicle they've ordered and receive a text message or telephone call when the driver arrives outside their door. At the end of the ride, the driver and passenger rate each other. Uber, not the driver, charges the person's credit card, which is on file. After the trip, the system sends the passenger an email receipt detailing the trip. This isn't your normal taxi experience. There is no guilt or anxiety associated with using a credit card or knowing what percentage tip should be left. Uber automatically calculates the tip and pays the bill. This also isn't an experience that is isolated to one region of the world; it's a global phenomenon. At this writing, Uber is available in 20 U.S. cities, plus London, Paris, Shanghai, Toronto, and Sydney. The company says, "For drivers, Uber is a revenue stream, allowing professional drivers to make more money by turning downtime into profits."[17] It also allows the average consumer to make money on the side.

Lyft is an extension of this idea, similar except more informal and potentially less expensive. None of the drivers are professional cabbies, and Lyft's cars are not officially cabs or limos. Rather, when a customer taps her smartphone app to request a ride, the app shows the driver's name, rating by past passengers, and photos of the driver and his car. Unlike Uber drivers, Lyft drivers accept donations instead of set fares. The app shows a suggested donation, which the passenger can increase to cover a tip. This donation model helps Lyft avoid issues with licenses for local transportation agencies.

Lyft requires a Facebook profile for both passengers and drivers to sign up for the service. "We make this a requirement because of the inherently social and inter-connected nature fundamental to the Lyft experience," says John Zimmer, the chief executive of Zimride, which runs Lyft. "We have found that requiring each user's personal Facebook to sign up has been the most effective tool to ensure accountability, recognition, and safety when it comes to passenger and driver interaction." Lyft kicks negligent drivers and lousy passengers off the system.

All this technology—from tracking individual cars on a phone to paying with a screen tap—allows a customer experience that was simply not available in the past. And these are just a few examples of how these technologies can be combined to deliver richer experiences at the point of need.

While many consumers focus on sexy devices, businesses need to focus on the mind-set shift that has led people to assume they'll be connected and serviced wherever they go. This obvious change in expectations means that a company must change its business processes to support business anywhere over many types of devices. If not, these companies will be run out of business by other enterprises and entrepreneurs that do recognize the implications and the opportunities.

Summary

Roughly every decade, there have been technology evolutions that fundamentally change computing. In the 1980s, it was the minicomputer; in the 1990s, it was the PC; in the 2000s, it was the Internet. In the 2010s, it has been mobile, social, and cloud computing. While technology will continue to evolve to alter the underlying infrastructure of business, companies face more than technology change. Over the past several decades, technological change has created business efficiencies. Today, technology has a broader impact by enabling behavioral changes that are empowered by technology such as social networks. Much like in the early days of the Internet, businesses face simultaneous changes in technology, society, and economic models.

The confluence of technology and resulting new consumer behavior has disrupted existing business models. Previous barriers to entry, such as access to capital, distribution channels, and supply chain dominance, have been significantly eroded. Start-ups across a wide range of industries have challenged established business practices and created new market dynamics. Industry boundaries have also dissolved, which means competitors can surface from anywhere.

The transitions we've experienced to date are simply a foreshadowing of the change to come. Businesses are competing in marketplaces where nearly anyone can become your competitor overnight. Companies that built large, expensive infrastructure businesses, such as AT&T and Verizon, never anticipated that Amazon would become a competitor in cloud computing. Regulated industries, such as taxi companies and hotels, didn't expect to be competing with consumers who would offer shared-ride services and accommodations in their homes. Google never anticipated it would compete with Facebook for a brand's advertising funds. Established software vendors never thought companies would buy mission-critical services from cloud start-ups.

The smartphone, tablet, and connected device landscape is disrupting one industry after another. In our personal lives, it will open up a world of opportunity for monitoring and managing everything from your health to your home. In the corporate domain, it will provide businesses with new data that can be turned into insight that creates economic value.

At one time, a large business may have been able to erect defensible barriers to entry that could take years—or even decades—to erode. Today, your business is standing on quicksand. No business is immune to unexpected competitors. Your competitive environment is a shifting landscape where the map is constantly changing. Unless you meet or exceed the offerings of your new competition, you'll lose business. You may have loyal customers, but your business won't grow. If your business isn't growing, it most likely won't survive.

Of course, this isn't the first time we've seen shifts in technology and in business models. Change has always happened. As Tony Robbins pointed out, "Change is inevitable. Progress is optional."[18] Change just happens faster now. Progress will be determined by how your business reacts to the current change while anticipating future shifts. Whether you are a business executive or technology leader, you must understand and adapt to these changes in order to build a viable twenty-first-century business.

In the next chapter, I discuss several of the issues that are holding businesses back and provide suggestions for removing these roadblocks. In the third chapter, I discuss the concept of right-time experiences and how it will enable your company to differentiate itself in a dynamic business environment.

Notes

1. The cost of the first cell phone, according to a Mashable article, http://mashable.com/2014/03/13/first-cellphone-on-sale/.
2. ITU mobile subscriber statistics, www.itu.int/en/ITU-D/Statistics/Pages/stat/default.aspx.
3. www.slideshare.net/JuxtConsult/juxt-india-mobile2013snapshot08-september.

4. http://www.achievement.org/autodoc/page/gat0int-1.
5. Matthew Braga, "Point, Shoot, Collapse: Why Big Camera Companies Are the Next BlackBerry," *Financial Post*, October 5, 2013.
6. Cisco stated, "More things are connecting to the Internet than people—over 12.5 billion devices in 2010 alone. Cisco's Internet Business Solutions Group (IBSG) predicts some 25 billion devices will be connected by 2015, and 50 billion by 2020," http://share.cisco.com/internet-of-things.html.
7. Steve Lohr, "Looking to Industry for the Next Digital Disruption," www.nytimes.com/2012/11/24/technology/Internet/ge-looks-to-industry-for-the-next-digital-disruption.html?pagewanted=all&_r=1&.
8. Nathan Ingraham, "Apple announces 1 million apps in the App Store, more than 1 billion songs played on iTunes radio, " http://www.theverge.com/2013/10/22/4866302/apple-announces-1-million-apps-in-the-app-store.
9. The current number of Android apps in the market on January 19, 2014, was 1,071,194, www.appbrain.com/stats/number-of-android-apps.
10. www.apple.com/pr/library/2014/01/07App-Store-Sales-Top-10-Billion-in-2013.html.
11. *Cloudonomics: The Business Value of Cloud Computing*, www.amazon.com/Cloudonomics-Website-Business-Value-Computing/dp/1118229967/ref=la_B007R9ZHPK_1_1?s=books&ie=UTF8&qid=1396747648&sr=1-1.
12. https://www.kickstarter.com/year/2013/?ref=footer.
13. Sonya Chudgar, "Can Square Change POS Forever?" *QSR*, May 2013, www.qsrmagazine.com.ttp://www.qsrmagazine.com/exclusives/can-square-change-pos-forever.
14. Jeremiah Owyang's blog, "The Next Phase of Social Business Is the Collaborative Economy," www.web-strategist.com/blog/2013/05/07/the-next-phase-of-social-business-is-the-collaborative-economy/.
15. http://seekingalpha.com/article/1790372-facebooks-ceo-discusses-q3-2013-results-earnings-call-transcript?part=single.
16. For more information about Uber, check out its website at www.uber.com; for Lyft, see www.lyft.com.
17. http://support.uber.com/entries/22344456-What-is-Uber-.
18. "Change vs. Progress: Making the Choices That Move You Forward," http://training.tonyrobbins.com/change-vs-progress-making-the-choices-that-move-you-forward/.

CHAPTER 2

Marching Backwards into the Future

Industry leaders recognize that many of today's products and services don't meet current customer expectations for usability and personalization, but they don't know how to fix these issues. In many cases, doing something requires a substantial change, which is always difficult, and rapid change with an unknown outcome is even more prickly. As a result, many businesses hold on to previous business practices instead of seeking out new ways of doing things. "When faced with a totally new situation, we tend always to attach ourselves to the objects, to the flavor of the most recent past," wrote Marshall McLuhan in *The Medium Is the Message.* "We look at the present through a rear view mirror. We march backwards into the future."[1]

In his book, *The End of Business as Usual,* Brian Solis called the evolution of consumer behavior, when society and technology evolve faster than the ability to adapt, "digital Darwinism."[2] Many businesses are experiencing this phenomenon today. It's not that business leaders are dim-witted and don't recognize that change has transpired. Companies understand that mobile, social, big data, and cloud computing are changing the business landscape. The question is, how can a company profit from these transformations?

In many cases, the required business transition forces a company to cannibalize an existing profitable business in favor of a model that initially offers lower sales or profits, or both. For example, many SaaS services that software vendors compete with offer "good enough" software at a fraction of the cost. Disruptors also frequently use cloud computing and mobile to minimize costs. In many cases, established companies attempted to create strategic advantage by building a highly customized set of IT solutions and business processes that can't be easily transitioned into a mobile and cloud computing world. Business leaders now face a challenging time where the company's IT systems and business models are at odds with growing the business.

Three Issues Stall Change

Virtually all business leaders recognize that change is important and necessary. Products change, customers change, and competitors change. The business world is in ceaseless flux. Of course, companies should be avoiding change for change's sake, but many simply want to avoid change entirely. In my dealings with senior executives, I've discovered at least three impediments to change within organizations:

1. Denial and/or unwillingness to take action
2. Lack of direction that prevents business leaders from getting started
3. Fear of external risks (privacy, security, and compliance) stalling change

Denial and Unwillingness to Take Action

In this case, business leaders acknowledge that there are new competitors, but they don't view these competitors as a threat. Or, they understand there is a threat, but they aren't willing to make the changes that are necessary to be successful.

Businesses can choose to adapt to new business models and create new markets. The problem is that most business leaders are approaching the change in the wrong fashion. They wait until the last possible moment to change. By then, a company has allowed its competitors to gain a strong foothold in the market and define what the new product or service experience should be. We've seen this happen time and again. Kodak reached $16 billion in revenue in 1996, but it missed the digital photography wave. By the time Kodak entered the digital market, it was already moving into a new era where mobile phones with cameras were replacing digital point-and-shoot cameras. By 2012, Kodak was bankrupt.

Netflix saw an opportunity to improve the customer movie rental experience by delivering DVDs to customers via the U.S. Postal Service and eliminating late fees. Blockbuster dismissed Netflix and the concept of renting DVDs by mail. In 2000, it had the opportunity to purchase Netflix for $50 million and refused.

Eventually it offered its own DVD-by-mail service, but it was too late. By 2010, Blockbuster filed for bankruptcy while Netflix was a thriving $2 billion concern that has continued to evolve, now challenging cable companies with streaming movies.

Change is difficult for most organizations, and rapid change with an unknown outcome is even harder. Many executives are risk averse. This aversion makes sense when the average C-level executive job tenure is two years or less. However, risk aversion leads to small incremental changes, and these usually produce market laggards.

When ride-sharing services, such as Uber and Lyft, began to take business away from taxi companies, the companies' first response was to ignore them. Instead of adjusting business practices to meet new consumer service opportunities, the regulations and the service remained the same. Once it was evident that these new transportation services were eating into profits, the first line of defense the San Francisco taxi industry pursued was legal action against Uber and other similar services. Rather than improving their value to their customers, the taxi companies tried to destroy the new competition by legal means and continue business as usual.

The same scenario occurred when Airbnb emerged in 2008. Airbnb is an online marketplace in which people can list and book unique accommodations around the world. Individuals use the service to rent a room or an entire home from another individual. These individuals aren't licensed to offer hotel-style services and aren't paying the taxes and fees associated with providing lodging services, which means their guests can be spared the 8 percent or more room tax local governments have levied. The official response: Regulators claim the businesses violate city occupancy laws and regulations.

These are examples in the consumer market for transportation and travel, but the same dynamics are present in enterprise software. Let's take Microsoft, for example. Microsoft's SharePoint was released in 2001. Over 13 years, it has evolved to offer content management, document management, and collaboration functions. It's used by large organizations around the globe. By all rights, it's a tremendously successful product that's continued to evolve to meet customers' ever-changing needs.

But cloud computing and mobile would also change Microsoft's fortunes in content and document management. New cloud-based services from Box.com, Dropbox, and Google came into the market to make it easier for consumers to share documents. Despite potential security concerns, employees gravitated to the simplicity of these consumer solutions for all of their personal and professional file-sharing needs.

While the services started as a way to store documents and share them between the web and PCs, they rapidly evolved to support document access and sharing from smartphones and tablets. Within a few years, Microsoft and other enterprise document-sharing companies were competing against consumer-oriented start-ups. How did this happen? These disruptors focused on removing the complexities of document sharing, such as file size, cumbersome navigation, and content synchronization across multiple devices. They created mobile apps that made it easy to access and share content from the device of your choice. They also made it easy and affordable for employees to share data across companies.

Businesses like Lyft, Airbnb, and Dropbox are software businesses that operate in the cloud. The product is largely a website or mobile application with a billing engine and a business model that makes something easier for the customer. It's highly adaptable and can often be changed to minimize legal issues or deliver new features. For example, Airbnb simply changed the company's website to enable donations instead of formal payment for services. Shifting to donations meant these businesses could continue to operate while they worked out issues with the regulators. Recognizing that security concerns were slowing enterprise adoption cloud service, Box.com added features such as AES encryption and audit tracking.

It's not just the software industry and services industries that are seeing this change. It can also happen in physical goods. Google recently spent $3 billion to buy Nest, a company that "reinvents unloved but important home products, like the thermostat and the smoke alarm." Honeywell, Johnson Controls, and others have been in the space for decades, but Nest makes thermostats and smoke detectors that are easy to program and monitor with a mobile phone.

What the taxi, hotel, industrial controls, and other industries didn't want to admit was that these services were filling a market void. The services are frequently cheaper. This is a common incentive to woo a customer. But cheaper services alone aren't enough to create a truly disruptive offering. These services must do something better to be successful. While it could be something revolutionary, such as creating digital music, many winning innovations simply take friction out of the process.

Square, a payment processing company, didn't change the credit card industry. It used mobile and cloud computing to make accepting credit cards easier for small businesses. Uber didn't invent a new way to transport people around the city. It invented an easier way for people to order, track, and pay for transportation services. Dropbox and Box.com didn't invent online file storage. They combined the economics of cloud computing with an easier user experience that could be synchronized across mobile devices and PCs. These services improved the customer's experience with value-added features such as convenience and better information.

Nevertheless, senior executives do have legitimate concerns about marching into the future. Reluctance to change internal processes and business models is not entirely due to inertia. Adopting a new business model often creates a short-term sales decline or causes certain types of revenue to disappear to match competitor prices. This disruption isn't a new phenomenon but is an ever-increasing trend. We saw this happen in the music industry, where the move from CDs to MP3 fundamentally changed the economics for record labels. Instead of paying $15 for an entire CD, consumers could buy just the songs they wanted.

Public companies are expected to constantly grow. Any shift that may lead to shrinking revenue or profits is a hard sell to the board of directors and stockholders, no matter what benefits the future promises. The willingness to risk a short-term loss for a long-term gain is one reason that private companies and start-ups can often outperform a publicly held competitor. Nevertheless, no business can continually approach the new market dynamics with old business practices. Amazon provides an example of a publicly held company that is willing to risk short-term loss for a long-term gain. It continues to innovate and its stock has continued to perform well.

The first step management must take is to acknowledge all new pricing and distribution models as credible threats. Management should evaluate the cost in terms of lost revenue and profits from adopting the same models within their own organization. If the decline in revenue or profits will be significant, management should be looking for ways to shave expenses in anticipation of declining sales.

Lack of Direction Stalls Action

Even if an organization's senior management decides the company should reinvent its products or define new ways of doing business, they still might not know what to do. After all, by the time the threat is blindingly obvious, they have typically allowed the competition to gain a foothold in the market. Usually the competition has already played the lower-price card and arguably done something that may be more convenient, more efficient, or more entertaining than what the company is doing.

At this point, management must decide if it should match its competitors or change its products. Is it enough to provide a "me too" product? Will that damage our brand? Will the company be admitting defeat and the superiority of another company's product? It's not just a financial decision. It's a decision that requires a certain finesse and coordination between marketing, product development, and finance. Customer support must also be included to manage any confusion around a billing or product change.

Major shifts in products frequently take two years or more to develop and create market momentum. For example, it took Apple two years to build the first iPhone and at least another year for it to take hold in the market. Mobile phone manufacturers didn't know what was coming, and telecom carriers had no idea how it would change the demand for wireless data connections. By the time companies like RIM and Microsoft had acknowledged how the iPhone was changing the industry, these companies were already competing against several years of innovations. The issue with innovation is that some companies are doing linear, or incremental, innovation while others are creating something brand new. The most successful organizations are able to do both.

Acknowledging there are new competitive threats is the first step in improving your market position. This risk always existed. What's new is that technologies such as mobile and social provide different challenges and opportunities to evaluate. We discussed how cloud computing helped fuel a new wave of competitors. We can also see that mobile and social provide new ways of connecting with our customers.

The second step requires understanding how to overcome inaction and lack of direction. To kick-start the process, a business leader must gain an understanding of the inefficiencies and weaknesses within the company's existing products and business processes. I call this finding your blind spots. I'll discuss finding and eliminating these blind spots in a moment, but first let's briefly discuss the third issue: external risks.

EXTERNAL RISKS   **INTERNAL RISKS**

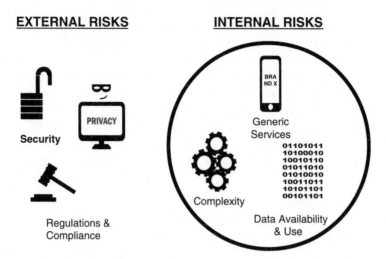

Security

Regulations &
Compliance

Generic
Services

Complexity

Data Availability
& Use

Figure 2.1   Understanding the Risks

Source: Lopez Research LLC.

Fear of External Risks Stalls Change

With all the new technologies available, companies are trying to strike a balance between maintaining customer privacy and delivering customized services. Sadly, the line between relevance and creepiness is very thin. Many consumers don't trust companies to safeguard the information they harvest and to use it wisely to improve the customer's experience. We come to what I call the external risks. In this case, you must address external challenges that are largely out of your control but must be considered as part of execution risk. These are the external risks of privacy concerns, regulatory compliance, and security considerations (see Figure 2.1).

1. **Privacy.** Will the customer and employees let us do it? (Many employers consider this an internal risk that they can control. I've listed it as external because it changes as people and society change.)
2. **Legality.** What regulatory issues are involved? Will the government allow us to do what we want or need to do? For example, a hospital has very strict regulations on the use of a patient's medical records, regardless of the benefits sharing data could provide to future patients and society.

3. Security. What security issues are involved? We have to secure our customers', employees', and partners' data.

There may be other, more prevalent, risks that your business faces. Financial instability, management transitions, or an aging workforce can also be issues that your company faces. I listed the challenges above because I've consistently seen organizations struggle with these areas in my work as an industry analyst. Now that I've outlined several of the risks an organization may face, I'd like to discuss how an organization should approach discovering and overcoming its own strategic blind spots.

Finding Your Blind Spots

If your car isn't functioning properly, you take it to the dealer for a diagnosis. Depending on what issues they find, you decide if it's worth fixing the car immediately or if you can wait until a later date. There are many questions a car owner will answer before agreeing to a repair. Is the issue critical or minor? Perhaps the owner evaluates the cost of buying a newer car versus the cost of repairing the older model. How will the repair impact the safety of the passengers and the longevity of the car? If a car is needed for transportation, eventually the problems must be fixed or a new vehicle must be found. This process of analysis is the same within a company.

If management is aware of a product or service issue, they normally try to fix it. It's a matter of having a strategy for resolution and the resources to accomplish the task. If it can't be easily fixed, the company tries to minimize the issue's impact on the business. Eventually the company resolves its issues, changes its business, or folds. The internal risks, such as a high-priced product or manufacturing issue, may already be known. These are easier to discover if the company is actively monitoring the competitive landscape.

The harder ones to catch are the ones that originate from a new set of competitors or technologies. In some cases, it can even be the act of simplifying a product instead of adding new features. When Apple introduced the iPhone in 2007, RIM (now renamed BlackBerry) and Nokia ridiculed Apple for the device's simple interface and curated list of features. But this simplicity kicked off a new wave of adoption and application design. In 2013, Apple owned over 20 percent of the global smartphone market with only a few smartphone models. Tablet sales for the iPad alone had exceeded 150 million units in two years, which proved there was a market for a new type of computing device. In 2013, Apple became the most valuable brand in the world,[3] while Nokia was sold to Microsoft and BlackBerry sought out a buyer for its ailing mobile business.

The rapid adoption of mobile and cloud computing has led to major and unexpected marketplace shifts. For example, three years ago everyone would've assumed mobile devices couldn't replace laptops. Today, this topic is open for debate. While there may not be "a problem" per se with your product or service, there may be a way for a competitor to make the offering better, faster, or cheaper.

Perhaps the competitor made a transaction frictionless (Square). Maybe it offered a new piece of critical information, such as location, or a way to order and pay for a service (Uber). Maybe it created a way to organize and easily access all of your important information on any device (Evernote). In each case, these companies used mobile, social, and cloud computing to exploit inefficiencies in an existing product or service. These risks may be less obvious but are equally damaging. These are the blind spots that every organization wrestles with.

How do you find the blind spots within your organization? The title of Andy Grove's book, *Only the Paranoid Survive*, says it best. Grove understood that the only way for a company to advance was to assume that what it has built today wouldn't be adequate for the long term. With the speed of innovation, the definition of *long term* may be only six months from now. If you look at the pace of innovation in mobile phones, there is something new every six to nine months.

A company must assume that its products and services are never complete. A business must constantly seek out and eliminate friction within its products and internal business processes. While it sells and upgrades its existing products, it should always be looking for ways that new technologies or changes in business models could destroy its crown jewels. Successful businesses won't wait to be disrupted. Leaders will work to create the disruption.

Most importantly, it must be willing to proactively destroy and rebuild at least a portion of its existing products. For example, BMW isn't waiting for ride sharing to replace the need for new cars. In 2011, it launched its own ridesharing service called DriveNow. This may sound radical. However, changing your products and processes is the only way to prevent another company from exploiting your inefficiencies. *You must be the disruptor or be disrupted.* While you may forgo a part of the company's existing revenue, you'll control your own destiny and influence the market's evolution.

Three Common Blind Spots

If anything could be wrong, where do you look? How do you get started? In my discussions with disruptive companies, I've seen three common blind spots businesses have and disruptors exploit. Note: I used the term *disruptors*, not *start-ups*. Almost any company can be a disruptor. It's a matter of defining what you want to disrupt and doing it.

The most common issues today are products, business workflows, and customer experiences that are generic and complex and use data poorly. While the company's processes may work, they're frequently inconvenient, which adds to complexity. Speed is also an issue but not a blind spot. Many executives acknowledge that their company is slow to change. Given that it's a pervasive issue, I address the issues of speed throughout the book.

Generic Services That Are Uninspiring or Annoying   Most businesses want to offer engaging and personalized experiences, but the messages and products that they deliver are frequently the same for everyone. A person may receive the same advertisement as anyone else who hits the website or mobile app. Many times customers will receive the same auto-attendant message from an interactive voice response (IVR), regardless of what number they are calling from. Even if the IVR recognizes the number, it doesn't necessarily mean it will offer any personalized messages. An employee can rarely customize the view of an enterprise application to make their job easier. Generic is simple, but it lacks engagement and differentiation.

The new world of mobile, social, and IoT gives organizations an opportunity to change generic functions and make them more relevant to the individuals who have to use them. I talk about how context from mobile, social, and IoT will provide a wealth of new information in Chapter 3.

Complex Products and Processes   In the quest to deliver the best products and enterprise services, a business frequently crams too many features into an application or product. A product, application, or website could have hundreds of features, but only a handful are used by the majority of a company's consumers. This normally translates into a cluttered and unsatisfying user experience. Microsoft Word provides an excellent example of this. It has hundreds of features but most people use only a handful of them.

On the business side, most applications that companies provide their employees tend to be unnecessarily complicated. The design principle seems to have been that every time someone needed something, it got thrown into the application. The developers continued to add features over the course of many years. Functionality took precedence over usability.

Neil Cohen, vice president of sales and marketing for Visage Mobile, say one reason complexity occurs in both consumer and enterprise products is that companies believe they can compete more effectively by augmenting existing products with newer features that the competition has added. Instead of innovating and leading the market, they're actually turning their products into a complicated and useless mess. Cohen said, "You can think of it as a mutually assured destruction through the addition of more and more features that *never* get used."[4]

As a result, when the organization tries to offer access to a memory-hungry and feature-dense application on one of the new mobile devices, it doesn't work. The screens are too small. The applications crash because they require consistent connectivity or fast data networks. The navigation doesn't work because the original applications weren't designed for touch screens. Attempting to shrink an application that was designed to run on a personal computer onto a four-inch screen is just a disaster. We therefore need to move to different experiences, because many of today's applications don't work well for employees. They annoy rather than empower.

From the consumer perspective, the situation is similar with websites and many mobile applications. It's often difficult to figure out how to navigate to reach where you want—or need—to go. Many people are frustrated by mobile websites either because they lack the information that's on the company's main website or because the company hasn't made the website easy to read on a mobile device. Search results often don't return what the consumer needs, leaving users frustrated and confused. The consumer cannot be sure if the item, answer, or contact exists or not. Is the failure the site's fault or mine?

Whether it's a mobile application or a website, too many choices have been presented in a format that is not user-friendly. Programmers have given more thought to what methods they will use to develop an app or a website than to what website visitors and mobile app users might need. I hear this debate with the apps development team all the time. It starts with "We'll build a native app" or "We'll build a web app." Most developers want a single method for programing and aren't interested in using multiple tools and development models. Developers that create winning experiences do so by working with a product owner and user to define the experience. The developer can then select the type of development model that delivers the best experience for a specific process and application.

Additionally, businesses frequently try to map the employee and customer experience to how their internal processes operate. It's not that the process is too complex for the customer or employee to understand. A person understands the flow of the process, but oftentimes it doesn't reflect the path an individual wants to take to complete a transaction. For example, you may want to know the shipping charge of an item before you reach the last stage of checkout. A salesperson may simply want to record a sale without adding additional data such as what the customer has purchased in the past.

These are items that focus on the convenience for the company, or they are manifestations of a business model that lacks user convenience. For example, your customer's legal team will only accept signed copies of contracts via email but not from a document-signing service such as Docusign or Echosign. Most likely the company selected this solution when electronic signatures weren't commonplace or weren't considered legally binding. These conditions have changed but the company's process has stood still.

Many disruptors focus on simplifying one part of a process, delivering a more flexible way of accomplishing tasks, or making the interface and workflow easier to use. The app or service gains traction as a result of the simplicity, and the disruptor adds functionality as it learns what's important.

Getting the Data to Add Up to Value   Ideally, every business wants to deliver the right information at the right time. The reality of the situation is very different. We have buckets of data in our systems, and our customers provide us with data. But our data can be our worst enemy.

In some cases, the information we want to share with our customers and employees is missing. It's frequently incomplete or inconsistent, or it doesn't translate between systems. For example, a product may be on back order but there is no estimated availability.

Or a customer checks the in-store availability of a product online, but the product is unavailable when he reaches the store. A customer calls a bank, enters her account information, and is forced to repeat it again verbally to the agent.

Along with poor-quality data, there is also an issue with misuse of data or poorly timed communications. Do I need an email or a text message every day? Am I really going to buy something from Williams-Sonoma every day? When is the right time to receive a message? Should I receive a "balance low" warning before I've bounced a check or after? Many email and SMS marketing campaigns fail to deliver relevant information at the right time. Many alerts are also sent at the wrong time or past a point where they will be useful. For example, a consumer may receive a gate change notification long after it has been announced on the airport. If your customer receives a message after his check has bounced or long after he's arrived at the new gate, the communication is worthless and annoying. It damages your brand and compromises your customers' trust.

In some cases, businesses are creating an experience that misses on all of the marks above. They provide generic, poorly timed communications that lack any insight on what you've done in the past and any predictions of what you might do in the future.

Taming the Beast of External Risks

But generic services, complexity, and bad data aren't the only issues executives have to contend with. Privacy concerns, regulatory compliance, and security considerations also plague senior management.

Problems of Privacy

Wherever there is a discussion of offering "personalized" service, there's also a debate about privacy. This debate started in the web world. A website can tell exactly which website pages a person visits, how long the person stays on a page, where he goes next, and, in the case of an online retailer, whether he buys today or returns at a later date. This is accomplished with a technology called cookies. Over the years, consumers have discovered what cookies are, and they have the opportunity to turn these services on or off.

Companies want to get the same data and more from a person's mobile device. Ideally a company can collect and integrate data from mobile device browsing, PC browsing, mobile application use, and sensor data. Just as in the early days of the Internet, the social norms for what you can track and how you can track it are in a state of constant flux.

A few years ago, people may have been up in arms to learn that smartphones track their location. In 2011, Apple ran into this concern when the media reported that Apple could track its users. Consumers wondered why Apple had their location data and how the company was using it.

Apple's press team had to write a formal response stating, "Apple is not tracking the location of your iPhone. Apple has never done so and has no plans to ever do so."[5] It went on to describe exactly what types of location information it used and how it was using it. Although Apple has made itself as clear as it could, I am sure many people still believed Apple was personally tracking them. Now, of course, consumers willingly turn on location tracking because they see value in the services. Google can help you pinpoint your location and give you turn-by-turn walking directions. Apple can help you find a lost iPhone. When it adds value to a consumer's life, the location feature isn't creepy.

According to a survey by TRUSTe, a San Francisco–based privacy management solutions provider, while 62 percent of smartphone users say they are aware that advertisers are tracking their mobile activities, only 1 percent say they like it and only 10 percent would willingly consent to sharing their location data with marketers.[6] It also does not help when the retailers point out that the technology does not identify a shopper's personal data like name or phone number. It's not clear exactly what they can infer from the data and how it will be tied back to a specific consumer. Companies can take this issue off the table by telling their customers exactly what they're collecting and why.

Another issue that's surfaced is that companies put in a blanket request for information in case they want to use data later. Recently, I wanted to register at a site. The form stated that if I signed in with my Facebook ID, the application had access to all my contacts, all my interests, and all my personal data—when all the site really needed was my email address and a password. I might have decided they could see my interests. Perhaps I would've shared my birthday. But why did they need my friends' information? Exactly what information would they have access to? I don't know if my friends want to release their information. In fact, I know many of them don't.

A business should give customers the ability to select which data a company can collect. For example, a travel application might need to know if you own a passport and if you have children, but a gaming application doesn't need this data. Does a news app need to collect my friends' birthdates or their religious views? Probably not.

Interestingly, some companies have more freedom to use private data than others. If a telecom company were to use consumers' private data without their knowledge or permission, people would be up in arms. If Facebook uses it, however, consumers may not be as upset, or they may complain. More than once Facebook has violated its users' privacy only to back off when people protested. But Facebook is always pushing the boundaries. If companies like your mobile phone provider made the same mistakes as Facebook, it would be disastrous. There would be lawsuits, if not pitchforks and torches.

Starts-ups frequently push the boundaries with privacy, while established companies may not be able to be as aggressive. There are several reasons for that difference: Laws were passed to regulate established companies, and users don't pay for Facebook, but they pay their cell bill. Most people, I suspect, don't look a gift horse in the mouth as carefully as they look at a service for which they have to pay.

Michael Becker, marketing development and strategic adviser for North America at Somo, a full-service mobile solutions company headquartered in Los Angeles, points out that privacy boundaries are personal. What one person finds to be a valuable service, another finds creepy and intrusive. "The best practice for any commercial entity to address the issues of privacy," says Becker, "is to start by following the core pillars of privacy management: choice (a consumer can choose to participate or not), control (he/she has control of the aspects of participating), transparency (the marketer is completely transparent as to what is going on and how it will use data) and security—the marketer is employing best practices in data security."[7]

Three Ways to Minimize Privacy Concerns

To overcome these fears, any organization that would like to gather information about individual behavior can adopt a number of strategies. The most basic is to allow customers to opt in rather than opt out. "Merchants need to be transparent with indoor location practices, and tracking consumer movement should be opt-in," says Dan Ryan, the cofounder of ByteLight, a Boston-based supplier of indoor positioning software. "An opt-in solution where consumers are in control, and ultimately receive a better shopping experience based on leveraging location data, is the most likely to succeed."[8]

A company can never fully eliminate a person's privacy concerns, but it can get a long way by improving transparency, relevancy, and value.

1. **Improve transparency, privacy settings, and the EULA.** Many privacy concerns are intimately tied to lack transparency. People want to know what data a company collects, why it's being collected, and how it's being used. Customers don't want to find out that Apple, Google, or their favorite store collects their location data and they don't know what the corporation does with it. Almost every company explains its policies in its end user licensing agreement (EULA). Every company tells users whether they are collecting their data and how they use it, but few people read the agreements because they are long documents written in legalese. Consumers click the button that says they agree to the site's policies and are then surprised and irate when they learn the implications of what they've actually agreed to share.

   EULAs are becoming more explicit. For example, many apps now say, "We have the right to see your email contacts, your address book, and your friends list." The user can decide whether that's okay. If it were not okay, of course, the person couldn't download the application. Ideally the application should give the user privacy setting options to choose what material he/she wants to allow the company to collect. It should also tell the user what they plan to do with the information.

2. **Provide relevancy and value.** The real issue with privacy seems to relate to relevance. If the data an organization wants to capture appears relevant and beneficial to the consumer, people don't have a problem with it. It's when the relevance is not clear, or if there's nothing in it for the individual, that people become angry. People will share their data if they see value in it and believe you'll protect it. If you tell me that I can turn on location services to find my phone if I lose it or automatically check in to a location, I'll be much more likely to share my information with you.

3. **Don't ask for more than you need.** Since we can now store and process vast amounts of data, some businesses want to collect everything. Executives believe they will be able use all this data somehow, at some point, even if today they don't know exactly how. Sometimes companies collect useless data because they are afraid that if they make people think too much about what they're doing, they won't opt in to give any data. But just because a program can vacuum up everything a person does with their phone and a certain app, does not mean it should.

But privacy concerns are not limited only to the way a business tracks the behaviors of its customers and prospects. Human resources departments across the globe are also debating the benefits and detriments of monitoring electronic communications and employee tracking. GPS tracking can yield incredible workforce productivity in industries such as field service, construction, and transportation.

George Karonis, founder and CEO of LiveViewGPS Inc., a Valencia, California, location-based service, points out that employee tracking "can give businesses solid data to analyze for initiatives such as improving efficiency. Businesses with lots of workers in the field making deliveries or service calls can optimize routes and schedules."

Tracking helps a business tell customers exactly where their package or service person is and how long the wait will be. It can improve response times. Karonis explains, "On-site coordinators can re-route workers in the field to respond to unscheduled calls in the most efficient way possible. The greater efficiency provided by tracking helps lower costs by reducing both downtime and overtime."[9]

A study conducted by Lamar Pierce of Washington University, Daniel Snow of Brigham Young University, and Andrew McAfee of the Massachusetts Institute of Technology looked at 392 locations of five restaurant chains. Under the surveillance cameras and software, these restaurants reported a 22 percent drop in theft and a 7 percent increase in revenue.[10] Both of these examples illustrate that some level of tracking helps improve business productivity.

Unlike the consumer examples, the people in these situations are being paid to do a job, and monitoring progress isn't new. Employers have always had tools to track certain aspects of employee behavior. Most companies have policies that state the firm can log and read emails and voice calls from all corporate accounts. However, workers started to take more notice when they discovered their employers might be able to use data from their personal cell phones to track their location. With people using personal devices for work, the rules are unclear on exactly what employers can legally access. Does my company have the right to see that I'm playing Angry Birds and posting on Facebook on my own iPhone during office hours?

To alleviate concerns over a company being able to monitor its employee's personal device use, companies can purchase a solution that allows the business to manage, track, and secure just the corporate data on the employee's personal device. All personal apps and data aren't viewed by the corporation. I discuss this software in further detail in Chapter 8.

While the law in this area is still evolving, it seems clear that employers can monitor employee Internet usage on company equipment and should be able to track its own vehicles. A business can record keystrokes on employee computers and capture all company email.[11] If the company purchased and supplied the employee with a mobile device, many of the same rules apply. Whether the company can track the location of the device is normally determined by the nature of the job. And in most cases, the device can only be tracked during business hours.

The same principles that would help consumers overcome privacy concerns will also work for a company's employees. As in the consumer world, employers must be transparent about what they are tracking and be careful that they are not monitoring employee personal time or personal communications. In each case, both customers and employees need to know what data you're collecting. In the case of employees, their employment contract may require them to forgo certain rights that a consumer would have. These exceptions should be discussed during an employment interview or before a policy change, such as GPS tracking of delivery trucks, takes place.

In the SMS and email domain, we've already created many good privacy policies and procedures that can be applied. Many of these would be applicable to new mobile communications. To get a sense of the most up-to-date information on the topic, I encourage people to review the latest published guidelines from CTIA and the GSMA.[12] This issue won't go away but it will evolve over time. It's crucial that an organization dedicates resources and creates procedures to ensure it is continually reviewing and updating its privacy policies based on what data is available.

Problems of Security and Compliance

Security concerns have existed since the dawn of e-commerce. The types of threats just continue to multiply and change over time. In the current landscape, businesses reasonably fear the security vulnerabilities that cloud computing and mobility may enable.

One challenge (among many) of this connected landscape and information torrent is protecting the data from those who should not have it. Mobile computing presents a new set of security challenges. In fact, over 75 percent of the IT leaders interviewed for the *Q2/2014 Lopez Research Enterprise Mobility Benchmark* ranked security as their top concern with mobility. With the variety of new devices and operating systems, mobile is proving difficult to manage. Ray Potter, CEO of the security company SafeLogic, summed up the issues and concerns when he told me, "Mobile security is all about controlling and protecting sensitive data that is accessible anywhere in the world from a low cost yet powerful device. Enterprises are concerned about confidentiality, availability, and integrity of data, which happen to be the three pillars of information security. Security is vitally important because company secrets, roadmaps, source code, etc. are all accessible by devices that can be easily lost, stolen, or hacked. True mobile security provides protection of data against unauthorized device users in all scenarios of this kind."[13]

This challenge also relates to another key technology trend—cloud computing. Many companies have stalled cloud computing deployments due to security fears. Compliance also inhibits the adoption of new technologies and richer use of data. One of my clients told me recently, "We have to comply with Sarbanes-Oxley regulation. These regulations are pretty loose and liberal in their language. When our security people look at something, they don't see any flexibility in it. All they see is the opportunity for risk. Given the way the regulations are written, if our security experts can't be absolutely sure that our process meets the security guidelines, they won't do anything. They just lock everything down."

However, there is debate in the industry as to the extent of potential security risks in the industry. Vijay Basani, the cofounder, president, and CEO of EiQ Networks, a security and compliance solution provider headquartered in Acton, Massachusetts, writes, "While cloud service providers (CSPs) are loath to disclose details of attacks against their networks, hackers are clearly paying attention." He adds that the cloud can be a safe place to keep data, but only when customers, who are ultimately responsible for the security and integrity of their own data, adopt proper measures to keep it safe.[14]

David Black, chief information security officer at Aon eSolutions, believes this feat may be overstated. He says, "The reality is that cloud vendors know that security is the big risk to their entire business model. If they were to experience a major breach, they're sure to go out of business."[15]

The Rightscale 2014 state-of-the-cloud survey of 1,068 professionals highlights that security concerns are lessened once a company has evaluated and used cloud services. It states, "Security remains the most-often cited challenge among Cloud Beginners (31 percent) but decreases to the fifth most cited (13 percent) among Cloud Focused organizations. As organizations become more experienced in cloud security options and best practices, the less of a concern cloud security becomes."[16]

For highly regulated industries compliance remains a common issue across countries. For example, many medical institutions have restrictions on how they store and use patient data. Financial institutions need auditable records of digital and voice conversations with clients. Over the past several years, many vendors have begun to offer special solutions that have been tested and certified as meeting regulatory guidelines. For example, Citrix ShareFile launched a service in late 2013 for healthcare providers. Global carriers, such as NTT and Vodaphone, offer cloud security and compliance services. One way to address compliance issues is to look for cloud services that meet these specific requirements. In the mobile arena specifically, a business should add mobile management and security software to secure data on mobile devices. In general, a business should always test its software to catch potential vulnerabilities that a hacker could exploit. In Chapter 8, I discuss some of the strategies to minimize the security and compliance risks associated with mobility.

Privacy and security concerns are valid issues, but executives sometimes use them as an excuse to avoid change. They say, "We can't do this because it violates privacy rules. We can't do that for security reasons." Some risk exists no matter what management decides to do—or not do. The risk of doing nothing, however, is often greater than doing something after investigating the dangers and requirements. Caution is required but there are various government and industry work groups that have published guidelines that can help companies build basic privacy and security policies. Businesses can't avoid the move to mobile and cloud because the bulk of technology innovation will be focused on advancing those solutions. A business needs to understand its risk tolerance and actively seek out solutions that provide the right level of protection for its risk profile.

Summary

Most businesses are holding onto the past. And the past has departed. Bridging services and goods from the past is a step in the right direction, but it's not enough to make the transition into the new world that is evolving before our eyes. For example, you can make your software accessible in the cloud, but if you don't change the user interface, it won't operate effectively on a wide range of devices.

Business differentiation also requires more than simply adapting to existing circumstances. Executives must acknowledge the shift in the market, adapt to the trend, and evolve the enterprise's products and services to the next logical state. But many industries' and businesses' executives tend to fight an undeniable shift in their marketplace rather than adopt the new possibilities.

The rise of mobile, big data, social media, and cloud computing has irreversibly changed customer and employee expectations. Customers expect companies to respond to issues and opportunities in real time. Employees expect the business to provide access to meaningful information on the go and at the time of a decision. Creating competitive differentiation requires an organization to deliver valuable insights from data in near-real time and eventually offer predicitive capabilities. It also requires agility that most companies don't have and that many businesses aren't capable of building.

The market dynamics in every industry have morphed and will continue to move in new and unpredictable ways. Businesses must change or risk extinction. A company's management must decide which path the company will follow. Is it the path of change or is it the path of least resistance? The path of change is difficult and fraught with danger. That path, however, offers the greatest opportunity for a long-standing and competitive business. Following the path of least resistance—that is, business as usual—may seem prudent. It's certainly less disruptive, but it cripples an organization's ability to thrive and grow.

Privacy, both consumer and employee, is an issue. Security is an issue. Generic service, complexity, and difficulty with data are all legitimate concerns. Decision makers will have to address these concerns. If they simply throw up their hands and do nothing, competitors who overcame the same concerns will overtake their organizations.

Organizations that thrive in this brave new world will be those that create the right experiences for customers, employees, partners, and other stakeholders. The next four chapters show why the new realities demand what I call right-time experiences. These chapters will also highlight three types of experiences—communications, care, and commerce—and what makes these experiences so valuable.

Notes

1. Marshall McLuhan, *The Medium Is the Message* (Berkeley, CA: Gingko Press, 2001), 74.
2. Brian Solis, *The End of Business as Usual: Rewire the Way You Work to Succeed in the Consumer Revolution* (Hoboken, NJ: John Wiley & Sons, 2011).
3. www.businessweek.com/articles/2013-10-01/the-most-valuable-brands-in-america-2000-to-2013.
4. January 13, 2014, phone interview with Neil Cohen.
5. www.apple.com/pr/library/2011/04/27Apple-Q-A-on-Location-Data.html.
6. www.marketwired.com/press-release/truste-releases-us-consumer-findings-from-2012-online-mobile-privacy-perceptions-report-1680156.htm.
7. Stephanie Miles, "Strategies for Overcoming Privacy Concerns with Indoor Navigation Apps," August 22, 2013, http://streetfightmag.com/2013/08/22/strategies-for-overcoming-privacy-concerns-with-indoor-navigation-apps/.
8. Stephanie Miles, "Strategies for Overcoming Privacy Concerns with Indoor Navigation Apps," http://streetfightmag.com/2013/08/22/strategies-for-overcoming-privacy-concerns-with-indoor-navigation-apps/.
9. George Karonis, "Are Businesses Crossing Lines by Tracking Employees?" *Life & Health Advisor*, June 28, 2013, www.lifehealth.com.
10. Joshua Brustein, "Your Boss Won't Stop Spying on You (Because It Works)," *Bloomberg Business Week*, August 27, 2013, www.businessweek.com.
11. Donna Ballman, "10 New (and Legal) Ways Your Employer Is Spying on You," Aol Jobs, September 29, 2013, http://jobs.aol.com/articles/2013/09/29/new-ways-employer-spy/.
12. Privacy policy guidelines on the CTIA website can be found at www.ctia.org/policy-initiatives/policy-topics/privacy. Privacy guidelines for the GSMA site can be found at www.gsma.com/publicpolicy/mobile-and-privacy.
13. In-person interview with Safe logic CEO Ray Potter in September 2013.
14. Vijay Basani, "Keeping Your Cloud Environment Safe," *Innovation Insights, Wired*, September 3, 2013.
15. Russ Banham, "Cloud Computing Data Breaches Are Currently Few," June 24, 2014, http://www.businessinsurance.com/article/99999999/NEWS070101/39999805/Russ.
16. Rightscale, "State of the Cloud Report," February 2014, http://assets.rightscale.com/uploads/pdfs/RightScale-2014-State-of-the-Cloud-Report.pdf.

PART II

WHY RIGHT-TIME EXPERIENCES ARE KEY

New market models offer both opportunities and threats for established businesses. Threats include:

- Shrinking revenue and profits
- Contraction and substitution
- Diminishing control over the market because an organization cannot force customers to do anything, nor can it keep competitors out of the market due to low barriers to entry

New technology—mobile, big data, cloud computing—creates new possibilities as well. Opportunities include improved efficiencies, one-to-one relationships, and real-time intelligence and action. Companies see the change in business, but many are still operating under the constraints of tired business processes even as they attempt to offer services for the new world.

Companies that hope to flourish will have to change their applications and services to take advantage of these new opportunities. Businesses will need to create what I'm calling right-time experiences (RTEs). Basically, this is providing information and services that consumers, employees, and partners need (or would like to have) when they need it.

Right-time experiences are products, services, and workflows that offer a person the right information and services at the point of need or desire.

As I've pointed out, technology has set massive forces in motion. Organizations have options to embrace efficiencies and offer opportunities to customers, employees, and partners that were not possible in the past. To do so, however, means leveraging the technology to create much more dynamic business processes or services based on this information and means of delivery the enterprise never had access to before.

The new realities demand right-time experiences. In the chapters ahead, I discuss ways in which communications, care for both employees and customers, and commerce are being transformed by mobile, big data, and cloud computing.

CHAPTER

3

New Realities Demand New Right-Time Experiences

In the Chapter 2, I discussed how many of today's Internet experiences and business processes are complex or generic or lack critical information that a person needs to make a decision. If existing business practices are becoming outdated—and many of them already are—what does a company need to be successful? Businesses need to leverage the new market forces to create right-time experiences.

These experiences are information and services that your customers, employees, and partners need to take the next logical action. That action could be making a purchase, reserving a flight, finding a purchase order, or submitting an expense report. Leading companies, regardless of the type of product or service, offer a winning brand experience. This experience permeates every aspect of how the customer interacts with that brand, from its ads to the packaging, the product, the customer service, and the sales processes. Today's great companies—from Coke to Apple to Salesforce—are doing this in various interesting ways.

There are countless ways that we can use information from mobile devices, social media, sensors, and transaction data to build better experiences. Smartphones, tablets, and other devices can be used to exploit the information conveniently, wherever a person may be.

The concept behind right-time experiences is to deliver the right information, to the right person, on their device of choice at the point of need or the point of desire. To do this, an organization needs to analyze the wealth of data that is now available and deliver something worthwhile to its customers, employees, and partners in a valuable format. I am not going to pretend for a moment this is simple. If it were easy, everyone would be doing it.

Instead of using generic processes that haven't changed significantly since the smartphone's introduction, we want to provide relevant services that adapt to the user and his or her current environment. If a person is driving, what does he need, and how does that compare to what a person needs while sitting in a meeting? How does gathering the right information change when I'm on a smartphone versus a tablet versus a PC? Companies will grow or get buried based on their ability to give users the right experience when they need it. This applies to a company's customers, employees, partners, or all three. Right-time experiences differ from what we generally have today because, unlike generic experiences, they are contextual, adaptive, and connected (see Figures 3.1a and 3.1b). I'll describe this in more detail in a moment, but first I'd like to provide several examples of right-time experiences.

Let's take an example of Coca-Cola and how it delivers on its brand promise by offering right-time experiences to its customers and partners. I'm thirsty. I need a Coke now. I'm at a vending machine, but I have no money. Can I purchase through my phone? Yes! What happens next is unknown to me but important for the next customer

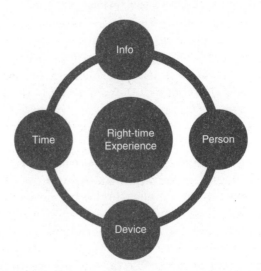

Figure 3.1a   RTEs Deliver the Right Info to the Right Person on Their Device of Choice

Source: Lopez Research LLC.

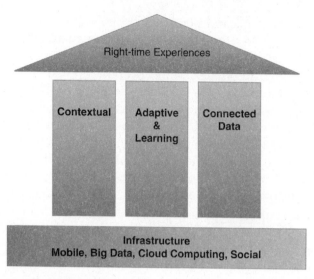

Figure 3.1b   The Three Pillars of RTE

Source: Lopez Research LLC.

and for Coca-Cola's bottle distribution partner: The vending machine can send a real-time message to the distribution center that it's low on Diet Coke.

A nearby driver with Diet Cokes in her truck will be alerted to this issue and sent to the vending machine to refill it. Instead of aimlessly sending the bottle distributor to every vending machine, the bottle distributor, Coca-Cola Enterprises, visits only the machines that need products. It doesn't waste fuel or employee resources. Coca-Cola, the beverage company, delights its customers by always having the right product where it is needed. The customer is happy because he could buy the right product without needing to use cash. These are three RTEs related to one transaction, and they create a great brand experience for Coca-Cola.

First Republic Bank offers an example of a right-time experience with a mobile application that is simple yet offers all of the necessary tasks a person needs. The interface is simple, with a few icons and a large font. The menu items are action oriented and easy to understand, such as "Transfer money," "Pay bills," and "Deposit checks." The app doesn't clutter the screen with features you won't use. It focuses on the basics of what a person may need to do on the go. It doesn't assume you'll want mortgage information on the home page or access to the entire website. Many people want to use a mobile app to find a branch location, so this has its own field.

Everything that isn't absolutely necessary is accessible from a "More" tab. First Republic's brand proposition is that it is customer focused and willing to service you via the method that works for you. The company used the "More" tab to deliver on its brand proposition by offering three ways for the user to connect to First Republic: email, phone, and the website. While strikingly simple, this leverages most of the features that are available from a mobile device. It uses the GPS to help a consumer locate a branch. It provides a way for the consumer to call or email the company. It uses the camera to offer deposits on the go. And if you need more detail, you can touch a button to get to the main website.

A First Republic client with a smartphone can have access to the right information at the right time wherever he or she may be. Now that you have some sense of what a right-time experience might look like, I'll describe the three elements of the experience.

Contextual Computing Leads to Insight

Not everyone needs or wants the same thing when using an application or visiting a website. Because of that reality, context becomes both interesting and useful. Who is the person visiting the site or the application? What time is it? Where is he? When did he visit in the past? What is he viewing or doing at this moment, and how does it relate to what he's recently done? All this contextual information can help the organization deliver the most meaningful, rewarding, and worthwhile experience. Theoretically, websites are supposed to offer these contextual and personalized services today. If I go to a website I've visited before, it might come up with "Hello, Maribel," but that's about the extent of the personalization one sees. For the most part, very little, if anything, changes as a result of the site knowing I visited it in the past or purchased certain items. The same is true with mobile apps.

Successful companies will deliver more compelling experiences by collecting and analyzing contextual data, including location, time of day, previous transactions, and device type. Sensors in the latest devices also furnish physical context, such as temperature, humidity, motion, and more. These data sources provide situational and environmental information about people, places, and things. By understanding an individual's current situation and previous history, a business can anticipate her immediate needs and offer experiences appropriate for the individual's situation. Most businesses have made limited use of context and customer records to date, but the collection and analysis of contextual data will supply the foundation for right-time experiences. This collection and analysis is where the new category of big data and analysis tools that I'll be discussing in Chapter 9 comes into play.

Mobility plays a key role in delivering right-time experiences. Mobile means more than just access to voice calls, email, and the Internet on the go. Sensors with these devices provide a foundation for contextual services, and connectivity provides a way to communicate data and delivery services. But while I find executives are much more familiar with the concept of context today than they were in the past, I don't believe many of them understand what that means for their business. And not everyone understands the definition of *context* or *contextual service.*

Marketing executives have discussed contextual services in the past, but these were usually focused on creating targeted advertising to consumers. Right-time experiences are contextual services that encompass far more than precisely tailored advertising messages. They expand to involve products and processes that meet the distinctive needs of different constituents:

- **Business to consumer (B2C).** The right information and services to live a richer, fuller life.
- **Business to employee (B2E).** The right information to perform efficiently and effectively at work.
- **Business to partners (B2P).** The right information and services to build a viable business ecosystem between companies.
- **Things to things (T2T) and things to people (T2C).** The right information sent from a connected device to a business system for automating tasks (for example, an alert from your basement to your smartphone saying you have a leak in the basement). Sensors in things can also communicate with individuals to provide information about how the device is functioning (for example, an alert from the HVAC system telling the building manager to order and install new air filters).

Context is one element of a right-time experience. However, many people think of context only as location: Where exactly is this employee, this customer, this package, this truck, or this container right now? Location is one of the most important contextual elements but not the only element. There are many other types of contextual elements, such as device type, transaction history, and time of day. Device type can be used to understand whether the device has a big or a small screen, and the application or web page can respond with the appropriate amount of text or imaging to fill the screen. Transaction history may mean an opportunity to cross-sell—or to demand payment on delivery. Time of day means marketers can send different types of messages at the times when they are most likely to be read *and* acted upon.

It's worth noting that smartphones and tablets are the most contextual devices that ever existed. Before we had these devices, we didn't have enough information to create contextual services. Today, even a low-end smartphone can capture multiples types of contextual information.

If we ask our customers, prospects, and employees to opt in, we have the opportunity to understand how people are using applications and services on a device. People will opt in for services that make their lives better and improve their everyday experiences. Social networks are an ideal example of how consumers are willing to exchange information, such as location and photos, for the value of communicating more efficiently with friends and loved ones.

There are at least nine types of contextual elements that organizations should consider incorporating into their business processes to deliver right-time experiences. These include, but are not limited to, location, time, and current process (see Figure 3.2). Let's investigate what each of these elements is and what type of right-time experiences they could possibly provide.

Location

Firms can use location to tailor the type and occasion of a right-time experience. Right-time experiences mean providing different services based on knowing if the user is at home, in the mall, at the office, or at a customer's site. Multiple types of location technologies—triangulation, Bluetooth, wireless location signatures (WLS), and GPS—may be combined to locate both people and things. As manufacturers outfit more devices with sensors and communications technology, everyday items will start communicating with people. We already live

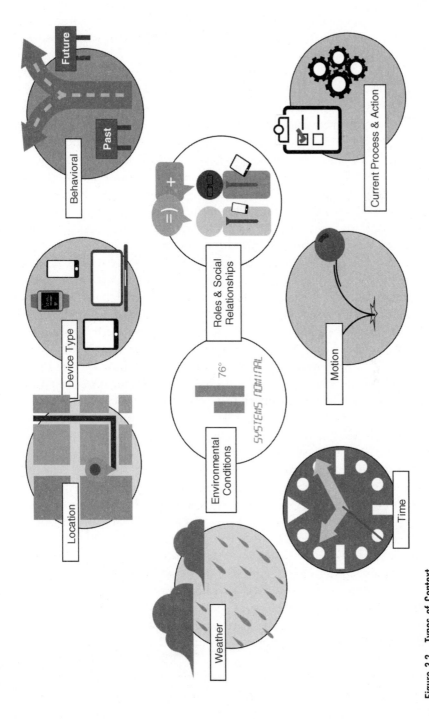

Figure 3.2 Types of Context

Source: Lopez Research LLC.

in a world in which, if you're driving to a meeting in downtown Los Angeles, your car can connect to a service that will identify available parking spots.

Google Now provides an example of a right-time experience that uses location, search history, and calendar services to create a smart interface with relevant data for consumers. It uses analytics to create both predictive and prescriptive experiences for the user. For example, it compiles information about what the user has searched for in the past and communicates suggestions and information based on a user's specific location. It might suggest a new Indian restaurant that is near the user's location based on previous search terms. Since it has access to the user's calendar and location, it can also offer prescriptive advice, such as when to leave for a meeting to avoid congestion and ensure the user reaches her appointment as scheduled.

A friend of mine told me how his iPhone knows that he teaches a class every Monday night (because it's in his calendar) and alerts him of the traffic conditions near the time he's supposed to depart. Since he's turned on location services, the phone is also aware of other places he goes regularly and can proactively alert him to the traffic conditions along that route. He said the first time this happened, it was strange, but he quickly grew to appreciate how his phone could now anticipate his needs. This is a perfect example of a right-time experience based on context. It's also an example of how right-time experiences can be predictive and prescriptive, which I'll discuss in a moment.

Companies can use location data to create a *geofence*, a sensor-based virtual boundary around physical spaces, such as a business, a mall, or a sporting venue. A business owner or manager has the opportunity to trigger communications and automate tasks based on a person entering or exiting the geofenced area. Retailers have been adding geofences for some time to track when customers are near their retail location or have entered the store. For those customers who have opted into the system, the retailer can use mobile SMS alerts or push messaging to promote upcoming in-store promotions or send an electronic coupon when the prospect is near its retail locations. Today, a majority of these push notifications are generic. In the future, as consumers become more comfortable with the technology, retailers will be able to build right-time experiences targeted to individuals.

Consumers can also use the concept of location to automate how they access their applications and services. Cover, acquired by Twitter in April 2014, offered a smartphone lock screen for Android that was contextually aware. The software learns when and where you use different apps and puts them on your phone's lock screen for easy access. It automatically recognizes when you're at home, at work, or in the car. If you're in the car, it brings the maps application front and center. At work, it might surface your calendar and document management app, such as Box.com. The user can also set a custom ring volume and wallpaper for each location. Cover markets itself as "the right apps at the right time." This is an example of a right-time experience in which an overlay application can use location and time to make it easier to use existing apps and services.

Businesses can also use location to provide better business-to-employee experiences. Geofences are becoming popular in all types of locations and industries. Geofencing is a type of location-based service that sends messages to smartphone users who enter a defined geographic area. You may be familiar with this from your shopping experience. Some stores have created geofences that will send a message or promotion to your smartphone when you enter the store or when you've walked past a certain item. Lets look at how this might also be used in a business-to-employee example. If an employee enters the geofence, a workflow could be initiated or a message delivered. A construction firm, for example, can link a mobile device's location to a timekeeping system to automatically log when a worker enters or leaves the work site.

Location services can also provide "things to people" alerts. For example, Elgato's Smart Key is a small device that can be connected to your keys or any number of devices. An app on an iPhone can notify the user whenever he leaves his key behind, let him know where it was last seen, or help him find it by playing a sound. Since it can be attached to many things, people have gotten very creative with the use of this technology. They use it to find their cars, notify them when their luggage arrives at the airport carrousel, and protect their bags against theft while traveling. Alerting you that you've left your keys before you leave the house or immediately letting you know that your bag has been stolen is the essence of a right-time experience. It's pertinent information that's delivered in a timely fashion.

These connected devices can also communicate with business systems to automate and enhance operations. If a data center's temperature rises above a certain level, for example, the cooling system software could access the data in order to determine if there is a problem and automatically send a repair request to the maintenance company.

Time

Creating an optimal experience frequently requires understanding the time of day. An experience that is welcomed at breakfast (for example, a business news summary) is a distraction during a customer meeting. While right-time experiences benefit from real-time data, they do not have to be in real time but can happen at the moment of need or at a specific time of day. An individual may desire different services or communications based on the time of day. She may need traffic conditions and school closing information before breakfast. The exact same information can be useless by lunchtime. Vishi Gopalakrishnan, product manager for AT&T's Unified Collaboration group, says, "We don't want to send somebody an ad for Cheerios at ten o'clock at night, or an ad for gin at seven in the morning."[1] On the other hand, a friend noted that Ernest Hemingway might've loved that. So the dimension of the right time can vary based on a person's behavior. Someone who works the night shift will arguably engage with services at a different time than someone who works from 9 A.M. to 5 P.M.

Companies can employ time data in conjunction with data about an individual's previous behaviors to understand the optimal type of communication and the optimal time to deliver it. A grocery store, for example, may send a text message at five o'clock to alert a commuting customer that the rotisserie chicken he's bought in the past is on sale.

Another dimension of time is based on providing the right information or service at the optimal moment. The optimal time for a communication or service relates to reacting to a change in situation. The director of sales, for example, wants to be alerted to a large customer win or loss before she enters a meeting with management. Truckers can use real-time traffic data in applications to reduce the time they spend in traffic, waiting for an open loading dock, and being on the road.

Current Process and Action

Process helps determine the flow of transaction and what information, product, or service may be most valuable in the context of completing that process or action. People frequently start and stop processes and workflows. Many processes aren't finished and are abandoned altogether because someone doesn't have enough information.

Right-time experiences will require businesses to link data across systems so the user has the right information at the point of need. For example, a procurement manager who is ordering a large quantity of a specific supply would want to know if the product is out of stock, whether the product's price will change before the order is approved, and what alternatives may be available. Before approving an employee's vacation request, a manager should know who's already on vacation and what job functions will need to be filled in the employee's absence.

Other times, a person may have started a process but doesn't want to go through the motions of completing the entire process over again from scratch. One thing the web world and e-commerce have taught us is the concept of maintaining persistence of a process across time. If you were interrupted during an online shopping process, many websites will save the items in your shopping cart in the hope that you will return. If you are signed in to a website, the site may send you an email reminder that you abandoned your cart and the items are still available.

One of the benefits of mobile is that you can accomplish a task when you are away from your home or office. However, a person may only have a few moments to complete a transaction. Delivering a right-time experience means that a person starts a transaction at one time and finishes at a later time when it's more convenient. For example, I might initiate a product refund request while I'm in line at Starbucks but I will need to stop the process while I order the coffee. In an ideal world, I'd be able to return to the app at a later time and pick up exactly where I left off.

Building a right-time experience will require a company to create this concept of persistence across a wide range of devices and processes. Netflix provides an early example of how to use persistence to create a right-time experience. You can start watching a program on your TV, stop the program, and return to it at exactly where you left off on another Netflix-connected device, such as a tablet. You could do this an hour later or days later. It's a seamless viewing (process) experience that is portable across devices and across time. It's the same case if you start an expense report or any work process. You'd like your data to be saved, and you'd like to return to exactly where you left off.

Speaking of devices, let's review some ways that device type and presence provide context to deliver right-time experiences.

Device Type, Device State, and Presence

Right-time experiences should recognize and adapt to the user's device and the quality of the network. The software should automatically adjust how it presents the information based on the screen size and what navigation methods (touch, voice, gesture) are available.

Given that people will be moving around with more than one connected device, device presence will highlight what a person is using at that moment. Presence will span across devices to include nontraditional devices such as cars, wearables, conference rooms, and videoconferencing equipment. A right-time experience can be as simple as using your smartphone to find out what conference rooms actually have people sitting in them versus what conference rooms have been reserved.

Right-time experiences will also make use of device-type capabilities (e.g., video, touch screen, accelerometers). For example, expense account software should sense the presence of a camera and prompt the user to photograph receipts. Today, the Plantronics Voyager Bluetooth headset knows if you've placed it on your ear and will automatically shift audio to the headset. If you take it off, the audio will switch back to your phone. Plantronics' Concept One headset can do head tracking and free-fall detection. This would be useful if, for example, a person fell; the headset could send a message to the phone to call a relative. If you're looking for a product in a store, the store's mobile app could pair with the device, gauge where you are looking based on your head's position, and guide you to a product with voice or image overlays. Another example of this is the new Amazon phone launched in June 2014. The Amazon phone screen has an interface called Dynamic Perspective to adjust the 3D image on the phone's screen to match users' head position.

A simple but powerful use of device context is understanding if a device's battery is charged and modifying the application functions to conserve battery life. New functions such as flexible screens, visual search, 3D imaging, holograms, and voice commands will change what types of experiences companies can offer on new smartphones, tablets, and other devices. These ways of interacting with each other and with computers were fictional a decade ago. Today, I can navigate web pages using eye tracking on a Samsung smartphone. The cinematic vision of the future has arrived, and it's available today on a smartphone near you.

Social and Behavioral

Behavioral context will help a business decide the next best action based on how the employee or customer has behaved in the past. One customer always responds to coupons for jeans, for example. One salesperson always opens her customer relationship software to the follow-up screen. Right-time experiences will learn how individuals routinely use their services and create preferences based on these behaviors and user-defined attributes.

In all of these communications, the company should be delivering on its brand proposition. Is the company a trusted partner, a low-cost provider, or an experience provider? For example, Virgin America is an airline that frequently offers low airfares, but it's actually selling a travel experience. One example of this is its interactive system, called RED. The airline uses the screens on the back of airline seats as ordering terminals for food, beverages, and entertainment. Instead of waiting for a flight attendant to arrive at their seat, passengers can order food and beverages when they want them. They can pay at their seat without providing the card to the flight attendant. If they desire, they can purchase and send a beverage to another person on board.

If you're a frequent flyer, the airline wants to use information from your previous transactions to customize your future experiences. If you purchased an animated movie or a cocktail on your last flight, Virgin America may decide to recommend other movies you may like and make it easy for you to order your favorite beverage. While air travel could be generic, Virgin America found a way to personalize it. With a customer's opt-in, the airline can build even more customized services based on contextual items, such as previous behaviors.

Environmental Conditions

Future devices will have embedded sensors that will provide environmental conditions to context-aware applications and services. Types of environmental context could include air quality, temperature, humidity, and weather forecast. For example, a transportation company can use sensors in trucks to ensure the delivery of fresh produce on time by monitoring temperature and humidity during the delivery process.

Connected sensors will be used by many industries, with utility, oil, and gas industries leading the way. In the future, a utility technician could use a device's sensor to tell if there is a gas leak in the building before entering it, and airport security could scan for hazardous toxins.

The agriculture and transportation industries are already using weather data to decide when to plant or how to route trucks around snowstorms in the Midwest. Other, less obvious industries will also use weather information. Public utility companies need to monitor extremes in weather to ensure they are prepared to deliver sufficient electricity or gas to the population. Commodity traders make a number of decisions based on weather data. A freeze in Florida is likely to affect the price of citrus or crops, for example.

Construction workers carefully observe data, looking for periods to pour concrete or operate a crane. One construction company told me they use weather data to minimize fraudulent workmen's compensations claims. For example, if a construction worker said she slipped on a roof due to rain, the company uses historical weather data to confirm it actually rained that day.

In your home, your thermostat will connect to the local hourly weather forecast to decide when it should begin heating the house. Weather data will also integrate with your calendar to predict when you should leave the house to reach the office on time or if your flight is likely to be delayed.

Roles and Social Relationships

Individuals play different roles among a wide variety of relationships. By combining and analyzing data from social networks and documents or information a person has shared, companies can understand how people feel about their personal and work experiences.

In the consumer landscape, there is a wide range of data being shared in public social networks. Companies are mining sources such as Twitter, Facebook, and LinkedIn to understand what topics people are interested in, how they feel about products, and how individuals are related to one another. New interest-based social networks, such as Pinterest and Houz, are visual discovery tools that you can use to find ideas for home projects or other interests such as fashion ideas. These interest-based social networks even provide methods for collecting both individual preferences (personal context) and market trends (group sentiment).

In the business world, the same concept of roles and relationships applies. Today, roles are defined by your job function. Within the organization, companies will use information from enterprise social business and collaboration tools, such as Yammer and Jive, to evaluate existing team structures, roles, and responsibilities. For example, a company could link its contact center solution to social software to discover hidden experts and content within the firm's collaboration systems.

A company can discover an employee's or customer's current needs and uncover latent desires. Understanding how an individual feels about an issue will help brands and organizations build services that are better suited to a customer's or employee's actual needs. Businesses have started to use sentiment analysis to improve business processes, customer care, and existing products. This trend will continue.

Motion

The presence or lack of motion can be used to define if and how an experience should proceed. A connected medicine bottle cap, such as those from Vitality, can sense when a patient last opened the bottle and will send reminders if the patient forgets to take the medication. For medications that lack caps, the company offers a connected pouch that has sensors in it. The pouch logs if it's been opened as a form of tracking whether the patient has taken his medication.

Sensors in the latest devices provide environmental conditions such as temperature and humidity as well as magnetometers and accelerometers for direction and orientation. Companies can use this data to monitor corporate asset health and improve service uptime. For example, motion sensors in machinery could transmit alerts to headquarters to schedule maintenance and prevent unplanned outages. GE is building these types of services today. It collects and analyzes high volumes of sensor data to predict product performance and maintenance needs and to avoid unplanned downtime in industrial equipment such as turbines, jet engines, and locomotives.

Brian Courtney from GE's Intelligent Data Platforms says, "When we sell a jet engine, in a way we sell up time. We don't actually sell the engine. We monitor the jet engine and we fix little issues before they become big issues. We've put systems in place to monitor tens of thousands of jet engines. This is what makes GE's jet engines better than anybody else's."[2]

Context Matters

Within the contexts outlined above, a business can assess intent, which helps it anticipate a customer's or an employee's future behavior. Context provides the situational awareness that doesn't exist in today's transactions. Situational awareness moves us from transactional processes with limited insight to meaningful engagement. Contextual services will pull in a multitude of data points, analyze this flood, and present individuals with a set of options for how to act or react.

Many businesses are already adding a single element of context, such as location, into business processes. Companies should enhance these products with additional layers of context to create more valuable and unique experiences. Right-time experiences combine information from different sources, such as time, location, and schedule, to improve an interaction. Southwest Airlines Cargo provides an example of how adding one element of context can improve a service—and adding multiple types can make a service indispensable.

The airline adopted sensor-enabled asset tracking to provide its customers with visibility into the location of cargo shipments in the air and on the ground. The airline also created a better right-time experience by adding other contextual data, such as temperature alerts during transit and response capabilities in the event of a breakage.

Right-time experiences shouldn't require customers or employees to change their behavior to enjoy a better experience. Food chain Pret A Manger provides an example of this with its mobile website. The chain has optimized its website to respond to the time of day and the user's proximity to a Pret shop and to reformat the screen automatically to fit the type of device the consumer is using. GPS functionality displays the details of the closest shop, including the manager's name, walking directions, opening hours, and contact details. Pret A Manger illustrates how a business can create a rich contextual experience on the web without requiring a consumer to download a specialized application.

Adaptive Makes Interactions Personal

Understanding context alone isn't enough to build a right-time experience. Business processes and products must be designed to adapt to context, such as behaviors and device type. A right-time experience should also be learning, predictive, and prescriptive.

Right-time experiences will automate workflows, streamline content discovery, and build knowledge iteratively over time as employees and customers use an application. Adaptive design will change a user's experience to accommodate the capabilities and limitations of the device or the user's role.

Today's applications and services were built for mass consumption and designed to work on a specific device. Right-time experiences will adapt as a person moves between devices such as from a laptop to a smartphone to a tablet. For example, while an entire product catalog could be displayed on a tablet, only the product name and price would be displayed on a smartphone. It will also change based on what the user is doing at that time. If a sales employee apparently tries to access a sensitive financial file at 3:00 A.M. from a tablet located in a hostile foreign nation, the security system should understand prior behavior and be smart enough to deny access permissions.

Or, the application could take another approach and tell me, "Hi, Maribel. In the past, you've eaten Italian food at our other properties. We have a great Italian restaurant here. Let me show you how to navigate to it." This is the concept of taking the context, analyzing it—in this case, a real-time analysis—and then making a suggestion as a result of it, a suggestion I can either follow or ignore.

The hotel can communicate with me and send me a push notification that says, in effect, we know you're here; you're probably looking for lunch, and here are some suggestions. That is the concept of being adaptive; it means that over time, the application can learn how people react to different messages or different suggestions.

It is possible to write software in a way that it learns and adapts to a user's behavior. In time it can, for example, take a customer to the screen showing the one-pound Earl Grey loose tea because it has learned that every two or three months, this customer reorders that product from the several hundred varieties and package sizes the site offers. Or, I might want to go directly to my watch list on eBay; the eBay mobile app learns this and always takes me there first. A salesperson may always start his day looking at his prospects list in Salesforce.com.

If the user's context changes, the right-time experience should automatically adapt. Right-time experiences will analyze a person's transaction history, analyze data from her current condition, and respond with data that is relevant to the individual or to a specific occurrence. The best right-time experiences will make the technology seemingly disappear, leaving people free to do their job or perform a task without learning how to use an application or a service.

What could a learning and predictive right-time experience look like? MGM's Bellagio hotel provides an example of this today. If I am standing at the restaurant row in a casino for any length of time, the casino has the opportunity to improve my experience. The Cisco wireless network at the Bellagio hotel in Las Vegas could recognize that I am standing in restaurant row (location) and that I've been standing there for 10 minutes (dwell time). It could then alert the marketing software of this. The marketing software would analyze this data and infer that I may be trying to decide what restaurant to select.

The system knows that it's 12:30 P.M. and all of the restaurants are packed (time of day and asset utilization). It knows from my hotel reservation that I am traveling with my family. If it's connected into the hotel's restaurant reservations system, it knows I like Chinese food based on my previous stay (customer records and behavior). It can use the hotel's mobile app that I've downloaded to my phone to send me a message that is targeted to my behavior at that time. The message could say, "Maribel, Noodles has a 1-hour wait for a table for four, but Café Bellagio has only a 15-minute wait. Would you like to make a reservation?" It's an assistive experience that helps me easily accomplish my goals (eating) and helps the hotel make an additional sale.

What could this look like in a business-to-employee scenario? Similar to consumer services, today's rigid employee apps will also be replaced by adaptive and predictive applications and cloud-resident services. Kana's contact center desktop experience provides an example on the enterprise side. Rather than burden agents with all sorts of options, the desktop presents the exact information that applies to the task at hand. If the conversation with the customer shifts, the software offers continuously updated options as events unfold. The system learns and adapts over time. With the right information at their fingertips, agents solve problems faster, often on first contact.

This is the concept of learning how customers and employees use an application and working overtime to make the experience seamless. It's happening as enterprise software moves to the cloud and it will continue as we develop new mobile software. My next car will probably recognize me by my smartphone, unlock the driver-side door, automatically adjust the seats, and queue up my favorite music playlist. It will adapt to me. It will effectively "know" me.

Predictive and Prescriptive Experiences Anticipate Behavior

Eventually, the program and/or service will start to be predictive. Predictive has largely been discussed in an advertising context. While predictive advertising is valuable, it is overplayed as a concept. You can predict that Maribel needs to buy toothpaste because she bought toothpaste two months ago. However, many people have bought toothpaste or diapers or any number of basic goods recently.

Everyone thinks about that type of thing as a predictive example, which is fine. However, it isn't very innovative since it takes into account only one data point—in this example, that I've bought toothpaste in the past. Frequently the advertisements aren't even targeted, let alone predictive.

Predictive right-time experiences will discover an individual's patterns and modify the user experience to make these patterns more accessible or more easily accomplished. This prevents issues and presents opportunities to the user. It combines historical data with predictive algorithms to define the probability of future events. It also takes in data from more than one source, which could include things such as transaction history, visits, customer care calls, and social networking feeds. Mobile-enabled business processes combine data from previous transactions with current contextual data to understand what a user is doing at this moment and what information or services will be useful.

A predictive example is pharmaceutical salespeople getting the data they need pushed to them when they are about to walk into a certain customer's site. They want to know what the doctor has ordered in the past, if he's received it, and if he's had any issues. The right time to receive this information is before the rep walks into the office. A pharmaceutical rep could automatically receive updated content in her sales management app tailored to the doctor she is about to meet and providing details about the practice and what products the doctor has prescribed in the past. If the news is bad, the rep would like to know this information more than a few minutes before she walks through the door. She wants and needs time to fix the problem. A right-time experience will predict not only what information would be useful but also when it needs to be delivered.

The app could also automatically log the sales call based on when the rep enters and exits the hospital as well as provide directions to the next appointment. This is predicting and automating what needs to be done next.

A simple example of a predictive service that exists today is maintenance alerts in the auto industry. Newer cars can communicate information with their owners and the service center. It can tell you based on your tire usage when you actually need to balance or replace your tires or check the air pressure. Instead of basing your maintenance on the number of miles you've driven, the car can tell you when to replace items based on the actual wear-and-tear of the parts. You may be due for a brake pad replacement at 16,000 miles, but your car can tell you that, based on your driving, you won't need to change them for another two months. The car has collected and analyzed sensor data, learned your driving patterns, and predicted when you'll need service.

Smart businesses will use analytics to create predictions that also improve customer care and deliver the right information to an employee. For example, companies like GE and Bosch are also building predictive services in industrial automation to minimize equipment failures and improve asset utilization.

In the past, contextual data wasn't readily available. Today it is, and we should be using it. The principle is for an application or service to take the contextual information from the device and combine it with other types of context, such as social networking behavior and previous transactions. It must analyze it, learn from it, and use all the available data to make better and better predictions of what the user wants and offer right-time experiences.

Predictive Experiences Offer Advice and Action (Prescription)

A right-time experience will not only predict what will happen but also provide guidelines for what the company or individual should do as a result of these predictions. These right-time experiences help companies learn from previous decisions and plan for upcoming issues.

An example of prescriptive right-time experience might be software a company uses to avoid mobile roaming expenses. If an employee schedules a business trip abroad with the company's travel agent, the company's mobile management software could automatically check to see if the user has an international roaming plan. If not, the software could launch a purchase order for the plan and set a reminder to cancel it at the trip's end. The service will learn what type of calling behavior the employee has had in the past. For example, Visage Mobile is designing a service that can predict if an employee will receive roaming charges based on information about booking a trip from the travel department; it prescribes a course of action accordingly.

Customer care can also be improved by adding context to business processes. An automobile service center could create a right-time experience by linking a customer's car sensor to the client's service record and the center's scheduling system. When the car drives into the service center, the scheduling software could automatically check in the vehicle, alert the service staff to which services are required, and suggest additional services.

Connected Makes Interactions Actionable

The experiences a company's customers, employees, and partners have in far too many situations are broken because they are complicated, generic, and irrelevant. In many cases, the company provides limited or poor-quality data or, worse yet, the wrong data. For example, Comcast's provisioning system may say a prospect's home can't get cable TV service. The home is a new build, but the prospect can see that the actual cable facilities are within 100 feet of the new home. In this case, the customer is frustrated and Comcast may lose a sale because it's using outdated records. If Comcast had connected its systems with those of the town's building department, it would've known about the new construction and could've sent a team to investigate if it was serviceable.

Today's technology offers organizations the opportunity to move into right-time experiences, which take into account all the context now available, analyze that context, and make these experiences less generic, more engaging, and more relevant. These experiences are also less complicated, because they present the right information without the user hunting for it.

I've discussed contextual and the adaptive, but these experiences should also be connected. This means the data flows smoothly to every system that needs it. If an order goes to manufacturing, there may be many systems that need access to that information. The information from the order should automatically be connected to systems that manage the warehouse, shipping, and accounts receivable, as an example.

Right-time experiences will bridge and integrate internal data sources and silos. Most applications operate in information silos, while right-time experiences integrate data across internal company departments. They will also link to partner and third-party data sources that reside outside the company. Weather, traffic, flight data, and parking spot availability are just a few examples of third-party web-accessible data sources.

Right-time experiences will link to application programming interface (API)–accessible data and services, such as reviews, product comparisons, transaction clearinghouses, authentication services, and click-to-call services. Other new third-party data sources are also becoming web-enabled, such as Data.gov, health care data, directories, and mobile application utilization. It's not just consumer-oriented data that is being made available, however. Businesses are also providing API-accessible data to their partners, and IT managers will use this data to create right-time experiences that optimize workflow. For example, a beverage manufacturer could make its inventory data accessible to its bottle distributor's dispatch systems with APIs.

Hertz Drives RTEs

A real opportunity exists today. Businesses are collecting data and turning it into information, information that can be a valuable asset. The Hertz Corporation is an interesting case study of how a company can use mobile and IoT to enhance and transform a customer's experience.

Hertz is one of the world's largest general-use airport car rental brands, with approximately 10,900 rental locations in about 150 countries. One thing that makes it interesting is how it is approaching mobile. It's an established company that is choosing to lead, not follow, in contextual services. According to Rob Moore, senior vice president and chief technology officer, the corporation is looking at several types of context: location, time, inventory and availability of cars, and customer history.

Not all that long ago, a Hertz customer would land at an airport, find the counter, give the agent her license and credit card, sign all the paperwork, and find the car. This then progressed to a more seamless experience for Gold members with a kiosk. How does mobile change that?

When a customer lands and turns on her smartphone, the Hertz app knows her plane has landed and whether it is early or late based on the customer's reservation information. It knows what type of car she's selected and can match that choice to the cars available on the lot at that time. The app will be able to route the customer right to her car, using the context of mapping to help her get there. She does not have to look at the board or search for the car, thanks to the use of the context of location and the context of time.

If a company ensures its systems are connected, it can then take advantage of real-time inventory. When a customer opens the Hertz app, he will see what cars are available. The app gives a person the option of a free upgrade to certain cars. Or, it can ask if the renter wants to upgrade to another class car for an additional charge. This is a more agile business process because it lets customers make the change on the fly, and it lets them do so without any human intervention.

Upgrading to a bigger, hotter car was always an option, but relatively few customers wanted to go through the process of finding a clerk and redoing the paperwork. Moore says that the Hertz mobile "Carfirmation" is now live to allow customers to view inventory to change the car at no charge or choose an upgrade, including a special "deal of the day." As one happy customer said, "I couldn't believe how awesome this was. I changed the car on my iPad while on the Hertz bus ride from the airport, and literally three minutes later I was at the Hertz lot and they'd already switched the car and had the correct slot on the board with my new rental."

That, of course, is nice to hear, but more significantly, the program meant over $1.14 million in additional revenue in the 18 months after the December 2011 launch.[3] Moore says that 26 percent of customers change the cars they reserved, at an average of $73.92 in revenue per transaction. Hertz is using mobility and context such as inventory availability and prior rental history to earn more from its existing assets.

On returning the car, customers can just park and go. Sensors in the car know when it has entered the Hertz lot. They can report what time the driver dropped it off and calculate the bill. Moore says a paperless eReceipt is zapped to customers' inboxes in less than 30 minutes. Paperless receipts are not new, but the savings in labor and improved accuracy quickly add up.

Another change: For some time, Hertz had its own GPS system, a small device of its own design called Neverlost. Today, many customers aren't purchasing this service because their smartphone already contains a navigation system. (That's a challenge for Garmin, TomTom, Magellan, and other GPS marketers as well.) So Hertz's challenge was to sell customers navigation for $10 a day when they have something very similar—and nearly free—in their smartphone.

Hertz has redesigned Neverlost to look more like an iPad and plans to put it in all its cars. If the customer's smartphone dies, or if the customer has only a basic cellphone, the Neverlost car tablet provides immediate access to on-demand GPS. It can put the driver in touch with a live agent for immediate help. It includes local restaurant guides, highlights of the area, and recommendations. Hertz can work with partners to sell advertising to local restaurants and other businesses. This creates a two-sided business model: The customer pays for the service, and the restaurants, hotels, and tour companies pay for the service to be available.

Here's where the Internet of Things comes into play in changing the business. The cars Hertz purchases have a wide variety of sensors. These sensors can enable functions such as vehicle tracking if the car is stolen. If the "check engine" light comes on while the customer has one of the Hertz cars, the renter can call Hertz and one of its employees can look at the data feed for the customer's car. The employee can then tell the customer whether she needs to return the car immediately or not. A fuel sensor can tell whether the gas tank is completely full when the customer returns the car. As a result, Hertz can automatically calculate to charge the customer for the gas she didn't replace. Hertz has gone from having higher fuel costs than it should have to charging customers for the fuel actually used. The savings on fuel pays for the cost of adding technology to manage the new sensor networks.

Moreover, the sensors give the corporation new and interesting information. For example, they give Hertz a sense of issues such as how the tires perform on their cars. If you have thousands of automobiles being driven all over the world and can capture the data, you can figure out how tire performance differs in, say, North America and Egypt.

You can also figure out whether the tire companies are living up to product performance guarantees. Hertz can take that information, understand how its cars are being driven by various characteristics (e.g., country, climate), recognize differences in tire behavior, and predict what maintenance the cars might need in the future. That's valuable information.

Hertz may decide to share some aggregated IoT (not individual renters') information, such as tire wear-and-tear, with tire manufacturers. The corporation could sell it, barter for information it doesn't have, or use it productively some other way. It's the concept of linking to internal data, partner data, and third-party data sources outside the company to build a better product and service. This is the concept of connected data across business partners. If Hertz partners with the tire company, the tire company would have access to information it doesn't currently have access to. Each party can make better business decisions as a result of this new data.

This is an example of the fourth use case I listed at the beginning of this chapter, business-to-things and things-to-consumer. We've changed what types of things are communicating with each other. It's not just businesses talking to customers. It's businesses trying to change how they work with employees and partners. It is taking in data from sensors, devices, and equipment and turning it into actionable information. We need to think about the conversation, whether business-to-consumer, business-to-employee, or business-to-partner, in terms of how can we use mobile—and big data and cloud computing—to give better experiences to our customers and employees. In the Hertz example, it can be seen that the company has business-to-consumer experiences but also has the potential to deliver a richer business-to-partner conversation.

Right-Time Experiences Don't Happen Overnight

Organizations should take a phased approach to building new customer and employee experiences. Regardless of the type of experience they are building, these will evolve into right-time experiences in three phases: extend, enhance, and evolve.

The first phase of building a right-time experience—extend—is to speed up an existing process using mobile, big data, cloud

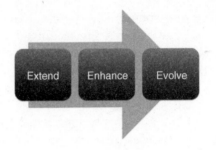

Figure 3.3   Businesses Evolve to Right-Time Experiences in Three Phases

computing, and other technology. It's basically getting your apps and processes to operate in a mobile and cloud computing world.

The second—enhance—is to make a process better with more information. This involves contextual information such as location, sensor data, image capture, and big data, all of which provide new information. Big data captures all the raw material about social media, previous transactions, context, and more, and it serves up a new piece of information—a right-time experience—as a result.

The third—evolve and transform—relates to the concept of predictive or adaptive services. The organization is able to do things with communications, customer care, and commerce that it could not do at all before or could not do economically (see Figure 3.3).

First, a business will extend its existing applications and services to mobile devices. Next, it will enhance these experiences using the different types of context I have mentioned in this chapter. In this second phase, the business will begin to use big data and analytics to turn context into insight that can enhance an experience. In the final phase, the company will create brand-new experiences that leverage context, mobility, and all the new tools that are available to it. I discuss this evolution in further detail in Chapter 7. But for now, I need to delve deeper into what right-time experiences look like and how we can create a framework for thinking about this transition.

The 3 *C*s of Right-Time Experience

As you can see from these examples, there are many types of right-time experiences that a business might want to create. It's always a challenge to figure out where to begin because we face so many options, possibilities, and complexities. To help categorize right-time experiences, we should begin by considering what I would call communication, care, and commerce.

- **Communication** is about trying to create a more continual dialogue that can improve engagement and customer care. It could lead to commerce but isn't always about commerce.
- **Care** is improving customer satisfaction while reducing the cost of customer care. It's about improving the customer experience so customers and partners want to do business with you. However, it's not limited to customers, prospects, and partners. Companies can also create care experiences for their employees by, for example, making an employee's job easier to do.
- **Commerce** right-time experiences make the sales process more convenient and valuable for consumers and easier for the employees and partners.

And that's what the next three chapters are about.

Summary

In summary, businesses need to deliver right-time experiences that deliver the right information at the point of need or desire. These experiences aren't just for consumers but are also for your employees and partners. What makes right-time experiences different is that they are contextual and adaptable to user preference, and eventually they will become predictive. To build these experiences, businesses must connect internal data sources for a consistent experience. To enhance the experience, leaders will connect to external data sources. Companies should think of right-time experiences as supporting communication, commerce, and customer care.

Right-time experiences aren't just reactions to situations. They enable versatility by anticipating customer and employee needs. Customer and partner RTEs drive revenue and improve the customer experience. Employee RTEs are about increasing productivity and reducing costs.

Companies that want to successfully compete will reshape their business models, increase collaboration, and improve customer relationships with right-time experiences. With proper planning, any industry can create right-time experiences to change its customer experience and to help drive growth.

Notes

1. In-person interview with Vishy Gopalakishnan, April 24, 2013.
2. Phone interview with Brian Courtney of GE's Intelligent Platforms on August 14, 2013.
3. In-person interview with Robert Moore of Hertz on September 17, 2013.

CHAPTER 4

Communications in a Right-Time Experience

We've continually created new and more meaningful ways to communicate over the ages. We've seen the invention of the telephone and the adoption of video chats over smartphones. With so many different ways to communicate, one must wonder, what's different about a right-time experience communication?

Communications in a right-time experience context has two components. The first is to create better, faster, and easier ways to communicate with customers, employees, prospects, and partners. One thing that's different today is our ability to communicate with an individual in many different ways, not only by email, but also by text, video, and social media. These new communications methods are present in and bridge both our personal lives and the business world. According to Microsoft, 72 percent of all companies are deploying at least one social software tool.[1]

The second difference is that connected sensors on a wide range of objects can transmit information that was never available or was difficult to gain access to before. This is data from what's frequently called the Internet of Things, and it opens up a world of possibilities for communications.

Communications Move from Generic to Contextual

So many of the communications we have today are generic: They are messages like "Save 20% on this" and "Buy this now." For example, Bed Bath & Beyond continually sends me the same text messages. It's rarely a message that says a certain item or type of product is on sale.

It's usually a 20-percent-off coupon. It's almost not worth opening the message because I've seen the same text so often.

There is an opportunity to send people relevant messages, such as "The store has different hours today" or "We are opening a new location" or "We have partnered with Nate Berkus, and his collection comes out in Target stores on September 16."

These communications need not be only from a business that wants to sell you something. San Diego has an application that alerts residents to fires, floods, and earthquakes—the sorts of natural disasters that strike people who live on the West Coast. Schools use SMS messages to announce school closings, and your bank can alert you when large transactions are made on your credit card.

A business can transform when, how, and what it communicates to its employees and customers by using context such as presence, social network status, location, and a wide range of data points from sensors such as motion, vibration, and orientation.

One danger in creating right-time communication experiences is that we may bring the same communications irrelevancy from email, web, and TV marketing to an even more personal channel—the mobile phone. If you sign up for email alerts from certain retail stores, the company might send you an email every day. This is annoying because you aren't shopping daily, but it's relatively easy to ignore (and delete) if it's in your email. It's not as easy to ignore if it's popping up as a notification on your phone. Worse yet, companies frequently offer only the option to unsubscribe, not to change the number of times they communicate with you. Right-time experiences mean consumers must be able to define when and how often they'd like an organization to communicate with them.

Part of building a communications RTE is deciding what to communicate, the device you want to communicate with, and the right time to communicate. It's thinking of the transaction holistically. It answers questions such as these:

- When will the person open the message?
- What device will she most likely be using at that time?
- What types of distraction may be present at the time he receives a communication?
- How will those distractions impact the amount of time she spends on viewing my message?
- How easy is it to act in this situation?

Answering these questions will help a company define what type of experience it should build.

New Devices Change Communications Opportunities

Ten years ago, life was simple from a device perspective. You had voice calls, email, and text messages. You had a laptop, and perhaps you were one of the lucky few who had a data-capable mobile phone. Today, the world is different, and that presents new opportunities.

As I mentioned, we now have the opportunity to tap into the contextual elements that a device provides, such as location, network speed, and connection quality. We can change what we communicate based on context, such as screen size. For example, it might not make sense to view engineering plans on a smaller smartphone screen, but it does make sense to design these apps for a tablet with a larger screen. For a business application, such as supply chain management, a company may offer a majority of functions on a tablet application, but only a subset of those on a smartphone application, such as inventory or order approvals.

Businesses will also integrate device context with third-party data, such as traffic information, to deliver new communications experiences. For example, when I checked in for my flight from Barcelona to San Francisco, the American Airlines application told me several things. First, it told me that my flight was delayed and what gate it was departing from. It also told me how long it would take me to get to the airport from my current location based on current traffic conditions. This is an example of integrating data from the company's systems (flight and gate information) with data from the device (location) and third-party data (traffic conditions) to deliver richer communications around the check-in process.

What Happens When Things Talk?

I first encountered the term *Internet of Things* in the early 2000s. I was working at Forrester Research and our group was keenly interested in the research Kevin Ashton had been working on at MIT's Auto-ID Center. The idea was if all objects in daily life were equipped with identifiers and wireless connectivity, these objects could communicate with each other and be managed by computers. In 1999, Ashton was searching for ways that Procter & Gamble could improve its business by linking RFID (radio frequency identification) information to the Internet. He went on to cofound and become director of the Auto-ID Center.

In a 2009 article for the *RFID Journal*, Ashton wrote, "If we had computers that knew everything there was to know about things—using data they gathered without any help from us—we would be able to track and count everything, and greatly reduce waste, loss and cost. We would know when things needed replacing, repairing or recalling, and whether they were fresh or past their best."[2]

The idea behind the Internet of Things described a system where the Internet connected to the physical world via ubiquitous sensors. These things, including everyday and industrial objects, would connect to each other and communicate in such a way as to make them programmable and more capable of interacting with humans. Ashton wrote, "We need to empower computers with their own means of gathering information, so they can see, hear and smell the world for themselves in all its random glory. RFID and sensor technology enable computers to observe, identify and understand the world—without the limitations of human-entered data."[3]

In the 2000s, this was an interesting idea that was difficult to accomplish. It required major technological improvements. After all, how would we connect everything on the planet? What type of wireless communications could be built into devices? What changes would we need for the existing Internet infrastructure to support billions of new devices communicating? How would we power these devices and make them cost-effective? There were more questions than answers at that time.

Today, many of these obstacles have been overcome. The size and cost of wireless has dropped tremendously. Manufacturing companies are building Wi-Fi and cellular wireless connectivity into a wide range of devices. While it is not perfect, battery technology has also improved, and solar recharging has been built into numerous devices.

The definition of the Internet of Things has expanded to include items such as automobiles, digital health devices, utility meters, and just about anything that can contain a sensor. IoT will also gather and transmit data from sensors connected to living objects, such as people, animals, and plants. It can share this data with systems and with people. Software that is accessible on mobile smartphones and tablets has become one of the primary interfaces for controlling and accessing information from IoT devices.

Business leaders will need to understand how mobile and the Internet of Things will change the types of devices that connect into their company's systems and what types of new data inputs these connected devices will provide.

Chad Jones, VP of product strategy at Xively, a division of LogMeIn Inc., shared an example of how IoT-based communications can be either helpful or useless depending on what's connected to what. Xively provides a cloud-based service that allows businesses to collect data from IoT devices and connect this information to other devices, applications, and users. It handles more than 200 million devices, 17 million users, and 1 million customers worldwide. Jones described a hypothetical situation where you could have a sensor on your snowblower connected via an app to your smartphone. How is this connectivity helpful to the owner? Say the snowblower app tells you that the motor's running at 700 RPM. Is this useful information? Do you know what to do with this data? A device simply communicating a fact about its health isn't necessarily useful.

Now, say your snowblower app is connected to Lowe's or Home Depot or your local franchised snowblower power equipment dealer. The retailer or cloud provider knows who you are because you've registered your machine. Imagine a cloud service at the retailer that monitors the statistics from many snowblowers. The service provider's software could review the statistics and automatically send you an alert that says it's time for some preventive maintenance and to change your spark plug. You now have the opportunity to order the spark plugs or set up a maintenance visit. The next time it snows, your snowblower is ready. The retailer has communicated valuable information at the right time.

In fact, Lowe's offers a product it calls Iris that is a remote control system for your home. It allows you to customize and monitor your home's functions. You can adjust the lights, control the thermostat, arm the security system, and even lock and unlock doors. The service will send email, text, or voice call alerts to you from your computer, tablet, or smartphone letting you know if your alarm is triggered, showing you a video from a camera in the home, alerting you when your child comes home from school, and unlocking the pet door when the dog approaches it. A kit that contains the basic set of connected devices is $300, and the basic service is free because the devices can communicate without requiring human intervention.

These new connected devices provide even more contextual data for applications and services to use to provide relevant and compelling communications experiences. These devices will connect with similar devices and other devices like smartphones to make this data consumable by people and other machines. It's a tremendous opportunity for organizations if a company expands its notion of what communicates (including things) and how it communicates. In the past, computing was a destination; today, computing and connectivity travel with a person. In fact, analysts and consumer electronics vendors have touted wearable computing as the next great wave in computing.

Adding Digital Data to the Physical World

There are new and creative wearable devices being introduced on a near-continuous basis. These include smartwatches, fitness bands, and even connected socks that can tell the wearer what her stride and impact were during a run. These devices are augmenting the physical world with digital data. Google Glass provides an example of one such device. It's the next generation of a heads-up display that can be used to provide information to people. It's shaped like a pair of glasses but is a wearable computer. With a voice command, the device can take a picture, take a video, provide directions, send messages, and answer questions (e.g., "How long is the Brooklyn Bridge?"). At the time I was writing this book, Google Glass was an intriguing prototype. After I interviewed Ray Potter, CEO of SafeLogic, he agreed to model the glasses for this book (see Figure 4.1).

Figure 4.1   Google Glass in Action

Source: Lopez Research photograph of Ray Potter, CEO of SafeLogic, using Google Glass.

Today, the glasses are considered awkward-looking and expensive, but we shouldn't discount the potential impact this type of technology will have in time. In a few years, a company may have created a more mainstream design. While Google Glass is a prototype today, it's a foreshadowing of the future of wearables. A wearable device will be very useful to people who must use their hands to do something else, such as surgeons, technicians, and crane operators. For example, a simple spoken "Okay, Glass" can turn on the device, and a few words could call up the status of a patient, including vital signs (body temperature, heart rate, and blood pressure), without requiring the wearer to glance over at a monitor.[4]

Dr. Pierre Theodore, a cardiothoracic surgeon at U.C. San Francisco, tested Google Glass in the operating room as a way to get the right information while he's operating. Google Glass allows him to review critical information, such as X-rays, without leaving the patient's side. In a *Fast Company* article, Theodore said, "Right now I have a 48-inch TV screen mounted in the back of the operating room that's 15 feet away. . . . Most surgeons will tell you that there have been times when they were not able to access the radiographic images when they needed it."[5]

This is just one example of the potential applications for Google Glass. To date, Google hasn't provided facial recognition software for the platform, but you can imagine a world in which you use something like Google Glass for visual recognition of an item or a person. Museums, municipalities, and retail locations could design services for Google Glass, or products like it, that will provide richer multimedia communications experiences. Google Glass could be your next virtual docent at a museum or travel guide as you walk through a city. If it has access to your social media profile, such as your Google+ account, it could begin to design customizable recommendations based on understanding what you've liked or commented on in the past.

Software, such as augmented reality software, is also being added to mobile applications. It can be used to overlay digital data on the physical view of an object from a device's camera. Imagine how this changes shopping, when you can use your camera to instantly recognize products and provide additional information, such as the nutritional content of food or the available sizes and colors of clothing.

I've already noted that wearable technology isn't just for consumer use, but let's take a look at an example of how it is being used by a company's employees. Tesco is performing a trial in London in which its employees can use a camera-equipped phone or tablet to capture what's on the shelves in a given store. The images are uploaded to the retailer's databases, analyzed, and compared to the ideal arrangement of products. The database sends back a suggestion of what products should be on the shelf and superimposes data on the image of the shelf. This helps employees easily identify any misplacements or gaps in products.[6]

Another example would be using mobile and augmented reality to assist with maintaining equipment. If you're standing in front of a piece of equipment, you can use the camera in your phone to detect what type of equipment it is from object recognition or by scanning a bar code. A right-time experience could connect this image to service repair records to understand when it had last been serviced and to a content repository that has manuals or video brochures on how to service that equipment.

Since the mobile phone or tablet has communications technology built into it, a field technician could connect to an expert for assistance or to the manager at headquarters for an approval. For example, if a technician has a question about the equipment that she's trying to repair, she could launch a voice-over-IP call using conferencing software like Skype or Microsoft Lync. Or, the technician could use her cell phone to connect directly to an expert. This is where the intersection of collaboration tools, mobile devices, and content management solutions all come together to provide the right information at the point of need.

From Personal Digital Assistants to Personal Concierges

In Chapter 3, I noted that right-time experiences are learning and adaptive. Technologies such as Google Glass are attempting to create these adaptive experiences today. In the 1990s, personal digital assistants, such as the Palm Pilot and Psion 3A, helped people organize their contacts and calendars. Today, we've advanced the concept to personal concierge services like Google Glass that deliver the right information exactly when you need it. This is the manifestation of a right-time experience, which combines a physical product (sensors, phones, glasses) with data to deliver a new and engaging experience.

Another example is that Tempo Smart Calendar app that uses artificial intelligence and semantic technology to anticipate and surface relevant data right in the calendar when you need it most.

Agenda View   Contextual Insights

Figure 4.2   Tempo Smart Calendar App

Source: Tempo Press Files App ScreenShots http://www.tempo.ai/press.

It will look at who you are meeting with, find relevant emails, and find contact information and company background. It can cull through social networks where you are both connected and pull that information into one unified view. It can also notify attendees if you're running late (see Figure 4.2). It's a right-time experience that integrates data from multiple apps (email and calendar), multiple social networks (Google+, LinkedIn, and Twitter), sensor data from your phone(location), and third-party app data like Maps to deliver to a user the right information at the point of need.

As in the Google Now example from Chapter 3 and the Tempo example above, companies are building apps and services that link information together and deliver it in one place. These applications and services are acting like virtual concierges that customize services based on a customer's immediate needs. A concierge-style experience could communicate today's weather, traffic, and school closings before a person starts her day as well as link to her TripIt account to discover if any friends will be traveling to her area this week. It's a right-time experience because it has predicted what information would be valuable to that person, and it communicates it at the best time for the data to be useful.

In hospitality, a hotel could build a concierge app for its guests. A hotel loyalty app could know what time a guest's flight landed, automatically check him in, and tap into his dining preferences from OpenTable to reserve a table at a nearby restaurant. Today, Ritz Carlton's app uses location data to know when a guest has arrived and provides special offers, local nightlife recommendations, and other interactive items, such as scavenger hunts.

In a business environment, we can also have personal concierge services that communicate the right information when needed. This may start out as alerts for items that are due, such as expense reports. Or, it may be the augment reality maintenance app that was mentioned above. But in many business examples, it often starts with the offering of richer communications and collaboration technologies.

Contextual Communications That Integrate Motion, Location, Social, and Other Data

Speaking of richer collaboration technologies, we've seen great strides in unified communications and collaboration software over the years. These will integrate motion, location, and calendar data to automatically decide the best way for an employee to communicate while on the go. Carriers such as Vodafone describe solutions that automate the process of switching between communications modes to make the user's life easier. For example, if I'm chatting on my smartphone as I walk to the car, it can automatically switch my call to a hands-free call once I begin driving. When I enter the office, the software transfers my call to my desk and, if appropriate, can launch a video session.[7]

As people use more and more devices, businesses will also need design experiences that are aware of the presence of multiple devices and allow the user to select preferences. In the PC world, my business calendar application may alert me to a meeting 10 minutes and five minutes before the meeting begins. I may not want my mobile app to do the same thing. I may want just one alert (or no alerts) sent to my phone to tell me my next meeting is about to start. If I have a phone and a smartwatch, I may want the phone or the smartwatch to send me an alert, not both. We run the risk of overmessaging in a personal environment.

Communications software is also evolving into what the collaboration industry termed social business software, which is an example of trying to create right-time experiences within one type of business software. We see this happening in our personal lives on social networks, and it's happening in the business domain as well. It's called *social* because we can communicate and collaborate on documents through microblogging and status updates that can be short sentences, video recordings, or audio files.

Mobile and social enable interesting, powerful, and valuable interactions within organizations. Updates to collaboration and document management tools make it easier to find and comment on documents, projects, and the like. Employees are sharing files, posts, and feeds. You can find associates within the organization to help solve a customer's problem. You can improve collaboration among employees by providing them with easy access to each other and easy access to the knowledge of what someone else is working on, which prevents (or reduces) the duplication of efforts on a project. With social software and mobile, we can collaborate at any time, with the right people and in the right way.

Solstice Mobile, a Chicago-based firm that specializes in mobile-based development and services, provides a real-world example of this. It has created a "Smart Office," utilizing contextual awareness, the Internet of Things, and natural user interfaces (see Figure 4.3). Solstice's conference rooms have connected-device motion sensors and cameras so employees can see which conference rooms are booked, empty, or occupied. "It's a great way for people to find a room for impromptu meetings, without having to circle the floors," says J. Schwan, Solstice's CEO and founder.[8] Employees can also book an open room with one tap from the Smart Office app. Attendees can see profiles of who's in the room and take pictures of whiteboards with mounted Internet-enabled cameras. Employees can reorder supplies, from office supplies to coffee, by snapping contextual QR codes around the office; they can also make requests, such as for a "fridge purge."

Although Schwan does not use the phrase "right-time experience," that's what Smart Office offers. It increases workplace productivity for employees and optimizes the guest experience for clients and visitors. "It enhances the user experience by enabling a set of contextual features that extend our Google Apps collaboration platform with Internet connected sensors, custom services and iOS and Android smartphone apps," says Schwan. The office directory contains contact details and skill sets of all firm members. Employees can locate others—whether in the office, near the office, or out of the

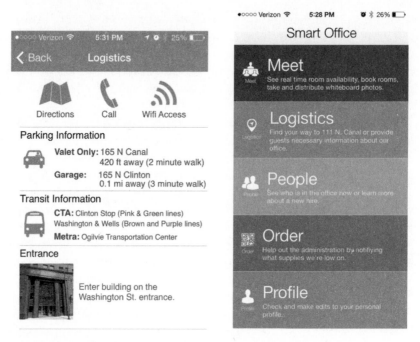

Figure 4.3   Smart Office Integrates the Right Information at the Point of Need

Source: Solstice Mobile.

office. "Through the use of low energy Bluetooth iBeacons, it also lets people know which floor someone is on in case they need to track them down for a quick conversation (face-to-face is the primary communication vehicle for people at Solstice)."

The day before a meeting, Solstice sends guests a link to download Smart Office. Guests can view details about their meeting, review logistical information, and may if they wish integrate their LinkedIn profile (see Figure 4.3). Contextual displays in the lobby show personalized content based on the guest's interest (for example, industry-specific case studies). A guest can navigate the content utilizing three-dimensional gestures (*Minority Report* style) via the integrated Leap Motion Sensor.[9] The display, in other words, communicates with the guest.

Solstice isn't alone in this endeavor. Companies such as Genentech and Intel have also built apps that allow employees to find available conference rooms, navigate the corporate campus, and have a richer employee directory on a mobile device.

Motion, location, vibration, and many types of sensor data are providing new information that apps didn't have access to in the past. When we combine sensor data with communications technologies, such as push notifications and SMS, a company can create the opportunity for smart consumer communications. For example, Fitbit is a digital fitness device that you wear on your wrist or hip. It's a pedometer that comes with an application. The mobile app syncs with the Fitbit sensor data to let you know things such as how many steps you've walked and how many calories you've burned. The Fitbit can send a note to your phone to motivate you. For example, it can say, "You need to walk only 2,000 more steps to meet your goal." You can also connect to other apps like social networks or to weight-loss apps like Loseit. By connecting and communicating data between apps and devices, Fitbit encourages use, reinforces its brand, and drives retention through social engagement.

In fact, a wide range of wearable or connected digital health devices are being worn by consumers today to track information such as weight, heart rate, body temperature, and environmental conditions, such as CO_2 levels. This data can be communicated to other apps or people, such as a weight-loss app or your health-care provider.

Instead of selling fitness apparel, companies such as Nike are creating a fitness communications experience that drives engagement. The Nike+ running app tracks your speed, distance, time, and calories burned with GPS and a sensor in your shoe. It then uses this information to help you track your progress and to motivate you with audio feedback as you run. This data can also be sent to a website where you can post the start of your run to social networks, such as Facebook or Path, and the app will provide real-time cheers for each like or comment you receive on social media.

This information was largely unavailable before smartphones, sensors, and wireless connectivity. Now consumers have the opportunity to collect and communicate that data. This has the potential to improve the health of billions of people, improve social connections, and change society.

Within a business environment, RTE communications provide faster and easier access to business information. It allows employees to make decisions faster by having the right information when and where they need it.

Oftentimes, it's about preventing a phone call by having information readily available at your fingertips. This could be information such as a product price list, product feature information, or the steps in a procedure. If a communications right-time experience can't eliminate a phone call, it should be able to route the call to the best person to answer without significant effort on the user's behalf. This is a good tie-in with existing collaboration/social business software applications, such as Yammer and Jive.

Companies use mobile solutions, like push notifications and SMS, to drive useful engagement by linking context to communications. An actionable push notification highlights what is needed and provides a path to the next available action. An example of an actionable business push notification would be, "Please sign in here to approve the submitted expense reports that are due today," with a link to the application where you can approve the expenses. There are multiple types of alerts you could send to an employee—about timesheets needing to be filled out, approving purchase orders, approving expenses or vacation requests, and more.

Communications Builds a Bridge to Commerce

Communications and commerce right-time experiences frequently overlap. Communications right-time experiences are often the first step in completing a commerce transaction.

Right-Time Communications Drive Engagement

Let's take a look at how Sephora, the $2 billion French brand and chain of cosmetics stores, is using communications and mobile to change its retail experience. It has a mobile application with loyalty program tracking and the ability to store Sephora gift cards in the app. It offers push notifications with the store location and number of Beauty Insider points available on the user's loyalty card. If the consumer has the app on her phone and is passing near the Sephora shop in the mall, Sephora can reach out to her through the app—or not. The real question is, what does the chain want to communicate? First, alerting the patron she's near the store is a good thing. This isn't revolutionary on its own, but it is the first step in providing a contextual experience. Second, Sephora wants to send a message targeted for that individual customer. Sephora can do this because it has captured what she's purchased in the past.

Sephora recently made a change that affects right-time experience communications. This is an example of how a small portable

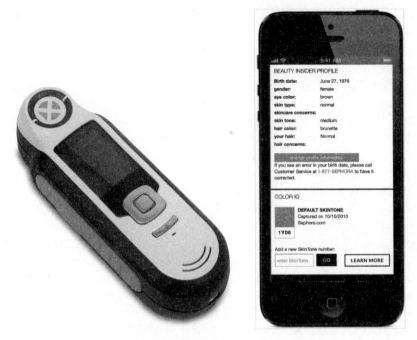

Figure 4.4   Sephora's Color IQ Device and Loyalty App
Source: Sephora.

device that isn't a cell phone can help create a right-time experience. Sephora has a small device store employees can use to scan a customer's skin color (see Figure 4.4).

Once the Sephora team member has scanned an individual's skin and established her "Color IQ," the device can determine which products in the store match her complexion. Bridget Dolan, vice president of interactive media at Sephora, said, "If a woman wanted to try every single foundation available to find the one that best complemented her complexion, it could take hours. With Color IQ, she can see all of the foundations that meet her criteria instantly on her smartphone and can then check them out in the store." Once a customer knows her Color IQ, she can save it in her Beauty Insider profile for easy reference while shopping in-store or on the go.[10]

Dolan says Sephora is using mobile to improve both the in-store and the online commerce experience. It can send a customer a message via the app when it adds new products to the catalog that meet her Color IQ. Indeed, Sephora can tell her this as she's walking by the store: "Maribel, there's a new hydrating skin foundation that matches your Color IQ." Because the application has access to the customer's history, it can also alert her if an item she's bought in the past is on sale.

The brilliance of this is that Sephora can use this application to make the in-store experience better or can use it to stimulate a purchase when customers are away from the store. This is the shift from generic advertising to targeted and relevant communications that happens at a point of decision. It impacts Sephora's ability to encourage the next best action.

Retailers and other companies across the globe are picking up on this trend of right-time communications, and telecom carriers are helping them do this. Rogers Communications, a Canadian telecommunications company, launched a service that will help advertisers know where their wireless subscribers are and speak to them more directly. "Rogers Alerts" let advertisers pay to know when people with a Rogers phone are near a store and to send them text messages with promotions to persuade them to shop there. The store's application alerts the store that the customer is in the building, knows what he has bought in the past, and can make a good guess why he might be stopping by based on time of day and history. Basically, it leverages multiple types of context to make advertising more relevant than it has been in the past.

According to *The Globe and Mail*, the service does not mean instant access to Rogers's entire pool of 9.4 million wireless subscribers. "Users have to opt-in to receive the messages, which Rogers says will not exceed four per week. Some national retailers have already signed up, including Sears Canada, Future Shop, Pizza Hut Canada, A&W, and Second Cup. Rogers Wireless will also use the service in its own marketing."[11]

"This is about increasing the relevance of marketing in a model where the consumer has opened up a door to greater intimacy, which is a one-on-one message," says Nyla Ahmad, vice president of local digital at Rogers. "With an SMS [text message], you notice it more and your likelihood to read it is far greater."

Retailers have found it is often challenging to convince a significant number of people to download an app, and it is even more difficult to get them to use an application once they've downloaded it. Asif Khan, founder and president of the Location Based Marketing Association in Toronto, says that "with a geo-targeted text message program, you have a much larger audience. The potential is large." But just knowing someone's location isn't enough; the communications must also be relevant. This is where combining data from previous transactions (if known) and context, such as location and time of day, is helpful.

The technology Rogers is using was developed by California-based Placecast. The program works by building geofences around a specific location, such as a storefront or a park near a store. When a user passes through that space, the technology recognizes her phone and can deliver a message. "It allows us to be more nimble and let people know about products that are more relevant to them," said John Rocco, vice president of marketing at Sears Canada, a Rogers client. "It could be a hot spell coming, and we have great air conditioners. Winter coats [when it gets cold]. This technology allows us to be more real-time." This would be an example of a right-time communications experience that uses weather and location.

Rogers has already had to play "referee" with some advertisers, however. "One advertiser wanted to geofence their competitor," to send an offer before a shopper walked into the competitor's shop, says Jack Tomik, chief sales officer for Rogers Media. "We don't feel that's a proper use of that service."

A SAS/Leger survey of Canadian smartphone owners in spring 2013 found that Canadians say they would buy more if presented with promotional offers on their smartphone while out shopping. When asked what they would do if they received a promotion on their smartphone that applied to either the item they were buying *or* a complementary product, 38 percent of Canadians said they would buy both items.[12] In addition, 58 percent said they'd be interested in receiving personalized promotions from nearby stores while out shopping.

"When you couple the power of the smartphone with really smart analytics, retailers have an opportunity to forge some really strong customer relationships and elevate their marketing to new levels," says Lori Bieda, executive lead for customer intelligence, SAS Americas. "Retailers who recognize the power of customer information and analytics and use it to deliver location-smart personalized offers to consumers, when and how customers want them, will win the lion's share of the shopping basket."[13]

Personalized promotions can also help improve customer loyalty, the SAS/Leger study reported. Some 47 percent of smartphone owners said they would be more likely to return to a store that sent them personalized promotions to their phone while they were out shopping. The under-55 crowd said they are more likely to return to the store (50 percent versus 29 percent for those 55-plus). Women were more likely than men to say they would return to a store that offered them smartphone-based, localized promotions (51 percent versus 43 percent of men). They were also more likely to cash in on smartphone-based in-store deals, with 44 percent saying they would buy multiple items when presented with relevant promotions (versus 31 percent of men).[14]

Most research on the subject suggests that people's willingness to receive these commercial messages is directly proportional to how relevant they are to the individual consumer. Rogers's service will let users specify the type of messages they want to receive and will also track user behavior over time to better target its offers. "This is not spam. This is not handing out handbills on the corner," says Rogers's Tomik. "This is very direct."

The Rogers system is a good start because it uses location to determine who is nearby. There is no need to send me a text if I'm 10 miles away from your store. Theoretically, this means the ads will be more relevant. I need to opt in so you can't decide to automatically spam me. Also, you send me only four ads a week.

However, these four ads are why the system is potentially problematic. What four ads per week? Can I tell them what I like? Can an advertiser buy all four and annoy me? This happened, and continues to occur, with ads that were placed in online TV shows. There may have been only four slots in a 40-minute show, but the same advertiser could choose to buy them all, or it would be the same four ads repeated at each commercial break. Perhaps more significantly, if an advertiser sends the same generic ads to everyone, is it actually contextual just because a person is near the store?

Location can be very powerful. It's one of the first elements you can use in defining context and prescribing the next best action. However, it can also be a very crude way of targeting people. Our call to action is to do more than use location to trigger a sales promotion.

Part of the challenge retailers faced in the past was knowing who was in the store. Now a mobile application that's using Wi-Fi and/or GPS can alert the store if a customer is nearby or has walked in. But what happens when the customer is inside? Other challenges quickly surface. Where is he within the store or property? What is he doing, and what should you communicate at that moment? This is where context from mobility can be linked with information on previous transactions and behaviors to build better communications.

Communications Isn't Just About Ads

Walgreens provides an example of how communications in retail doesn't always have to start with an advertisement. A retailer can add value and relevancy with other types of notifications. Walgreens is creating simplicity and new interactions with mobile. It interacts with about 12 million people per week online and via mobile, and it sees 1.8 million digital visits (nine websites, 10 mobile apps) every day, half of them (900,000) via mobile.

Furthermore, half of Walgreens's mobile traffic (450,000) is by people accessing the company's mobile apps or websites while in-store. "We're focusing on thinking about the customer, not about the channel because our customers think of Walgreens as an entity wherever they want to interact with us," says Graham Atkinson, CMO of Walgreens.[15]

"Anyone can innovate," said Deepika Pandley, VP of online strategy and customer experience at Walgreens. "The best ideas have come from people hyperfocused on what they are working on. The biggest lesson we've learned on mobile is, it's okay to take risks with new technology or ideas as long as you're ready to get feedback and react to it quickly."

For example, Walgreens offers a mobile app that enables both communications and sales opportunities. The customer enters all her prescriptions and the app helps her set up reminders and track when she has taken her medication. Prescription quantities now count down as users mark their reminders as "taken" and automatically update the prescription quantity. Users can export their prescription data and take pictures of their prescriptions. They can email prescription history and the app can access the entire FDA drug database. (Note this is an example of connecting to third-party data, as discussed in Chapter 3.)

The application provides value by making the customer's life easier. Walgreens can send you alerts to let you know that your photos are ready to be picked up or to remind you that flu shots are available. Sales and coupon alerts are available, but they aren't the main focus of the app. Walgreens's app provides a perfect example of a right-time experience. It provides a person the right information when it is needed. It delivers convenience through timely communication.

Location and Personal Points of Interest Drive Relevancy

Qualcomm Technologies Inc. is one of the world's largest fabless semiconductor producers and the largest provider of wireless chipset and software technology. Qualcomm Retail Solutions Inc. (QRS), the Qualcomm subsidiary responsible for creating the Gimbal platform prior to the unit's transition to a standalone company. Gimbal is a context-aware and proximity platform that helps retailers and brands to engage consumers with relevant, timely, and personalized communications sent to their mobile devices. The platform includes Gimbal proximity beacons and a development kit for iOS and Android devices. Gimbal provides an always-on, low-power, geo-fence-based location awareness. This enables an application to become aware of an end user's location, including arrival, departure, and dwell times (e.g., Maribel entered the building at 9:10 A.M. and was here for an hour).

It also uses Bluetooth beacons to provide a granular level of location awareness, enabling applications to determine with a high degree of accuracy their relative proximity to the beacons. For example, a retailer could see if a person is standing in aisle 9 in front of the toothpaste, not aisle 12. Depending on whether I've opted-in to the store's location tracking, it may even know that it's Maribel who is standing there. The store can also track if I've been there for 5 minutes or 15 minutes. If I'm standing there too long, I may need more information to make a decision, or I may not be able to find what I'm looking for. Either way, the retailer has context on how a customer's shopping experience is progressing. If the retailer knows who the customer is, the information can be used to create a tailored service for me. This concept of smart beacons is relatively new and revolutionary. Before its introduction, it was difficult and costly to achieve accurate indoor location.

One of the items that is particularly interesting in the Qualcomm platform is what it calls Gimbal Interest Sensing, which provides applications with inferred end-user interests based on mobile phone usage. I interviewed Kevin Hunter, Gimbal's chief operating officer, about Gimbal and its ability to enhance the retail experience with contextual communications.

Hunter discussed the concept of personal points of interest and interest sensing. Personal points of interest are places that people visit that provide context about where they go. From these points of interest, we can define a picture of what they do and what they might like. He said, "Let's imagine you want to provide me with a more meaningful experience. The phone knows where I work and where I live. It knows that Kevin goes to the gym every morning at 5:30, and he drops his kids off at school. These are all different locations. If you have a good understanding of the environment that a phone has visited, it gives you understanding of who that person is and what their interests may be.

"If I frequently stop at sporting goods stores, a retailer could decide to send me targeted offers for soccer clothes. Once you understand the person better, you are going to have to start to make things more relevant. This relevancy is not based on just location but on timing and interests as well." Hunter's vision of building contextual communications is exactly what I call a right-time experience.

For the end users, Qualcomm and Gimbal call this the concept of a digital sixth sense that can provide you with the right information at the point of desire or need—exactly what I'm defining as a right-time experience. In case all of this sounds too creepy, you must remember that consumers have chosen to opt-in for these services. Gimbal's privacy features are designed to protect consumers' personal information while giving them command over what and when they share. With access to this type of information, companies have the opportunity to deliver new and meaningful experiences. This type of information wasn't available before we had smartphones. Any business that learns to use this context wisely will have the opportunity to revolutionize the way it communicates with its customers and prospects. This will change retail as we know it. But it isn't applicable only in retail. Entertainment venues, transportation facilities, and any company that wants to provide a personalized experience can start to leverage these technologies. Let's look at an example of how a leader in the hospitality and entertainment market, MGM Resorts, is deploying contextual solutions to improve communications and commerce today.

Target Time, Location, and Previous Behavior Change Communications

Consumers have high expectations for connectivity as they bring multiple devices into venues such as hotels, convention centers, and retail stores. Reliable and fast connectivity, such as Wi-Fi, is becoming a requirement for venues of all sizes. Casinos are an intensely competitive industry that is based on delivering the right experience at the right time to a set of customers with wildly divergent needs—convention attendees, gamblers, diners, and shoppers.

John Bollen, vice president for technology, MGM Resorts, understood how consumers were engaging with MGM's properties online. He wanted to create a seamless and consistent guest experience that spanned all digital devices and screens. He views the lifecycle of an experience with MGM Resorts as having four components:

1. **Plan the trip.** This is primarily a consumer using the Internet or mobile web to book a room, make a restaurant reservation, book a show, and review hotel offers.
2. **Pre-trip.** This involves a consumer using the mobile web or a mobile application to review reservations, check in, find property and event information, and review recent offers.
3. **In-trip.** Within the property, MGM uses a Wi-Fi portal page, a mobile app, IPTV, and digital signage to deliver a wide range of information. Guests can log onto Wi-Fi using the portal page. If guests download the property's app, they can find maps, directions, offers, and venue information. They can also receive messages from MGM.
4. **Post-trip.** Customers can review their bill, check out, check flight status, and review their loyalty program status.

Once thought of as tool for convention rooms, the Wi-Fi (and apps) MGM uses provides an example of how mobility can be used to effectively engage customers, provide the right content at the right time, and generate revenue. MGM Resorts visitors have access to the information they need. The MGM Resorts Bellagio app uses Cisco's Wi-Fi network, Meridian, and Connected Mobile Experiences product to search the property's amenities—dining, shopping, and entertainment. With this app, guests can become loyalty members and be alerted to discounts at local restaurants, shops, and wine bars. Another feature includes indoor location–based services, offering turn-by-turn directions as visitors roam through the venue. It also provides personalized content and experiences that build loyalty and boost sales.

MGM's system detects presence, locates, and tracks all Wi-Fi signals—anonymously, to ensure privacy—and then aggregates and enhances the data for location analytics and reporting. Based on this data, the engine delivers detailed analysis of customer on-site behaviors. The analytics engine classifies and groups the data based on defined criteria to provide thresholds and configure policy-based alerts for use with CRM systems. The resulting intelligence helps create right-time experiences by joining existing customer data, location data, and web data such as Yelp reviews and social feeds.

The example I provided earlier of helping a hotel guest find a restaurant with availability and routing him to the destination is now a reality at the Bellagio. The property is using a mobile app to provide relevant and timely communications that can help me shop, dine, and purchase for a show. The goal isn't to digitally stalk me and push irrelevant ads. The goal is to use to app to provide me with information that helps create a delightful and friction-free stay at the property.

The New Fan Experience

Just as a resort wants to enhance guest experiences, so does a stadium. The sports industry has changed dramatically over the past five years. There's never been a better opportunity or a more challenging time to create engaging sports fan experiences in the home and in the stadium. The experience of watching sports at home continues to improve with the adoption of HDTVs, multiple camera angles, and advanced on-screen statistics. Social media has changed the way teams engage with fans by creating a second-screen experience on the tablet or PC in the home. Fans can actively participate in a dialogue with other fans while they're at home.

With the advent of new technology, the stadium experience began to lag behind the home fan experience. Fans had access to the Internet and a wide range of sports scores and camera angles on a variety of devices. Sports teams want to bring innovative and personalized experiences into the stadium to drive revenue and fan loyalty. Loyalty isn't just a function of how much a fan spends but is also a function of a fan's engagement with the team online, at home, and within the stadium. Fans expect to interact, and interaction gives brands the real-time opportunity to understand the consumer and react immediately. Instead of waiting a week or a month to change a marketing campaign, a team can try various ads on the fly.

The burning question for the San Francisco 49ers was how the team could provide an in-stadium experience that exceeded the convenience and engagement of the couch experience. The answer was to create a new fan experience that uses mobile, social, big data, and analytics to create personalized experiences that offer the right information and service at the point of desire. As the team set out to build a new $1.2 billion stadium, management dedicated over $100 million for technology to create a best-in-class fan experience. The fan experience can be divided into three parts: before, during, and after the game. The phase that requires the most work for sports teams today is creating the right experience during the game.

Most sports teams with mobile applications offer the same information: news, scores, and player statistics. This is the first phase of mobility that extends existing content to an app. The real win is to move beyond existing functionality.

For sports teams, next-generation mobile fan apps should offer a wide range of game-enhancing activities. These could include the ability to download tickets to devices; traffic-avoiding directions to the stadium and to a seat; the ability to buy food and merchandise from the seat; in-stadium promotions and contests as well as end-of-game promotions; polling and voting; half-time show content, such as Super Bowl ads, that aren't visible in the stadium; the ability to interact with other fans; precise directions for leaving the stadium and navigating stadium traffic; information on nearby attractions and promotions; and more.

These contextual apps will integrate location data, social data, and other third-party data such as traffic and local sales promotions. The 49ers will use what is known about their fans to provide the right content to the right users at the right time. Teams can create an experience that makes use of social and mobile to connect fans with players in a unique way, something that can't be experienced at home. For example, as part of the social media campaign, fans in the stadium could tweet questions to the coaches and players. Players and coaches could respond at half-time with tweets, photographs, or video posts answering fan questions on the big screens. Teams could reward attendees who participate in contests and social campaigns with opportunities to meet players after the game. Other enhancements could include cashless transactions to order food and drinks from a seat or the use of big data to explore player stats and what-if analyses in real time on their mobile devices. Some stadiums have discussed providing information on restroom wait times and directions to the rest room with the shortest lines.

The 49ers partnered with SAP to create a fan experience that gathers and analyzes data from all existing digital fan touch-points such as 49ers.com, Twitter, Facebook, and Instagram. It also integrated existing customer records and sales data. In mid-2013, the team had 394,224 Twitter followers, 1.8 million Facebook fans, and 334,000 Instagram friends. In the week before the Super Bowl XLVII game, the 49ers had 133,480 tweets and the Ravens had 80,789.[16] Imagine the power of being able to harness all of this data and turn it into meaningful insights for the team.

The combination of all the social network traffic over a year's worth of games would create millions of unstructured pieces of information—big data—that would need to be analyzed in near-real time or real time to provide new experiences. By combining big data from mobile, social, and other business systems, such as point-of-sale terminals, the team will create new applications and features within the stadium on game day to improve engagement, customer service, and customer communication during and after a game.

A common complaint among sports fans is about the poor quality of wireless connectivity within the stadium. Game attendees want to send text messages and share photos and video clips with friends and other fans. During a game, a majority of the attendees will hit the wireless network at the same time. In the case of the 49ers, the new stadium will seat 68,500 fans. Wireless LAN and wireless cellular networks normally crater when hit with a large usage spike. The 49ers are partnering with Aruba Networks and AT&T to build networks that can perform under the pressure of nearly 70,000 fans all hitting the network at the same time. One of the first areas any business must master is delivering robust wireless connectivity on site with a mixture of comprehensive Wi-Fi and boosted cellular capability. The San Francisco Giants have faced similar concerns. The team has upgraded its wireless LAN network three times since AT&T park opened. Today, the ballPark's network supports over 500 Mbps of traffic every game but the fans are always connected.

Aside from the technical aspects of connectivity, teams must also address several business factors. They need to know who is in the seat on game day. More than 75 percent of the seats for 49ers' regular season games in 2014 had been sold by mid-summer 2013, but this does not mean the person who bought the ticket is sitting in that seat on game day. Understanding who's in the seat is critical to providing the best game-day experience. Next-generation fan experiences require teams to break down internal data silos to provide a complete 360-degree view of their fans.

For example, a team should be able to integrate information on who attended a game, whether they have attended a game in the past or are season's ticket holders, and what they purchased at the game. The integrated view should include whether the fans participated in any social networks and any of the on-site social activities. Social sentiment analysis, concession history, ticket purchases, and other systems are all separate data stores with minimal, if any, interaction among these systems.

San Francisco's cochairman, Dr. John York, believes in designing a software-driven stadium that capitalizes on mobile. "Everyone is used to having information at their fingertips and fans are no exception. With the right software, fans can look up player data in real-time, figure out what questions to ask, and get involved in the game further," says York.[17]

But it's not just a software solution for statistics. Given the pace of change in mobile phones and tablets, York believes fans will spend $1,000 (in smartphones and tablets, not including subsidies) every 18 months to have the latest technology. He therefore does not believe the 49ers need to splurge on hardware, like screens, that will be obsolete in a few years. He believes the 49ers should empower fans to do whatever they want on whatever device they have. This shifts the consideration to understanding what software-related services and network infrastructure services a sports team should provide its fans with today, which leads us to mobile apps.

ESPN provides another example of a company in the sports industry that is using mobile to create fan engagement by delivering content in new ways. Instead of just being on television or on the web, ESPN wants to drive new loyalty experiences on smartphones by using a mobile application. The ESPN app can gather data from a customer's previous history to understand that he is a Red Sox fan and that he happens to be in Fenway Park. With this knowledge, ESPN can offer special commentary such as videos, photos, or stats about his favorite ballplayer. It's a right-time experience through communications.

Build a Better Team and Increase Competitiveness with Right-Time Communications

The actual experience in the stadium is just one aspect of building a better fan experience; the team also wants to win games. The 49ers, like every franchise, must build a world-class team to retain a competitive advantage. According to John York, "We asked ourselves how we can get an edge in a game with salary caps? It's about the data you have and how you use it. We asked, tell me what you want to see as a head coach, a scout and we'll build it. We can make the league a better product with a smarter, more efficient game."[18] York worked with SAP to help design an application to analyze game film, support clock management, and assess what the 49ers should look for to find the best matches for the team. The solutions will change how the 49ers scout and train. It's an example of a right-time experience that provides the coaches with the right information to make the right decision by leveraging next-generation analytics. It changes how the 49ers recruit new talent, and it will change how the team plays the sport.

Building a better team at the outset is important, but you can also dramatically improve the existing team's performance with right-time communications. A German soccer club is using a combination of mobile and big data to change player training. Sensors in the players' clothing and in the soccer ball communicate data such as speed, movement, perspiration, vital signs, the speed and direction of the ball, and more. The team can apply big data and analytics solutions—in this case SAP HANA—to learn how different players perform. How the player kicks the ball, the ball's position, and the force of the kick can change the game. This data, which is available in near-real time, helps the training coaches build more personalized programs.

In the past, the coaches would use video and take the information from the video and put it into a tool to track player performance. The advantage of the new system is that it augments an existing process and communicates key data much faster—the difference between a team winning or losing. Similar work has been done in other sports, such as tennis, to analyze the serves and player movement. This provides quantitative information to players about what they're doing and how it impacts their performance on the field. It communicates the information that allows them to understand and change their performance dynamically.

The Red Bull Racing team provides an example of how mobile, sensors, video, and big data are being used in Formula One racing. There are cameras in the cars and throughout the racetrack, all feeding data back to a main station to be analyzed. Once the technicians have analyzed the video and the sensor information from the car, they can—in virtual real time—suggest modifications to the car or to driver tactics. Split seconds matter in Formula One racing, so the ability to take in video and sensor data and analyze the unstructured data for patterns is key. After the machine analyzes the patterns, experts in the field can look at the information and make strategic decisions about the driver's moves or what might be changed in the next pit stop.

Keeping on the sports theme for a moment, let's look at how the NBA is changing the communications experience by opening up access to its wealth of current and historical data.

Let Customers Drive the Conversation

Adam Silver, deputy commissioner and COO of the NBA, wants to unlock data and create fans by allowing them to cocreate the next generation of products and services. Silver says, "Our hundreds of millions to billions of fans around the world are the next generation of innovators. We want to empower them with software to bring back new ways to use our data." The NBA worked with SAP to develop a website[19] where fans can obtain real-time data on players and teams. The site uses big data and in-memory processing to let fans analyze data from as far back as 1946 to create their own statistics, get answers to specific questions, and plot player and team performances on their mobile devices. Future enhancements will pair video clips with performance data instantly. Silver claims, "Technology helps unleash the passion fans have for the game." They can get a better understanding of what's happening by instantaneously seeing how their favorite player is doing and being able to assess how that player performs with certain team-mates and different combinations of players on competitive teams.[20]

Improve the Quality of Civic Life

Local governments can create right-time communications experiences that improve the quality of life. One example is community alerts. Governments such as San Diego County are using mobile apps to alert people to street closures, forest fires, earthquake activity, and other disasters. By using sensors embedded in a wide array of systems serving the public, such as traffic lights, public transport vehicles, and parking spaces, machine-to-machine technology can communicate the status of the system being monitored via the Internet in real time.

Zia Yusef, the CEO of Streetline Networks Inc., headquartered in Foster City, California, had a vision of how the Internet of Things could change the cities with smart parking. The company began work with a very simple premise: Parking is broken and the Internet of Things can fix it. A lack of (or perceived lack of) parking is a real problem for drivers, business owners, and municipal governments. Streetline estimates that 30 percent of urban traffic is caused by motorists looking for parking. In a study that measured traffic in one Los Angeles 15-block area for a year, researchers found that drivers drove more than 950,000 miles, produced 730 tons of carbon dioxide, and used 47,000 gallons of gas searching for parking.[21]

If a person could use an application to find an available parking spot, this could fundamentally change traffic patterns and consumer behavior. Smarter parking could minimize traffic congestion, reduce carbon emissions, and eliminate labor inefficiencies associated with parking enforcement. By helping drivers understand what parking is available near a place of business, smarter parking solutions could increase visits for companies in highly congested areas.

According to a Randall Stross, a professor of business at San Jose State University, "Smart-parking technology for on-street spaces is expensive, and still in its early stages. The largest examples are pilot projects with costs covered primarily by grants from the federal Department of Transportation." The SFpark pilot project "uses sensors from StreetSmart Technology for 7,000 of San Francisco's 28,000 meters while LA Express Park has installed sensors from Streetline for 6,000 parking spots on downtown Los Angeles streets."[22]

Yusef believes that the Internet of Things is going to become the next big thing because data from devices can create intelligent services. The adoption of mobile devices makes it easier for people to obtain services wherever they are, including in their cars. Streetline Networks uses wireless sensors embedded in parking spots to gather the real-time status of municipal and garage metered parking spots. The sensor tracks if a spot is occupied, empty, or expired. It sends this information to a data management system, which links to a mobile application for drivers. The application provides voice-based directions to nearby open spaces. It also offers additional information such as rates, hours, locations of EV charging stations, locations of handicapped parking spaces, and specific payment options. Drivers can set a time in the application to remind them their meter is about to expire. They can also use the application to locate their car and optimize parking decisions based on availability or price—and, of course, they can pay for the parking with their phone.

"Parking is an area where no one expected any innovation," says Yusef. "No one was thinking about technology in this space. Parking is an area where you could provide multiple interesting use cases for the data. As the data becomes more available, there are different apps and use cases for the various constituents." He described this as new data versus big data. IoT generates new streams of data that didn't exist before. While it aids drivers by helping them view available parking spots, Streetline offers a solution designed for city leaders to help them manage and analyze the use of parking through real-time and historical analytics applications. The solution is an integrated offering that provides sensors, middleware, a platform, and applications.

One of the principles of building right-time experiences is that data becomes interconnected. This interconnected nature isn't just connecting to data within your organizations. Businesses will build better services by connecting to third-party data and by sharing their data. Streetline practices this philosophy by offering a platform with an API and different apps that can share data such as pricing, hours, and parking available with a community. A retailer, restaurant, or theater can use this data to display a map on its website that indicates parking locations near the business. The merchant can also have access to real-time parking availability for a separate fee. "One of the fascinating things is the art of what is possible" in IoT data, says Yusef. "We can open up the off-street parking data to the development community and see how they will use it."

As we'll see in a minute, many cities are creating strategies to build connected—or smarter—cities. These projects can equate to years for deployment and billions of dollars. Parking is the first step toward smarter cities in a bite-sized fashion. Streetline believes parking is a killer first application of the Internet of Things for cities because it generates the revenue and eliminates labor inefficiencies. A city can start with a few blocks, prove the value, and expand over time. It's the base application for building a sensor-based network in cities. Smart parking is a communications experience for consumers and a commerce experience for parking spot owners. It's a win-win for both sides.

Sensor-based networks can provide city officials with access to data that was either impossible or too costly to collect any other way. City officials can use these new data sources to understand a parking space's turnover and at what times the space rents. By analyzing parking patterns by time, location, and price, cities can create demand-based pricing for parking or enable parking incentives. A parking spot has two sources of revenue: fees to rent the space and fines for expired meters. A city or a garage owner can change the price based on analysis of occupancy data. After reviewing six months of data, cities are creating demand-based pricing that changes every month. In some garages, we've already seen the move to dynamic pricing, which can change daily.

Parking enforcement can know exactly which cars have been parked too long and can reduce the inefficiency of having officers drive around the city seeking expired meters. Enforcement revenue may go up because officers can know exactly who has been parked illegally. It may also go down as drivers become more sensitive to meter limits and are provided with apps that allow them to pay for additional parking. The combination of improved ticketing, more efficient labor, and dynamic pricing can produce an ROI for the sensor network within six months to a year, says Streetline. You can imagine parking as a right-time experience that supports three constituents: the driver, the parking spot owner, and a business owner. The experience collects big data from sensors and from applications and uses analytics to understand consumer parking patterns. Yusef observes that "the ROI discussion is up front and center, but reduction of congestion and sustainability is a key driver for other areas."

This is just the beginning. Once a city has a mesh-enabled sensor network, it can enable additional sensing capabilities to improve its return on investment. With minimal hardware changes, Streetline believes it can capture other types of data and deliver new services. The first category of services could use existing sensors in new ways, such as using the light sensor in the parking solution to understand if a streetlamp needs replacement. There may be a parking sensor under the streetlamp. The company can collect information over time and use this data to determine if a streetlamp is broken or if lights need to be replaced. With this knowledge, a city could eliminate random maintenance checks and dispatch a crew only to repair a problem or perform preventive maintenance. The second category would require different sensors. For example, the city could put pressure sensors in fire hydrants to determine water pressure or add pollution sensors to streetlamps to detect carbon dioxide.

Use IoT and Mobile to Drive Efficiencies

Right-time experiences can be created by connecting to third-party data, such as the data cities can now provide. Technology is empowering this movement by providing apps for people to self-report conditions. For example, Waze is an app that allows individuals to report issues or bad traffic conditions along their commute, which helps others route around trouble spots, reducing commuter travel times, but also helping urban traffic run more efficiently. SeeClickFix is a Boston-based communications platform for citizens to report nonemergency issues and for governments to track, manage, and reply to these issues. For example, if an individual sees a pothole, she can report it using geotagging in her phone.

As Mark Alarcon, the mayor of Stockbridge, Georgia, notes, "I think one of the most difficult things for a city to do is to capture the needs of the citizens. Everyone in our community has different perspectives of their neighborhood, roads they travel and time of day they commute." Speaking at a town meeting, Alarcon said, "There's a lot of convoluted things that can happen in trying to serve the community. . . . The SeeClickFix program, this application, is free of charge and you can download it on your smartphone. It's GPS driven and captures whatever it is—your neighbor's tall grass you've asked to have cut for three weeks and it's over your head or the car that's sitting on the curb and is unsightly."[23] These are two examples of how social, sensor data, and mobile apps can provide a right-time communications experience.

According to Ben Berkowitz, SeeClickFix's CEO and founder, "We have also seen that having a centralized listing of community concerns is a helpful resource for fixers with limited resources who must prioritize certain issues to be addressed earlier than others. The basic tools—for fixers as well as reporters—are available for free."[24]

The Spanish port city of Santander (population 180,000) has buried 12,000 sensors under the asphalt and attached them to streetlamps and city buses. The sensors measure everything from air pollution to open parking spaces. They tell trash collectors which dumpsters are full.

Luis Muñoz, an IT professor at the University of Cantabria, won an $11 million grant from the European Commission in 2010 to pay for the sensors and hardware such as street signs equipped with digital panels that display real-time parking information for every block. Citizens can upload a photo of a pothole or broken streetlight and send it directly to City Hall.

"You send us a photograph, and we try to solve that incident in about five or six days," says Iñigo de la Serna, mayor of Santander. "It took like three weeks to solve that project before having the applications." According to the report, the city saves about 25 percent on electricity bills and 20 percent on garbage collection—and utility companies pay for the sensors' upkeep, because they save money.[25]

These technologies are also helping cities improve workforce management and safety. The City of Memphis adopted Xora's StreetSmart mobility solution in 2013 to increase city worker safety and reduce numerous man-hours of redundant paperwork as it enacts programs to restructure neglected areas of the city and manage code violations more efficiently. After the death of an employee on the job and reports of citizens violating ordinances, Memphis officials sought to improve zoning regulation enforcement, neighborhood cleanups, and knowledge of city worker whereabouts.

Xora, acquired by ClickSoftware in March 2014, has an application that is designed to help cities eliminate or reduce paper-based processes that typically accompany urban restoration programs and it provides a city's employees with better information in a timely manner. "Using StreetSmart can help us tighten our work processes, reduce errors, and allow us to devote more time to address other citizen concerns," said Michael Jones, Memphis deputy chief information officer.[26]

The workforce management solution offers pull-down menus on mobile devices that allow city workers to fill out forms quickly and print documents from a mobile printer. This replaces a two-step paper-based process in which workers input data and transcribed it later. The application continuously feeds GPS locations of each city worker to a display monitored by supervisors. A time-and-location stamp feature for photographs and customer signatures allows workers to document information and be accountable for their work. "Harnessing the latest technology and advanced wireless broadband networks can help our city government work more efficiently and effectively to serve Memphians," said Memphis mayor A. C. Wharton. "We continue to evaluate and innovate around our operations to best meet the growing needs of our city as we attract new businesses and citizens every year."

IOT Keeps the Trains on Time

Yarra Trams, operator of Melbourne, Australia's 100-year-old tram network, is working with IBM to improve day-to-day tram operations and passenger experience. It's the largest operating tram network in the world, with more than 250 kilometers of double tracks. It manages more than 91,000 pieces of equipment and 487 trams traveling on 29 different routes. Neil Roberts, director of ICT for Yarra, says, "We are committed to delivering a world-class service to all our passengers, but keeping our trams running is no simple task. Our greatest asset in tackling this challenge is data and smarter infrastructure software."

One challenge obviously is that older trams have very different maintenance needs than new. In addition to managing repairs across new and aging infrastructure, Yarra's operations center and maintenance teams are charged with keeping trams running and rerouting passengers even when streets are flooded. When major events like the Australian Open are held in Melbourne, Yarra increases tram service in specific areas to accommodate heavy passenger traffic.

To ensure trams are available when and where passengers need them, says Roberts, "we have turned 91,000 pieces of tram equipment into 91,000 data points. Sensors and reports from our employees and passengers provide information in real-time about tram equipment, services and maintenance issues." For example, an automated wheel-measuring machine housed at a tram depot detects the condition of a tram's wheel. The data allows Yarra to alert maintenance teams to potential issues and ensure necessary repairs are made before service is disrupted. Certainly this is a right-time communications experience for any rail traveler and for Yarra rail employees.

"With this kind of data, as well as mobile technology," says Roberts, "we can prevent service disruptions, schedule predictive maintenance, quickly re-route trams and better communicate information about tram services to passengers. When an incident occurs, we use IBM Smarter Infrastructure Software to log details about the incident, create a work order and ensure all is well on the tracks."[27]

Again, the power of everything from trams to trash to communicate with each other and with mobile devices opens endless possibilities. Imagine you're a trash collection company. You have a route and you pick up the trash regardless of the dumpster's condition. What if the dumpster could tell you when it was full and you could send out a crew to empty it only then? What could you save in fuel and in labor? Enevo makes a smart sensor that can do this. When it is placed in the trash container, it can alert the waste management company when the container needs to be emptied. In addition to alerting the garbage collectors, Enevo One also analyzes data from the sensor to understand the time it takes for each can to fill up.[28]

What we see from these examples is that sensors can be used to deliver value and timely communications across a wide range of areas, from finding a parking space to helping the trains run on time. These types of communications weren't possible or were too costly to provide in the past. With these new technologies and a bit of creativity, a business can move from generic communications to targeted relevant communications that will improve engagement, customer care, and commerce.

Summary

Right-time experiences come from likely and unlikely places. RTE communications experiences can include messages from people to people, businesses to people, and things to people. They make our lives easier by simplifying the process of gathering information. Occasionally they tell us things before we know we need to know them. Or, they can delight us with new information.

Using context such as time, location, past behavior, and more, a business can transform when, how, and what it communicates to its employees and customers. Right-time communications will promote commercial transactions, improve care experiences, and drive engagement with consumers, employees, partners, and other stakeholders.

Right-time communications can improve after-sale service for businesses, in-store events for consumers, and in-stadium game experiences for fans. Eventually, right-time experiences powered by mobile, big data, and cloud computing will improve civic life for virtually everyone.

The next chapter shows how a diverse group of organizations improve customer and employee care through right-time experiences.

Notes

1. www.microsoft.com/enterprise/it-trends/social-enterprise/articles/Microsofts-Vision-for-Enterprise-Social.aspx#fbid=_PW6Nas3PJa.
2. Kevin Ashton, "That 'Internet of Things,' Thing," *RFID Journal*, June 22, 2009, www.rfidjournal.com/articles/view?4986.
3. Ibid.
4. http://mashable.com/2013/10/03/philips-google-glass/?utm_cid=mash-prod-email-topstories&utm_emailalert=daily&utm_source=newsletter&utm_medium=email&utm_campaign=daily.
5. www.fastcompany.com/3022534/internet-of-things/a-surgeons-review-of-google-glass-in-the-operating-room#3.

6. www.itpro.co.uk/strategy/21735/augmented-reality-set-to-boost-shopping-experience-for-tesco-customers#ixzz2uwQSoKS9.
7. Vodafone video on the future of enterprise communications, www.youtube.com/watch?v=Ej0I4axEC1s&list=TLy4QM7Xso1RW7jCKVKEMflQpkasmGldMq.
8. J. Schwan, "Feeding the Innovation Culture—Practicing What We Preach," August13,2013,http://jsblog.solstice-mobile.com/2013/08/mobile-innovationsolstice-smart-office.html.
9. Ibid.
10. Interview with Bridget Dolan at the GigaOm Mobile Event on October 21, 2013.
11. Susan Krashinsky, "Rogers to Offer Promotional Ads by Text," *The Globe and Mail*, October 2, 2013, www.theglobeandmail.com/report-on-business/industry-news/marketing/rogers-to-offer-promotional-ads-by-text/article14646004/.
12. *The 2013 SAS Digital Wallet Report*, http://www.sas.com/offices/NA/canada/downloads/Mobile-Survey2013/SAS-Digital-Wallet-report-July-2-2013-EN.pdf.
13. July 19, 2013, press release, "Mobile Marketing Key to Increased Sales, Improved Customer Loyalty: SAS Survey Reveals," http://www.newswire.ca/en/story/1200755/mobile-marketing-key-to-increased-sales-improved-customer-loyalty-sas-survey-reveals.
14. "Mobile Marketing Key to Increased Sales, Improved Customer Loyalty: SAS Survey Reveals," www.sas.com/offices/NA/canada/en/news/preleases/mobile-marketing-survey-2013.html.
15. www.digiday.com/brands/walgreens-cmo-focus-on-the-consumer-not-channel/.
16. James Cifuentes, "Infographic: 49ers Win the Social Media Super Bowl," February 7, 2013, www.pcmag.com/article2/0,2817,2415187,00.asp.
17. http://en.sap.info/sap-hana-powers-ultimate-fan-experience/93836.
18. Ibid.
19. www.nba.com/stats.
20. "SAP Keynote: Bill McDermott & Bob Calderoni," Orlando 2013, www.sap.com/events/sapphirenow/index.epx.
21. "Becoming a Smarter City," p. 4, www.streetline.com/smart-cities/smart-city-whitepaper/.
22. Randall Stross, "The Learning Curve of Smart Parking," *New York Times*, December 23, 2012, p. B-4.
23. Rachel Shirey, "Stockbridge Second City to Consider Interactive Phone App," *Henry Daily Herald*, August 13, 2013, www.henryherald.com/news/2013/aug/13/stockbridge-second-city-to-consider-interactive/#h0-p2.
24. http://seeclickfix.com/faq.
25. Lauren Frayer, "High-Tech Sensors Help Old Port City Leap Into Smart Future," NPR, June 4, 2013, www.npr.org/blogs/parallels/2013/06/04/188370672/Sensors-Transform-Old-Spanish-Port-Into-New-Smart-City.
26. "AT&T Mobility Solution Helps City of Memphis Efficiently Manage Programs to Improve Zoning Enforcement and Fight Urban Blight," June 18, 2013, http://www.att.com/gen/press-room?pid=24412&cdvn=news&newsarticleid=36631.
27. Neil Roberts. "How Big Data Keeps Yarra Trams Running on Time, Rain or Shine," September 16, 2013, http://asmarterplanet.com/blog/2013/09/yarra.html.
28. www.enevo.com.

5

Care in a Right-Time Experience

Enterprises that excel at customer experience understand that aspects of customer care exist in every part of a transaction, from presale through postsale service. As we've seen, technology now enables organizations to deliver experiences that were not possible in the past. If a business is listening, it can learn about problems and potential service and product opportunities on social media faster than it can through existing customer care channels.

Mobile provides a channel for companies to create one-to-one relationships and tap into contextual data from mobile devices. It provides the opportunity to deliver care at any time, from any location to a wide range of devices. Customer care in a right-time experience is everything from having a useful mobile-friendly website to being able to answer a customer's problem with the first call or no call at all. This chapter shows how a diverse group of organizations improve customer and employee care through right-time experiences.

Mobile Extends Options and Information to Everyone

Once again, the principles of a good customer care experience apply to internal customers (business-to-employee experiences), business partners, prospects, and customers. As consumers, we have an idea of what care means from a customer's perspective. And I discuss how right-time experiences can improve that experience in a moment. However, what does good customer care mean from an employee's perspective? It means that the employee will not only have access to the right information but can act on this information.

For example, a knowledge worker who travels is often in meetings, on airplanes, or in a car much of the day. This person works all day and during the evening has to deal with the administrative chores that have accumulated. She may have to record sales contacts, approve orders for supplies, file an expense account, and more. While this employee may have received an approval request in an email or within a PC-based application, the authorization process stops while it waits for the manager or the employee to return to the PC to approve the request.

In the past, employee customer care related to how quickly IT solved your problem when you called the help desk. Today, employee care can be defined as delivering actionable business processes, workflows, and applications that make it easier and faster for an employee to get work done. Mobile provides an opportunity to simplify and streamline business processes. The manager no longer needs to lug around a laptop to work on the road. The business can build mobile applications that enable workflow approvals on the go or buy the mobile versions of these applications from its existing application providers.

If Helen needs her vacation approved, the manager can select "yes" or "no" in the human resources app on a smartphone. Howard needs to know if he can order a dozen cartons of printer paper. His boss can see the order and approve or deny it on his mobile device. Julie's expense report is in the queue. A click from the email on your smartphone can log you into the Concur mobile expense application or mobile website to approve or question an item. This is the equivalent of providing better customer care to your employees. It also benefits the top and bottom line by making your processes run hours, if not days, faster. Of course, a business might not be thrilled to spend the time and energy to mobile-enable all of its processes out of the gate. Perhaps approving vacations is an unnecessary feature to have right away because it doesn't increase revenue or cost. However, filing expenses in a timely manner can help accounting accurately reconcile the books and eliminate other paper-based processes.

Mobile allows organizations to reduce paper-based processes. This helps salespeople, service technicians, inspectors, surveyors, and many more—those who do their job during the day and return home or to their hotel room to do some kind of paperwork as a result of the day's activities. In the past, they might have collected the information on paper while standing in front of somebody and have to type it into a system manually at a later time.

Now a mobile device can replace a paper form. It can capture a signature, which eliminates the need to scan a document later. It can capture the time and location of the signature. This exists today with the UPS or FedEx delivery person recording our signatures on a portable handheld. These types of functions once required specialized hardware and software. However, the availability of cheaper and easy-to-use mobile handsets and workforce management applications has made it possible for a wide range of industries and roles to embrace these functions. A health inspector can record a site visit on a tablet. Truck drivers can log and file how many hours they've driven on a smartphone or a rugged handheld. A nurse can log a patient's vital signs on an iPad. The data can be transmitted immediately or filed electronically at a designated time. Either way, no one is redoing work at the end of the day. It is possible to fill a book with just examples of how eliminating paper processes can improve a business.

Enterprises can automate more and more processes, and that makes life easier for everyone, whether a road warrior or a back-office clerk. Not to mention that doing so speeds up business processes and saves money by eliminating the wasted hours and reducing mistakes. Wasted time is squandered money; fewer mistakes is saved money.

Some companies will create right-time experiences that focus on servicing the customer more effectively by providing a company's employees with better access to corporate data. Lowe's provides an example of this. As mentioned in the last chapter, data availability and right-time communications are part of the first step in providing winning customer care, employee services, and commerce experiences.

The Lowe's chain operates in more than 1,725 locations throughout North America and has approximately 160,000 employees, the vast majority of whom, of course, are working in the stores. Every day, customers approach employees who want to know "anything from how to start a project to how to think about it and what products to buy," says Dennis Knowles, senior vice president of specialty sales and store operations. With hundreds of thousands of products in-store and online, Lowe's employees now meet the challenge to help customers find the right inspiration, materials, and tools with an iPhone and two custom apps.

The Lowe's Employee app gives store staff access to key product information, while the Store Manager app allows managers to handle administrative tasks. Every iPhone for employees includes a barcode scanner, a credit card reader, and an additional battery. In the past, a Lowe's employee needing to look up product availability or inventory had to walk to a fixed terminal in the store and possibly wait in line to use it.

Now store staff can scan a product and immediately access vital information right on an iPhone, including product pricing, inventory, and location in the store, without having to leave the customer's side. If a product is out of stock, the Employee app indicates when more will arrive and whether any nearby Lowe's stores have it in their inventory. Employees are able to place an order for a product and use the credit card reader to process payment. This is a right-time experience that changes both customer care and commerce.

Lowe's former executive vice president and CIO Mike Brown related a story about a customer who needed a large quantity of an out-of-stock product: "A store manager was able to look where the inventory was, order the product in ten seconds, and solve the customer's problem. The customer was absolutely blown away at the simplicity and how fast that could happen in a Lowe's store."[1] Satisfied and happy customers tend to result in positive staff morale, which tends to reduce turnover.

Before the iPhone, Lowe's managers would find themselves trapped in the back office for hours at a time, pulling up reports on a terminal and printing out reams of data. Now they can access that information anywhere with the Store Manager app on iPhone, allowing them to spend more time with customers and employees. They can double-check the accuracy of price changes, view sales reports, see when new products are due to arrive, arrange product transfers between stores, view employee schedules, and also access corporate email and calendars. "With iPhone, our managers are able to keep their fingers on the pulse of the store because they're out in the aisles," says Knowles. This is the first wave of customer care experiences in which businesses improve both efficiency and customer care by extending data that exists today in the PC system to employees' mobile devices.

Closing the Deal Faster

The business division of Comcast sells Internet and phone services to companies of all sizes. Its sales people visit customers, and it often took days for customers to review and sign a contract for service installation. The company has created a service experience that makes life easier for its customers and its sales staff. It provided its sales team with a tablet and a mobile-enabled workflow that integrated Docusign's electronic signature into its CRM software.

With Docusign, the salesperson could get the customer signature earlier in the process. Signing the contract automatically created a record in the CRM system, which is also connected to the company's ordering and provisioning system.[2] This provides a seamless flow-through where the customer signs a document and the service can be automatically entered into the provisioning systems for scheduling. It shrinks days off of the process and delights the company's customers and employees.

Enhance and Transform Customer Care Experiences

Let's talk about enhancing a customer care experience with more information, such as prior behaviors and device type. Let's look at how device type can change a care experience. Does the device have voice command or touch-screen capability? If it has voice capability with natural language processing, you could ask the mobile application to call technical support. Can it take a photograph? If so, an insurance application can prompt the user to take a picture of the damage a storm created and file a claim from his phone. Do you have a record of the user's previous behavior? This is where mobile, customer data, and context from sensors can come together.

Groupama, a €1 billion insurance and banking company in France, set out to improve how its customers submit claims and obtain assistance at an accident site. Philippe Vayssac, the customer interaction project owner for Groupama, believed he could fix this by "rescuing his customers from interactive voice recording hell."[3]

First, Groupama found that, in line with interactive voice systems used across all industries, between 10 and 25 percent of such calls failed because customers didn't push the right button or didn't say the right word or sentence to proceed to the next step (which could be a vocal, dual-tone multifrequency signaling, or speech recognition technology issue).

A second problem was structuring an interactive voice systems menu that would accurately arrange the wide range of Groupama's services into a simple set of menus. Instead of focusing on the 30-second industry standard for answering a call, Groupama wanted to provide customers with access to all the functions of the company, from sales to support, in a visual, rather than a voice, interface on a smartphone. Vayssac says, "If customers don't have a good experience when calling us, we probably won't be able to convince them to buy or renew with us. This applies to whether customers are contacting us to buy insurance or to make a claim."[4]

How many times have you called a company and been asked to enter your account number only to be asked for the same information five minutes later? Imagine you've just been in an automobile crash and now you have to look for your insurance provider's telephone number and your policy account number and wait on hold.

Vayssac and his team thought of this scenario when they designed their mobile app, an Interactive Visual Callback Response application that visually guides customers through menus to identify why they need to contact the company. The application collects the account information, such as a customer's policy number, the first time the customer opens the application. As a result, the information is already in the application when a customer needs it. In the first 19 months after Groupama introduced the app, customers downloaded it almost 24,000 times.

Once the system understands why the customer is calling, it can select the right agent to help the customer address the problem. It also provides customers with one-touch access to the appropriate department without the customers needing to know which number they should dial. The service gives them exactly the right information at the point of need in the most seamless way possible.

Vayssac says that 58 percent of the users allow their GPS position to be sent to Groupama and 84 percent give their email address (the field is not mandatory when they register). Application downloads picked up strongly when the company decided to insert a note into the classic waiting queue: "Your wait will be about XX minutes. Save your time and get a quick response in making your request (or making a claim) with our iPhone and Android app Groupama toujours là. A Groupama agent will call you back as soon as possible."

The application ties into the contact center system to provide the estimated time it will take for an agent to call back the customer. The customer can either choose to wait or have the agent call her back at a prescheduled time that is convenient for the policyholder or sales prospect. After the initial setup, the application can send all of the customer's account data, including GPS location, from her smartphone to the agent.

The app passes the customer's identity to Groupama's contact center software from Genesys, which can then direct the customer relationship management system to automatically display the customer's records to the agent as the callback is placed. It's also used to ensure that the customer gets a callback from an agent with the proper knowledge to handle the situation. This eliminates the annoying need for customers to repeat their name, address, and policy number to the agent.

Also, as Vayssac points out, "If a company has one phone number to reach the contact center, a toll-free phone number like many companies, you may have many calls in the waiting queue. Prospects who want a quote to buy insurance are mixed with customer claims, and that's not good." A more significant point is that the app improves Groupama's service quality. Vayssac adds, "Customers are happy because they don't have to wait on the line and agents are happy because customers are happy."

Often people don't know exactly where they are when they have an accident or an automobile failure. The Groupama app taps into the GPS information from the phone to identify where the customer is calling from, making it easier to send medical or roadside assistance. The application also has a feature that allows the customer to snap a photograph of the damage and send the photo from his smartphone to the agent. This shortens the claims process for the agent and for the customer.

Groupama wanted to introduce new communication and care channels that work for the customer, not just the company. It built a right-time experience that could deliver real customer satisfaction by linking location, photo capture, time of day, and agent knowledge together in one easy-to-use application. As an added bonus, the application delivers cost savings through efficiencies and increases sales revenues through effectiveness.

The mobile application also helps Groupama cope with sudden peaks in call volumes to the contact center in the event of a widespread emergency. Groupama can push information in real time to customers and redirect them away from calling the contact center to special areas of the company's website set up to handle this specific incident. Over time, Groupama can use data gathered from customers who use the application to redesign its processes to be even more efficient.

"While other insurance companies have launched smartphone apps, many are simply dumbed-down versions of their existing websites," Vayssac points out. "By contrast, Groupama's app allows customers to interact more easily with agents in Groupama's contact centers."

Putting The People Back In Care

Groupama isn't the only company that is looking for ways to use technology to improve customer experience by making it easier to connect with a person to resolve issues. Amazon and Salesforce have also introduced new mobile-firendly ways of connecting to support.

As Amazon looked to introduce tablets and other mobile devices, the company thought long and hard about how it could provide a customer care solution that would minimize the frustration of learning how to use a mobile device. The company launched a new customer care model for its Kindle Fire HDX tablets called Mayday. It's an electronic "button" on the device that connects the user to an Amazon expert who can co-pilot them through any device feature. The support person can draw on your screen, walk you through how to do something yourself, or do it for you. Mayday is available 24x7, 365 days a year, and it's free. Throughout the process, you will be able to see your Amazon Tech advisor live on your screen, but they won't see you. Amazon's goal was to connect a user to an agent within 15 seconds or less. The day after Christmas it announced that its actual response time was 9 seconds. Effectively Amazon used the Mayday button to eliminate purchasing fear but also delivered on its promise of rapid response time, a perfect example of an RTE that impacts both care and commerce.

In April 2014, Salesforce.com announced a new service called Salesforce1 Service Cloud SOS. Service SOS allows Salesforce.com customers to put an SOS button, similar to Amazon's Mayday, directly inside any mobile app. Pushing the button in the apps enables live video support and on-screen guided assistance. Alex Bard, EVP and GM of Service Cloud, salesforce.com, said, "The mobile phone has become the dashboard of our lives—we use it to manage how we interact with not only people, but products and companies. As the mobile device becomes every consumer's channel of choice, it is important companies meet their customers where they are."[5] The press release also noted that "companies need to reimagine how they deliver service across every channel, over any device and within the mobile app experience. Currently, when mobile users need assistance, they must exit the app or wait until they get to back to a desktop to find help." The concept of enabling an SOS button that allows one-touch access to rich communications for customers, such as video, is a perfect example of a right-time experience.

Contact Solutions provides another example of this. It offers customer care software that can be embedded within a mobile app. Instead of leaving a brand's mobile app to ask for care via phone or SMS, the customer will be able to send a text, leave a voice memo, or place a call from within the app. If he can't complete the transaction at that time, it will remind where he left off. It will also retain history of chats. These solutions deliver a right-time experience by giving the users a choice of communicating in the method they choose (text, voice, video), at the time they desire, over the device of their choice.

Making Travel Easier with Mobile

The Groupama experience suggests that company managers should look for ways that new technology (in this case, mobile) can coexist with and enhance existing IT services (call center). The organization should let customers—internal and external—pick the right time for a communication. Mobile devices provide the opportunity to capture new data points, such as location and images. Existing processes need to be redesigned to use these inputs effectively. There are examples in the airline industry that also highlight how a company can extend and enhance its care processes.

Today, self-service kiosks and mobile boarding passes are common, but this wasn't always the case. These were the first examples of customer right-time experiences being created in the travel industry, and we can now see the return on investment these early investments have delivered. In Montréal, Patrice Ouellette is director of customer solutions and innovations for Air Canada. He calls himself and his team "data-driven." Air Canada's systems allow it to get an accurate and up-to-date report on how many people are using each of Air Canada's multiple self-service channels, what the trends are over time, and what each check-in costs on a unit basis. Under his leadership, Air Canada was one of the first airlines to place kiosks outside the airport.

Air Canada consolidates all self-service channels to enable a seamless right-time experience in care. The airline delivers proactive travel services via smartphones. According to the company, the solution enables Air Canada to process transactions such as check-ins more cost-effectively than those done at the customer service counter. In addition, the system increases customer loyalty by virtue of more compelling and "stickier" self-service options like real-time notification. It reduces costs, improves customer service quality, and enhances productivity. This is phase one of a mobile initiative, in which you extend an existing service, such as check-in, to devices. By moving passengers from counter check-in to web, kiosk, and mobile device check-in, Air Canada has produced efficiency improvements in the neighborhood of 80 percent for those transactions.[6]

In Chapter 3, I mentioned that mobile provides new context that can enhance a customer care process. I also talked about evolving to right-time experiences in three phases. From what I've discussed above with Air Canada, we can see a real-world example of the benefits of extending existing services, such as flight check-in, to mobile devices. We can see how airlines have enhanced the process of air travel with right-time communications of flight delays and improved commerce with the ability to purchase airfare. But how do you transform the customer care experience of air travel?

Merging Wearables and Data to Transform Care

American Airlines provides an example of how one airline is thinking of this challenge. American Airlines plans to use mobile devices and context such as location and membership status to deliver new customer care experiences to its passengers. When a passenger with the AA app walks into the airport, the app can inform her of changes to her flight and also route her to the nearest airline club lounge. American Airlines (AA) is looking for solutions that could minimize or eliminate check-in lines at the club lounge. One potential solution could be to outfit its club attendants with new wearables, such as Google Glass. As the traveler enters the lounge, the club member's AA app could send an alert to the attendant that says the guest has arrived. The attendant can acknowledge the guest and wave him in. In the future, baggage handlers may use Google Glass to help them route packages more effectively.[7]

In February 2014, Virgin Atlantic was the first airline to use Google Glass as part of a program to improve customer service. In the trial, the Concierge staff for the airline's Upper Class Wing used Google Glass to deliver personalized customer services. In a press release, the airline said, "From the minute Upper Class passengers step out of their chauffeured limousine at Heathrow's T3 and are greeted by name, Virgin Atlantic staff wearing the technology will start the check-in process. At the same time, staff will be able to update passengers on their latest flight information, weather and local events at their destination and translate any foreign language information. In future, the technology could also tell Virgin Atlantic staff their passengers' dietary and refreshment preferences—anything that provides a better and more personalised service."[8]

These are just some of the ways the airline believes mobile connectivity, wearables, and context can help the company deliver better customer and employee experiences.[9]

Walt Disney World has consistently pushed the envelope in using technology to provide compelling customer care experiences. The company is an early adopter and leader in leveraging mobile, contextual services and big data to provide a best-in-class hospitality experience. Disney spent roughly a year and $1 billion to roll out its MyMagic + service in April 2014.[10]

Visitors can plan aspects of the trip online and can opt-in to share information with Disney on why they are visiting, how many times they've visited, and what they plan on doing while they are there. But the real magic happens when they enter the park. The company has introduced a wearable device called the Magicband.

The band is a waterproof wristband that looks similar to a fitness band or wristwatch. Vistors can use a MagicBand to:

- Unlock the door of their Disney Resort hotel room.
- Enter theme and water parks (with valid admission) and check in at FastPass+ entrances.
- Check in at the Disney's Magical Express transportation from Orlando International Airport.
- Connect Disney PhotoPass images to their account.
- Charge food and merchandise purchases to their Disney Resort hotel room during their hotel stay.

The MagicBand system is completely voluntary, but visitors who opt into using the band and its companion mobile app will have access to many advantages, such as skipping lines, pre-booking rides, changing reservations on-the-go via smartphones, and being personally addressed with their name by the characters. From Disney's perspective, the company can collect a wealth of information (big data) on any visitor who opts into the program. The company can track where their visitors go. It can understand which rides they visit and how many times they visit a ride. It can gain information on how they spend their money and what they like to eat. By analyzing this massive torrent of data, the company has the ability to deliver highly personalized experiences and customized messages. While consumers know they are being tracked, they still opt-in because the technology makes their vacation experience seamless.

Using IoT to Improve the Employee and Customer Experience

Utilities are also looking at how IoT can deliver operational efficiencies while improving care. BC Hydro, the Vancouver-based electric utility, provides an example of how connected smart meters (an IoT device) can improve customer service while saving the company money.

Until recently, BC Hydro did not know a customer had lost power until someone reported the outage. The utility could not tell if the problem originated at the house, on the line from the house to the pole, or on a pole upstream from that. BC Hydro lacked the basic visibility to deliver rapid problem resolution. Customers were upset and service calls were an expensive trial-and-error process.

BC Hydro also had a problem with theft. If the utility could not tell whether an individual customer's electricity was on or off, it could not tell if electricity was going to a paying customer. Aside from the lost revenue, theft caused strain on the distribution infrastructure, which resulted in as many as 100 premature transformer failures a year.[11]

To correct these problems, BC Hydro began installing smart meters. These offer the utility a number of benefits. The technology allows better analysis, improved notification tools, and automated decision-making that results in improved employee safety and shorter outage restoration times. The meters provide real-time outage notifications that can quickly pinpoint problems, which reduces the travel time it takes a crew to reach a site and accelerates the restoration process.

With reliable restoration notification, field crews can confirm the outage has been addressed instead of having to drive along the lines to look for secondary failures. The meters mean fewer outages from electricity theft by helping identify potential electricity diversions consistently and automatically, thereby improving safety and reducing customer outages caused by premature transformer failures, not to mention lost revenue. Smart meters also mean the utility doesn't need to send someone to your home to read meters, reducing labor costs.

Smart meters offer BC Hydro's customers other rewards as well. The new meters capture more accurate and detailed electricity use information on an hourly basis—rather than bimonthly meter readings or estimated bills. BC Hydro can bill customers based on actual electricity use, not from estimated readings based on historic profiles.

Smart meters also give BC Hydro's customers some control over their electricity consumption. Before the meters, customers had few tools to manage their electricity use because the old meters did not capture enough information. "Without specific and timely information, it is difficult for customers to take advantage of new service options or make informed decisions to actively manage electricity in their own circumstances," says the company literature. "Research has shown that electricity is typically not something customers regularly think about, and that increasing customer awareness by enabling them to view their own consumption in a timely manner can achieve electricity savings of up to 15 percent."[12]

To help customers, BC Hydro offered in-home displays, programmable thermostats, and energy management software products. These helped customers answer questions such as, "What happens if I run the dishwasher before bedtime instead of after lunch?" and "What's the cost of an elaborate outdoor Christmas light display?" Customers who do not want to buy an in-home display can access their own secure consumption information through BC Hydro's expanded Power Smart website. Smart meters capture information that enables the utility to design rate structures that encourage conservation during peak periods.

BC Hydro provides an example of phases one and two of evolving to transformative right-time experiences. Smart meters enhance the existing billing and maintenance business process with better information that is accessible in real time. It saves the company money while providing a superior way of troubleshooting problems and extending billing information to its clients. I've discussed examples of how insurance, airtravel, hospitality, and energy are using technologies such as mobile and big data to extend enhance and evolve processes, but what does a transformative right-time experience look like in health care?

Transform the Organization with New Options

Transformation means you are changing something completely, usually in a positive way. Let's look at how health care is using mobility, cloud computing, big data, and analytics to transform care.

Health-care companies were behind the technology curve until a few years ago. Now, they are using mobile devices, applications, and location services to improve and transform patient care. Doctors and nurses are using mobile devices, such as smartphones and tablets, to capture vital information at the point of care, improve patient data accuracy, and minimize paperwork. For example, RehabCare Group uses smartphones and iPads to improve the patient care experience with paperless patient preadmission and screening processes.[13] It also captures vital information at the point of care to provide better documentation such as treatment delivered, the time spent, and any other relevant clinical information. Medical professionals can avoid treatment mistakes by having an up-to-date record readily available at their fingertips on smartphones and tablets. These are examples of how the health-care industry is using mobile to enhance customer care while driving internal efficiencies.

Every hospital wants to improve the quality of care and patient outcomes. Washington Hospital Center (WHC) was no exception. The difference with WHC is that it wanted to provide the best care before patients even entered the building: It wanted to extend its world-class care to emergency vehicles. WHC worked with AT&T to develop CodeHeart, a secure application that allows first responders to initiate a real-time video and audio session remotely with hospital cardiologists to share a patient's condition and ECGs within moments after reaching the patient.

The mobile application can be used by hospital cardiologists to view, in real time, a patient's condition while simultaneously speaking with the patient's first responder or the attending emergency department physician. With access to this data, hospital staff can guide the first responder on interim treatment and prepare the hospital to provide appropriate care while the patient is en route to the emergency room.

CodeHeart is a right-time experience because it helps Washington Hospital Center determine in advance how to prepare for treatment—either with immediate preparation in the emergency department, by dispatching physicians to a patient in the field who cannot be readily transported, or by allocating physicians to the most critical patients once they arrive. "When it comes to treating a patient who appears to be suffering from chest pain or other heart attack symptoms, every second counts. CodeHeart helps us provide optimal care as quickly as possible and effectively treat every heart patient that comes to our facility," says Lowell Satler, MD, director of interventional cardiology at WHC.[14]

These are examples of how mobile apps and connectivity everywhere are changing health care. But big data and a different take on artificial intelligence (AI) will also revolutionize care. This new wave of AI is called *cognitive computing*. IBM's Watson is one example of this.

Curing Cancer with Cognitive Computing

Like many others, I grew up watching game shows on TV: *The Price Is Right, Wheel of Fortune,* and *Jeopardy!* I never imagined I'd see a computer competing against humans in shows like these. A computer might beat a human at chess because the rules and the moves and the possibilities, while mind-bogglingly complex, follow a certain rigid logic.

Enter IBM's Watson in 2011. Not only was a computer competing on a TV show against *Jeopardy*'s best contestants, but it won. Of course, Watson wasn't just any computer. It is one of the first in a series of the new cognitive computing systems. Cognitive computing refers to the development of computer systems that are designed to think like a human mind, rather than developing an artificial system. Cognitive computing integrates technology and biology in an attempt to engineer a computer that can learn from experiences like the human brain does. Early artificial intelligence programs could be taught a set of parameters, but they weren't capable of making decisions for themselves or intelligently analyzing various types of unstructured data to provide a solution for a problem.

I knew that this event would change the world, but I didn't know how. Shortly after Watson won *Jeopardy!*, IBM announced that it would work with Memorial Sloan Kettering to improve cancer care and research. Watson will help the hospital's experts use a wide range of medical information more effectively to help oncologists build personalized cancer treatments.

Watson is a computer system that is able to interpret queries in natural language and uses statistical analysis and advanced analytics to search millions of data sources in seconds and deliver statistically ranked responses to queries. Watson provides a majority of the technology foundation tools to provide a right-time experience in cancer treatments that is learning, predictive, and prescriptive. It can collect, store, and analyze a wide variety of data sources, including medical journals, patient records, images, and best practices from the National Comprehensive Cancer Network.

Watson's ability to absorb vast amounts of information means it can access and analyze every research study in the world. It can also review this data at lightning speed and suggest recommended treatment plans for individual patients in real time. To date, Watson has incorporated into its database more than 600,000-plus pieces of medical evidence and 2 million pages of text from 42 medical journals and clinical trials in the area of oncology research.[15] This is the essence of big data. The volume is massive, and the types of data vary from images to text to audio and video. It's not in any consistent format that would make it easy to store and manage.

Watson can collect abstract, unstructured data, such as how the patient feels, and integrate this with highly structured documents such as a patient's vital sign reports. One aspect of a right-time experience service is that it can learn and adapt over time. Watson is a system that learns over time, which enables it to make increasingly better predictions about possible treatment plans or how a plan could be improved based on new research theories and actual patient results.

Cognitive systems like Watson aren't meant to replace human judgment in treatment. These systems will be used to augment a medical professional's knowledge. They can provide physicians with the most up-to-date research and theories so they can make better decisions. They can improve care for the patient but also improve the process for the employee. Watson, for example, will point out areas in which more information is needed and will update its suggestions as new data is added. It also helps doctors find and connect with other experts for consultations.

Cancer treatment can be a long, involved process. You may therefore wonder why this is an example of a right-time experience. Keep in mind that right-time experiences are developed for the point of need or desire. In the case of cancer treatments, the point of need is ongoing and what's needed changes over time. Many businesses offer products and services that are ongoing or that will increasingly have some service aspect associated with them. Even manufactured hardware products, such as automobiles and television sets, are offering services and applications that are ongoing experiences and must be continually updated. Companies must build right-time experiences that are more than one-hit wonders. A great experience that happens once but fails to materialize again is only slightly better than a poor experience.

Unlike many business problems, treating cancer is effectively serving a market of one. It is the ultimate case study for mass customization. Each patient is different. Textbook cancer treatments alone can't address the various biological and environmental differences that impact the course and aggressiveness of a specific patient's cancer. For example, the recommended treatment may be chemotherapy, but there may be at least 10 or more possible chemotherapy options. In many cases, doctors learn what works best for a patient through trial and error or previous experiences with other patients. Physicians want to make evidence-based decisions but have difficulty keeping up with the volume of medical information, which doubles every five years. If this type of information is available and can be analyzed with Watson, it may be possible for doctors to quickly narrow the field of treatment options down to a list that would have the highest likelihood of success based on that specific patient's issues.

Memorial Sloan Kettering's work with Watson also qualifies as a right-time experience for its patients because it is a connected experience that links to data and services outside of its hospital network. This goes beyond medical data to include a connected business process across companies. In this case, Memorial Sloan Kettering is working with insurance provider WellPoint to reduce the time and documentation required to get an approval to start a treatment.

Memorial Sloan Kettering is one of the providers working with WellPoint on its Interactive Care Guide and Interactive Care Reviewer systems. WellPoint used Watson to store and analyze more than 25,000 test case scenarios and 1,500 real-life cases, including a mix of complex medical data and human language.[16] In addition, nurses spent over 14,700 hours training Watson on medical treatments.

The WellPoint system now analyzes treatment requests and matches them to WellPoint's medical policies and clinical guidelines to present consistent, evidence-based responses for clinical staff to review. It enables WellPoint to make faster and better-informed decisions about a patient's care. The insurance provider has deployed Interactive Care Reviewer to a select number of providers in the Midwest and believes that more than 1,600 providers will be using the product by the end of the year.

Dr. Craig Thompson, president and CEO of Memorial Sloan Kettering Cancer Center, observes, "Watson's capability to analyze huge volumes of data and reduce it down to critical decision points is absolutely essential to improve our ability to deliver effective therapies and disseminate them to the world."[17]

Cognitive computing has the opportunity to become accessible to the business masses. While the original Watson system filled three large racks of equipment and was quite expensive, the new system can be run on a single server that reduces the cost of the systems while improving the substantially higher performance. If this current computing trajectory continues, cognitive computing systems will be available as low-cost cloud services that could be rented by the month by a wide range of industries.

Watson takes in large volumes of information from everywhere. However, you can still create a great right-time experience by utilizing your existing data more effectively. Let's review how Texas Health Resources, a group of 25 acute-care and short-stay hospitals in the United States, is doing this today. It has more than 21,100 employees in 16 counties in north central Texas. Like all hospitals, it is trying to reduce avoidable hospital readmissions. The organization is using the Parkland Intelligent e-Coordination and Evaluation System, or PIECES—a software application developed by Ruben Amarasingham—to reduce readmissions.

When Amarasingham was assistant medical director for medical services at Parkland Hospital in 2007, he noticed demographic similarities in patients who were readmitted to the hospital. For example, frequent changes of home address in the past year or a low number of emergency contacts or family relationships were leading indicators of a possible readmission. He believed the medical records could be mined for those demographic and behavioral clues to alert providers to take extra caution with certain patients.

Amarasingham and his colleagues developed a software model that would scan patient data prior to discharge, and in 2009, he launched what he likens to a smartphone app that sits atop a health system's electronic health record to identify high-risk patients. The algorithm digitally analyzes the clinical and social factors in patients' records and uses advanced predictive modeling to predict "when a current or former patient may take a turn for the worse. It monitors patients and compares patients' stats to enormous amounts of data from a hospital system's electronic medical record, and lets hospital executives and clinicians know whether a patient is likely to die, return to the hospital, have a heart attack or experience another adverse event."[18]

By the end of 2012, the Parkland facility had cut its 30-day readmissions for Medicare patients with heart failure, including readmissions to all hospitals, by 31 percent, with an estimated savings to the hospital of $500,000 with no increase in staffing.[19] It's also collaborating with many facilities like Texas Health Resources and UT Southwestern to use predictive modeling software to achieve better patient outcomes.

In other areas, web portals and mobile apps are playing a major role in helping patients gain access to information and communicate with their doctors. For example, Electronic Medical Record software provider Epic offers a service called MyChart. It gives patients controlled access to the same Epic medical records their doctors use, via browser or mobile app (for iOS and Android). The free app allows users to view select parts of their electronic health record at home or anywhere else and to send a secure message to their physician about non-urgent health questions, such as about allergies and immunizations or requesting prescription refills. This is where the combination of cloud computing and mobile come together to create a new solution. The data is secure and complies with government regulations because nothing sensitive is stored on the device. Users have to log into a secure cloud service with a user name and password to access their records.

These are just some of many examples of how mobile, big data, and cloud computing are changing the health-care industry and patient care. Many of these same principles will apply in other industries.

Big Data and Mobile Deliver Predictive Knowledge

Again, with mobile, big data, and cloud computing, organizations can provide right-time experiences that were impossible in the past. These are things like General Electric being able to alert the company to an impending equipment failure. Or John Deere being able to look at what fertilizer a farmer's bought, what the farm's crop performance has been in the past, and what the weather will be to advise whether to plant now or wait a week.

Industrial manufacturing, such as aviation, locomotive, and heavy machinery, are evolving. Over the next decade, the Internet will create shifts in the industrial business that are on par with the transformations we've seen in other industries. Bill Ruh, vice president and corporate technology officer at General Electric, speaking at the Cloud Connect in 2013, said, "The change we see is movement from an analog business to a digital business. We see an architectural shift in how products and services are built."[20]

Table 1: Industrial Internet: The Power of 1 Percent

What if... Potential Performance Gains in Key Sectors			
Industry	Segment	Type of Savings	Estimated Value Over 15 Years (Billion nominal US dollars)
Aviation	Commercial	1% Fuel Savings	$30B
Power	Gas-fired Generation	1% Fuel Savings	$66B
Healthcare	System-wide	1% Reduction in System Inefficiency	$63B
Rail	Freight	1% Reduction in System Inefficiency	$27B
Oil & Gas	Exploration & Development	1% Reduction in Capital Expenditures	$90B

Figure 5.1   GE Predicts Savings for the Industrial Internet

Note: Illustrative examples based on potential 1 percent savings applied across specific global industry sectors.

Source: General Electric.

The team at GE is attempting to solve meaningful business problems, such as improving resources and fuel efficiency in aviation and locomotive industries. GE estimates these businesses can save roughly $1 trillion per year by improving how assets are used and how operations and maintenance are performed within the industrial industries that GE serves (see Figure 5.1).[21]

For example, the airline industry spends $200 billion a year in fuel. The ability to develop a new aircraft engine takes years, but the ability to tune the engine and give the pilot insight into how to operate the engine can create huge savings. Even a 1 percent change would equate to $2 billion a year in industry-wide savings. Integrating new technologies, such as sensor data, cloud computing, and analytics, could help industries deliver new efficiencies with existing processes.

Ruh says that machines will become intelligent as they get connected and software becomes available to analyze the data these machines generate. He believes this will require a foundational shift in how GE's systems need to be built to take advantage of this opportunity. He says, "If we collected all the data from our gas turbines every day, it's petabytes of data that we'd have to collect, store, manage and manipulate. In order to unlock the value of this data, a business must re-imagine how systems are built."[22]

How is this an example of customer care? One sensor on a GE gas turbine generates 500 gigabytes of data per day, and there are 20 sensors on each turbine. GE has 12,000 turbines globally. Its challenge is how to collect and manage this volume of data. GE would also like to perform real-time analysis on the data to decide if a piece of equipment is reaching a critical failure point, such as a blade breaking. Care isn't just about when a problem occurs. It's about preventing problems.

Ruh offered three pieces of advice. First, the machines must become more intelligent. Sensor technology is the cornerstone of this intelligence. Second, a business must have a strategy to store, manage, and analyze this data. Real-time analysis and insight also takes on a new meaning. Real-time data could provide GE with the ability to decide if a component is reaching a critical failure point and alert the company to shut down the equipment before the event occurs. A business needs to get the information in a timely fashion that allows it to predict, prevent, and act upon the data. Ruh says, "The analytics part is beyond the capabilities of most organizations and has to be done by the world of data scientists, which are hard to find."

Third, it's not about shrinking headcount. It's about providing not just information but actionable insight to your employees. For example, a pilot is going to fly a plane, but how does the airline provide information that allows the pilot to decide if it is more important to land on time or save fuel costs? All of this data must be completely distributed and accessible as well. Ruh believes the cloud, big data, and insightful analytics will be the underpinnings of successful business. This is where IoT, big data analytics, and mobile come together to provide a right-time care experience.

GE has started down the path of delivering predictive and prescriptive right-time experiences to its industrial clients with a set of services it calls *real-time operational intelligence* (RtOI). The company's Intelligent Platforms business set out to address the challenge of making sense of the complex and extensive data available to its customers in the oil and gas, manufacturing, power, water, and metal industries. RtOI helps managers sort through vast amounts of data using simple mobile apps that offer real-time access to operational information, such as plant efficiency metrics, alarms, and outages. It also provides companies with the option of allowing employees to use their own devices quickly, easily, and securely.

"It allows geographically dispersed assets to be monitored securely over company or employee-owned devices. Information is delivered by role allowing for reduced travel times, better informed decisions, and fewer execution errors," said Mark Pipher, general manager of knowledge services for GE Intelligent Platforms.[23] In some cases, plant operators who are using the solution have seen their efficiency and productivity up to a level of 20 percent, according to GE. This is providing a form of employee care that uses mobile to make their jobs easier and provides efficiency gains to the business.

The program uses current mobile app and web technologies to empower workers according to their roles and locations—in real time. It accesses structured information through equipment models that can be configured specifically to a company's operations, allowing users to find the information they need quickly and easily. Once data is mapped into the model, users can add intelligence through easy-to-use tools that can outline relationships and connections to multiple dispersed systems, transforming it to information. With GE's geo-intelligence technology, the system automatically navigates and provides information based on user location, role, and asset condition and context.

Earlier, I discussed how businesses would evolve to right-time experiences in three phases. I said that the first stage, extend, brought existing business processes to mobile devices and the second phase used mobile to enhance these original processes. GE's RtOI does just this. It extends data from existing legacy systems such as Supervisory Control and Data Acquisition (SCADA) and Manufacturing Execution Systems (MES) to mobile devices. It then enhances the process by allowing the people who need to make decisions (operators, engineers, and executives) access to new real-time visualization, analytics, and collaboration tools for legacy systems over mobile devices.

Respond to Problems and Opportunities in Real Time

So, while mobile and business intelligence/analytics can be used in industrial automation, we can also use context such as social to improve care. One element of customer care and mobility is always timeliness. In the past, people would call a company if they had a problem. Now, managers have the opportunity to see if there is a problem in real time with feeds from Twitter or Facebook. People will complain immediately about things, such as the service on the bus and if a product works poorly. People will also share their joy when products delight them. If we have social media monitoring tools, we have access to this data in near-real time.

Businesses can also discover the lead influencers for their products or services. Until now, we used brute force to reach and persuade the influencers. We put ads in what we hoped was the appropriate media, either in print or on TV. We hoped we reached the influencers and hoped the influencers would say nice things about us. Now we have an opportunity to know and reach, at least electronically, these influencers. Once we've discovered them, we can reach out to those people directly to give them special experiences, better experiences. We can start to impact and shape the conversation of our brand. If these influencers have a good customer experience with us, they talk about that experience and interest other people in us—they influence opinion.

And it's not just data about our organization; we can also have these tools monitor data about our competitors. We can start to benchmark our customer care against the competition. We can understand the perception of our brand versus a competitor's. There is a wealth of information out there that people are giving away for free. If we have the right solutions to capture and analyze this data, we can understand what kind of experiences customers are having with our products and our competitors' products. Companies, especially if they are a business-to-consumer sales enterprise, need these tools to learn what is happening in the market. This gives a business an opportunity to provide a better-quality product in the future or to provide a better customer experience than in the past.

Virgin America is one airline that listens to customer comments. If I send a Twitter message to Virgin America, it will send a Twitter message back to me. That kind of direct connection with a customer was rare in the past. Now, you might not know the customer's name, because the Twitter profile name doesn't have to be the name of the end user. But you at least know what type of experience your customers are having with your product or service.

Summary

Care in right-time experiences exists in every part of the transaction, whether the transaction is with a customer, a prospect, an employee, a partner, or another stakeholder. It applies across verticals that are wildly different, from retail to health care to general business. Mobile, big data, and cloud computing can improve care by reducing paperwork, increasing workflows, and automating processes. We've seen how a variety of enterprises have embraced the new technology and the options to improve the care they offer. What effect does all this have on commerce?

That's the subject of the next chapter.

Notes

1. www.apple.com/iphone/business/profiles/lowes/.
2. www.youtube.com/watch?v=JDArkLdmVoE.
3. In-person interview with Phillipe Vayssac on October 24, 2013.
4. www.genesyslab.com/Genesys—Brochure/docs/SS_Groupama_screen.pdf and in-person interview with Mr. Vayssac.
5. http://www.salesforce.com/company/news-press/press-releases/2014/04/140424.jsp.
6. www.ibm.com/smarterplanet/us/en/leadership/aircanada/assets/pdf/Air Canada_Paper.pdf.
7. January 2014 interview with Philip Easter, director of mobility.
8. http://www.virgin-atlantic.com/us/en/footer/media-centre/press-releases/google-glass.html.
9. Brook Barnes, "*A Billion-Dollar Bracelet Is the Key to a Disney Park,*" *April 1 2014,* http://www.nytimes.com/2014/04/02/business/billion-dollar-bracelet-is-key-to-magical-kingdom.html?partner=socialflow&smid=tw-nytimesbusiness&_r=2.
10. "Smart Metering & Infrastructure Program Business Case," BChydro, n.d., p. 5.
11. "Smart Metering & Infrastructure Program Business Case," https://www.bchydro.com/content/dam/BCHydro/customer-portal/documents/projects/smart-metering/smi-program-business-case.pdf.
12. www.apple.com/ipad/business/profiles/rehabcare/.
13. www.att.com/gen/press–room?pid=21775&cdvn=news&newsarticleid=33117.
14. Interview with Michael Holmes, Program Director IBM Watson Solutions on July 22, 2013, and www.theatlantic.com/sponsored/ibm-watson/archive/2013/04/how-memorial-sloan-kettering-is-training-watson-to-personalize-cancer-care/274556/#ixzz2dQQZ7JTC.
15. www.mskcc.org/pressroom/press/ibm-watson-hard-work-new-breakthroughs-transform-quality-care-patients.
16. www-03.ibm.com/innovation/us/watson/pdf/MSK_Case_Study_IMC14794.pdf.
17. Bill Hethcock, "Texas Health Resources Aims to Cut Hospital Readmissions by 25 Percent," *Dallas Business Journal,* May 2, 2013, www.bizjournals.com.
18. http://healthcare.dmagazine.com/2012/12/10/young-parkland-physician-makes-a-splash-with-predictive-modeling-software/.
19. William Ruh, Vice President and Global Technology Director, General Electric, speaking at Cloud Connect, May 2013, which can be viewed at www.youtube.com/watch?v=cS_fxhax16s.

20. www.ge.com/docs/chapters/Industrial_Internet.pdf.
21. William Ruh, Vice President and Global Technology Director, General Electric, speaking at Cloud Connect, May 2013, which can be viewed at www.youtube.com/watch?v=cS_fxhax16s.
22. Interview with Mark Pipher, general manager, knowledge services, GE Intelligent Platforms, on May 23, 2013.
23. Interview with Mark Pipher, general manager, knowledge services, GE Intelligent Platforms, on May 23, 2013.

CHAPTER 6

Commerce in a Right-Time Experience

In some ways, commerce hasn't changed in hundreds of years. Businesses must still bring the right goods to market and price these wares competitively. In other ways, technologies like the Internet and mobile have fundamentally changed how we experience commerce. They allow virtual marketplaces that allow buyers and sellers to connect instantly across the globe. They also enable us to buy at any time of day and on the go. This trend, first with the Internet and then with mobile, has had a profound effect on brick-and-mortar retailers and all types of businesses. Even Internet heavyweights, such as eBay, have seen shifts in commerce as a result of mobile.

At the end of 2012, eBay was selling an average of 9,200 cars and 383,982 car parts each week through its mobile application.[1] Granted, these buyers may have initially found the cars and parts on the company's website, but they were using the mobile channel to complete transactions on the go.

Given the nature of eBay's auction process, the ability to participate in an auction while out of the home or office is a huge process improvement. Consumers don't have to be sitting at a computer to win an auction, discover new products, or purchase items. This is just one example of the change technologies such as mobile are driving in the area of transactions. This chapter will highlight how a diverse group of organizations have improved or plan to improve commerce through right-time experiences.

Mobile and Context Change Commerce

Mobile has revolutionized countless industries, although the widespread adoption of smartphones and tablets has impacted some more than others. Every type of business, from brick-and-mortar retailers to B2B suppliers, is feeling new pressures and opportunities as a result of mobile access, social referrals, and easier access to information. Consumers and business buyers expect to research, locate, and purchase products wherever they are. They also expect accurate and consistent real-time data throughout a seller's website and its physical locations. The retail industry has discussed the concept of omni-channel in retail before, but mobile makes it more apparent if there are inconsistencies in pricing, service, and product availability.

But it's not just B2C retail experiencing changes in commerce. Connectivity, portability, and context are the three elements that make commerce different in both B2C and B2B commerce. In the past, we had a certain amount of portability with laptops, but our business applications weren't truly portable the way they are today. Also in the past, we had connectivity, but it was often spotty and slow. The hassles of portability and connectivity alone made commerce and business difficult to conduct on the go. Both of those issues have largely gone away. As discussed in Chapter 3, mobile and IoT have created a third significant factor after portability and connectivity: context. Once we marry portability and connectivity to context, it opens up a new world of possible right-time experiences based on location, interaction history, time, and more. The benefits of these are readily apparent in the consumer market, but we must also remember that the same dynamics can apply to B2B commerce as well. This chapter will briefly address these changes for both markets.

As discussed in the Gimbal example in Chapter 4, context is not just location. However, location is one of the more important contextual items and is often one of the first elements a company will use to create new communications, care, and commerce experiences. Here are a few quick examples of how we might use context in commerce.

- **Time.** It's two hours before a performance of *The Lion King*, and tickets haven't yet sold out. A loyal theater patron who happens to be dining in the neighborhood receives an offer for half off the evening's tickets.
- **Weather.** It's the final soccer game of the FIFA World Cup and it's begun pouring rain. A team can send a push notification offering fans that have the team's app 20 percent off any team-branded rain gear.

- **Location.** Priceline's research found that mobile travel bookers are typically closer to the hotel of their choice, often in the same city, and they book last-minute more often than other travelers. This led the firm to invest in a mobile website strategy, which in turn increased unique visitors by 13.9 percent, tripled page views, and grew the mobile site's share of business 31 percent.[2]
- **Behavior.** It's three weeks into February and a gym's mobile app data shows its customers are falling behind their new workout regimens. It can then offer special programs and incentives to encourage customers to return. If you couple these alerts with location, it's even more powerful. When a member is a few blocks away from the health club, the club's app can automatically send a push notification encouraging him to get back on track by signing up for a complimentary visit with a personal trainer.
- **Expertise.** Business leaders will tap into human resources and collaboration software to identify who has certain skills and where they might be utilized in new and creative ways. In construction, for example, we might have employees who have experience with a specific type of wall treatment or asbestos abatement. We may need to send them to a worksite on short notice to make a project run smoothly. Having a real understanding of our workers' location and skills is another way management can speed up processes and make commerce function better for employees and partners.

The real benefit for commerce in a right-time experience world is taking advantage of the connectivity, portability, and context we didn't have before. Let's look at three examples of how retailers are leveraging these three items in stores.

Reach and Engage Consumers Wherever They Are

Consumers now use their mobile devices to access information, to decide where to eat, shop, visit, or buy. Today consumers are using smartphones in the store to check pricing, inventory availability, and product reviews. Retailers have to contend with showrooming—the phenomenon of a customer viewing merchandise and checking prices in a physical store only to purchase online or from another retailer. While showrooming has created challenges, mobile also provides an opportunity to reach consumers wherever they are—frequently at the point of decision.

Numerous forward-thinking retail stores are turning to mobile to engage with their customers on the go, drive foot traffic into their stores, and make the overall shopping experience more convenient. Leading retailers will use new computing solutions, such as big data and analytics, to create adaptive and personalized services that will get smarter over time through customer-specific data analysis.

Companies will create more engaging commerce experiences by integrating data from a customer's prior behaviors, listed preferences, and sentiment analysis and information crafted from users that are viewed to be similar. For example, a retailer could provide an application with check-in that provides relevant offers based on the user's prior transactions, reviews, and combined web and app browsing history.

Shopkick provides an early example of a communications and commerce app that uses mobile to help engagement. Shopkick is a shopping rewards program that automatically collects points, called kicks, for certain actions, such as walking into a store. It's the equivalent of a multistore loyalty card. You can walk into stores such as Target, Macy's, and Mobil convenience stores with your smartphone and instantly earn kicks. The app also gives you points for buying. Retailers are using it as a way to drive foot traffic, which is another way of saying engagement with the store. Shopkick lets you use your phone to scan and save products to the app. When you enter the store or are near it, it will remind you what you liked and of deals you wanted to take advantage of—leveraging the power of mobile (camera and location) to send you a right-time communication.

Shopkick has updated the app so shoppers can now access virtual catalogs from brands and retailers within the Shopkick universe, and then tap and drag items to save them to a shopping list. Then, when the shopper enters a store that sells an item she has saved, the app will remind the person of the product or promotion that she previously saved. Another update groups participating stores by location to help users plan shopping trips that will reward them with the most points. Shopkick says it decided to update its app after becoming aware that, on average, consumers who have it log on to the app nine days a month, but on six of those days, they are not at the store. They may be at home or at work, browsing new offers and planning their next shopping trip using Shopkick. The app also offers rewards points for browsing products and discounts from catalogs in the app.

The idea, of course, is to drive commerce, but it's also meant to encourage someone to walk into the store to see what's available. Shopkick's app uses mobile and location to nudge you into the store. You may not buy something, but there's a higher likelihood that you will if you're in the shop. Earning additional kicks for purchasing while in the shop makes consumers more likely to buy. What's even better is that users can redeem the kicks at any Shopkick store, not necessarily the one from which they earned the kicks. Retailers like this because they get the reinforcing effect of leveraging multiple stores to drive traffic.

This was the first wave of creating engagement, but it doesn't end there. The Holy Grail for retail is using indoor location to provide a customized service. Shopkick is one of many companies that's working with retailers to deliver these more personalized in-store experiences. It has integrated with Apple's iBeacon technology, which uses Bluetooth Low Energy (BLE) to send notifications to users when they're inside a physical store. It calls the new service shopBeacon and is currently in a closed beta trial with several Macy's stores and deploying technology in 100 American Eagle stores.[3] ShopBeacon can welcome a shopper when he enters a store and show him location-specific deals, discounts, recommendations, and rewards. This can happen automatically without the shopper having to remember to open his app. It can also tie at-home browsing within the app to in-store shopping by reminding the shopper if the store sells items that he was previously viewing. This is a right-time experience that integrates previous behaviors (browsing and buying) with current context, such as location and store promotions, to deliver a personalized real-time experience.

Tesco provides an example of a company that is transforming retail with technologies using mobile and big data. It uses these technologies to provide right-time experiences in commerce, customer care, and workforce optimization. I mentioned earlier how Tesco was testing a form of augmented reality to provide store associates with better information on creating displays. The company has also used mobile to bring the retail experience to new places. In Korea, the corporation's Homeplus stores realized that weekly grocery shopping was a major chore for many people and decided to "let the store come to the people."[4]

Like many train stations, Seoul metro stations have walls between the platform and the tracks. Homeplus papered the walls of Korean metro stations with life-size photographs of the supermarket aisle displays, which look astonishingly realistic, to create a virtual supermarket. While waiting for their subway train, shoppers can use their smartphones to scan QR codes on products, add them to their virtual shopping carts, check out, and have the entire order delivered to their homes. They've turned waiting time into shopping time. Tesco noted that online shopping increased 130 percent during the introductory campaign.[5] This also allowed Tesco to increase its presence without increasing the number of Homeplus stores. At the time, Homeplus's online sales had surpassed those of its largest competitor—with fewer stores.

As early as 2010, Tesco in the United Kingdom was encouraging consumers to scan barcodes with their smartphones and add them to a shopping cart. Shoppers can either have their orders be delivered or pick them up at the checkout. At London's Gatwick Airport, British tourists leaving on vacation were using a system similar to Seoul's to order their groceries—including meats, fruit, and vegetables—from a kiosk. The order would be delivered when they returned home. Grocers are creating right-time experiences where you can buy online, buy by phone, pick up in-store, or have it delivered. All of this makes commerce unbounded and engages customers wherever they go. It's the essence of creating an omni-channel experience. The customer is dealing with the brand, not a single channel. So, Tesco used mobile to take retail everywhere. Kohl's, a department store chain in the United States, provides an example of using mobile to improve the in-store experience.

The Connected Fitting Room   Kohl's was looking for a way to improve its customers' care experience in stores while increasing the amount of goods a shopper purchased. One area of the shopping experience that has remained underutilized until now is the fitting room. Kohl's worked with Accenture, Avanade, and Microsoft to design what it calls a "connected fitting room" and is piloting the program throughout the United States at the time I'm writing this book.

Kohl's recently added RFID tags to a portion of its clothing line to track inventory. When a shopper enters a connected fitting room, the system uses the RFID tags to recognize the items the customer has brought into the room. The system displays these items on a flat panel touchscreen within the fitting room. The article's description and features are onscreen as well as the other colors and sizes available. The fitting room system can suggest complementary items based on the articles the customer has brought into the fitting room.

In addition to suggesting other clothing options, the fitting room allows the user to request other sizes and colors and have them brought to the fitting area. These requests are sent in real time to sales associates who are using Windows 8 handheld devices on the floor. It's a better customer care experience because the customer no longer has to get dressed to find a different size and/or color of a certain item. It also provides a right-time commerce experience for the retailer and the customer because it helps the shopper easily find and purchase additional items.

The system tracks all of the items brought into the fitting room and can provide analytics on that merchandise. Information is gathered and analyzed to provide new insights, such as average time customers spend in the fitting room, how many items are brought in, or store associate response times. The solution will provide a wealth of anonymous data from all shoppers' visits but could also provide information from specific customers if the shopper is using the Kohl's app.

This is a great example of how mobile can enhance a business process. However, none of this can happen without a concerted effort across departments. Kohl's needed to design a strategy that integrated multiple systems such as RFID tags and readers, supply chain information, analytics, mobile point of sale, and workforce optimization software. It worked closely with Avanade, Accenture, and Microsoft to evaluate and integrate technologies and understand the interdependencies between the different applications. In order to make a solution like this happen, it's imperative that the company connects to existing back-end systems but provides an employee and customer interface that is mobile-friendly. The result is a connected right-time experience that allows Kohl's to offer services, such as recommendations, that were difficult to employ in the past.[6]

Move from Generic to Targeted Experiences

In many cases, companies are still sending out generic communications in which everyone receives the same experience, whether appropriate or not. In fact, the point of right-time experiences is to reduce the number of generic events. This is particularly relevant in business-to-consumer communications but also relevant in speaking with our partners and employees. People don't want the same advertisement, the same coupon, the same offer as everybody else. They also don't want to be tagged as having certain interests based on one event. Just because I buy a book on child care doesn't mean I'm pregnant or that I want to see ads about strollers, cribs, and disposable diapers.

This is an issue Amazon and Netflix, among others in the retail sector, have struggled with. In the first wave of online commerce, companies simply obtained information about customers and their purchases. If you bought a book on Amazon, it would suggest similar titles that the company thought you would like. Perhaps you hated the book or the genre or were buying it for a friend and would never buy something like it again. You don't want suggestions for products you will never buy. It was similar when Netflix profiled the movies you watched and provided recommendations. If a couple's husband likes zombie movies and the wife likes Jane Eyre movies, Netflix has to figure out what to recommend, because recommending *Pride and Prejudice* to the husband is a waste of time and an irritation.

The best and the brightest have struggled with this question and are now starting to use big data to draw much more accurate recommendations based on the purchasing habits of many clients. Netflix and Amazon are both using big data technologies to improve their recommendations. By analyzing large volumes of data, a business can uncover hidden correlations that help with recommendations.

Everyone from brick-and-mortar retailers to small businesses will be using some form of big data processing, combined with sensor data and mobile app usage data, to provide a more contextual, customized, and relevant commerce experience. We will first obtain a basic contextual experience. Your company may provide slightly different options based on knowing just a little bit more about the prospect, such as location or time of day. After a while, big data will help the retailer or the employer who is trying to provide information to its employees to learn over time what these users like or do regularly on mobile devices.

I've talked about salespeople needing to know what's happening with customers—delayed shipments, weak earnings, layoffs. Those are examples of context. If you look in the retail environment, context extends to knowing what devices individuals use, where they are, browsing history, the time of day, purchase history, and much more.

One of the hot issues now in retail, as I suggested earlier, is showrooming. Prospects visit a retailer like Best Buy to look at a TV. The prospect types in the brand and model number to see if it's cheaper elsewhere (Amazon, for example). Sometimes prospects use their smartphone to obtain more information about the TV because the TV doesn't have the right information sitting in front of it. In some cases, retailers are combatting the perception of poor customer service and inflated prices by encouraging consumers to gather more information while they are on the floor by offering spec sheets with codes (QR). If the consumer scans the code, it will take her to a site where she can get more details.

There are many reasons why someone might use his phone to get access to information, be it about the product or about the pricing. Retailers want to have context to know that an individual is in the store searching for a certain Samsung or Sony TV on Amazon. With a mobile application, location info, and opt-in, retailers have the opportunity to offer more customized shopping experiences.

You know the person is in the store and what they are standing in front of. If Best Buy knows that an individual is standing thoughtfully in front of a TV and knows from her browsing history that she left the Best Buy site for Amazon, the chain knows what it needs to compete against.

What should a retailer do with this information? Should the store staff walk over to tell her why it's better to purchase from Best Buy and remind her that she can have it immediately? The retailer could offer to waive the sales tax or offer a discount, or it could suggest an alternative product. The more we know about the prospect, the greater the odds that we can suggest a meaningful incentive. Armed with this new knowledge, the salesperson can inform that customer that they'll automatically match a competitor's pricing. One prospect will be influenced by price, while another may want immediate delivery, and a third may desire a free product with purchase, such as a movie or DVD player.

This is using contextual information to change what would have been a generic shopping experience into a targeted shopping experience for this prospect. If the customer happens to be a member of the chain's loyalty program, the store's salesperson can also note this in a conversation. For example, "I see you've bought a Blu-ray player and you're looking at a 3-D TV. You're going to need an upgraded Blu-ray player to enjoy the full effect of the 3-D. If you buy both today, we can give you a 10 percent discount." A business can also start to create predictive right-time experiences if it knows what its customers have done in the past and understands what they are doing at the moment.

Changing the Game with Contextual Pricing

In the past, pricing strategies tended to be inflexible, and managers often lacked the data to make real-time or frequent price changes.

This is changing with the combination of mobile, big data, and the Internet of Things. Businesses often lacked competitive pricing data in the past. Now there are services that will monitor all of your competitors' pricing, and they will either give it to you as a web portal or add it into your existing pricing system to understand an item's current market price across competitors. Businesses now have the option of using big data platforms to analyze a wide range of pricing data or buy a service to do this.

Armed with new knowledge of a competitor's pricing, business managers can decide what type of action they'd like to take. If management decides it would like to change prices, the question morphs to how quickly a retailer can change the prices of a product across the various channels. Today, it's largely manual labor in the store. However, certain companies are embracing IoT to save labor and improve pricing flexibility with electronic shelf labels. Instead of having a paper shelf label, retailers can have an electronic shelf price label that allows headquarters—or a service provider—to set prices regionally and distribute the price changes automatically.

Tesco is an example of a retailer that has done exactly this. Before electronic shelf labels, Tesco would manually change between 5 and 10 million shelf-edge labels. This was time-consuming and didn't offer any additional value to the customers or the store. With new shelf labels, Tesco can change prices within an hour. This provides the flexibility for Tesco to respond to changes in inventory and shifts in competitor pricing and run short-term promotions.

But what's interesting about this capability is not only the ability to change prices instantly (and save hours of hand labor), but that a chain can run flash sales on items. Say the chain receives a large order of strawberries, and in one store or one area, not many customers want organic strawberries. If they don't sell, they're going to perish. Management now has the opportunity to cut the price of organic strawberries for the next six hours in this store or this group of stores—as opposed to the entire chain. It can change the price the shopper sees at the display or in the app, which will be reflected at the register. It's an example of taking an inflexible pricing strategy—notifying store management, creating new price tags, sending employees to change the tags—and making pricing much more flexible.

With mobile, a chain now has another option, even if it doesn't have electronic shelf labels. Management can send a promotion to every consumer in the store who has the chain's mobile application.

This can say, in effect, "Loyal shopper, for the next six hours, strawberries are on sale; get your organic strawberries now. Only $3.99 a pound with your loyalty card or app."

Other retailers, such as Safeway, are offering special promotions for individual users within the company's mobile app. Safeway's "Just For You" program allows users to see promotional pricing based on previous purchases and save these promotions to their electronic loyalty card. Once at the register, the discounts are automatically applied by entering the customer's loyalty number. Either way, a business has the opportunity to employ near-real flexibility pricing. Over time, a business can also learn which promotions resonated with customers and adjust promotions on the fly. This is moving from generic to contextual to personalized pricing experiences.

Staying on the theme of pricing for a moment, let's look at how a company can use contextual pricing to improve its business. When companies and customers think of pricing, we often consider price cuts. But many price cuts are responsive measures instead of proactive strategies. Like Safeway and its "Just for You" program, Progressive Insurance built a right-time experience that improves pricing by using context to match pricing to particular behaviors. Progressive Insurance's "Pay As You Drive" program provided a fundamentally new way of looking at pricing strategies. Instead of using demographics such as age or years driving to calculate its pricing, Progressive offers its policyholders the chance to lower their premiums based on an analysis of their actual driving habits (context) over a specific period.

The Snapshot device plugs into a car's diagnostic port (usually below the steering column) and automatically keeps track of the driving. Snapshot records how often the driver slams on the brakes, how many miles he regularly drives, and how often he drives between midnight and 4 A.M. Based on a 30-day trial, Progressive extends a personalized rate, then requires Snapshot to stay plugged in for five more months to set an ongoing renewal discount.[7] (Conceivably, a driver could drive uncharacteristically conservatively during the trial period.) Instead of offering a generic price cut to all buyers, Progressive can target a specific buyer.

According to Progressive, "Test driving Snapshot is an easy way to find out if your good driving would save you any extra money on your Progressive car insurance." Prospects can sign up for Snapshot when they get their auto insurance quote—which they can do online, over the phone, or from a mobile device. Or, if the driver is not ready to switch insurance carriers, she can sign up online or from a mobile device for a 30-day test drive. For the test, Progressive collects the driver's name, contact information, birthdate, and details about the household's vehicles. Once a driver plugs in the Snapshot device, Progressive collects the vehicle identification number and notes whether the device stays plugged in so the firm can alert the driver if Snapshot is disconnected. "The Snapshot device doesn't track your location or whether you're speeding, and it doesn't contain GPS technology," the company assures prospects.[8]

The Progressive website also provides suggestions on how to alter driving habits to save even more on insurance premiums and other expenses. It's a win-win for both parties. Drivers get lower premiums, and Progressive can better match pricing to actual versus perceived risk. The company can communicate valuable information to its customers when they want it. To build this right-time experience, Progressive Insurance had to change its business processes to take in new data inputs from the connected sensors. It had to translate data from Snapshots into metrics that would correlate a person's driving patterns to the risk of an accident. The company had to take these algorithms and change its pricing to reflect the new assessment of risk. It then had to market this new creative approach to prospects and customers.

Snapshot was revolutionary for the insurance industry. Risk is a major issue, and risk assessment has normally been based on demographics. The notion of creating pricing based on actual behavioral characteristics changes commerce. It gave Progressive Insurance something to market. It arguably changes the economics of risk for them. The firm can potentially attract more profitable customers because typically the people who are willing to go through the Snapshot test drive exercise tend to be the safer drivers.

Use Partnerships and Mobile to Drive Sales

Pricing is only one of many strategies that a business can take to create a commerce-related right-time experience. Many types of business can benefit from real-time data access and capture, such as retrieving and updating customer records, checking inventory and prices, and processing sales transactions. But businesses can also combine mobile context and partnerships to increase transactions and sales.

The Société de transport de Montréal (STM), the main metropolitan bus and rail transportation for Montreal, Quebec, provides an example of using partnerships to create a right-time experience. It faced a unique challenge. The transportation system receives government subsidies based on ridership, but ridership growth had stagnated. Without new growth, funding for capital improvements and other expenses would be difficult to obtain. The STM aims to deliver 540 million trips in 2020, and improving customer experience is central to its strategy for achieving that goal. To stimulate increased ridership, the company launched an innovative loyalty program in the form of an iPhone application called STM Merci in May 2013.[9]

Developed jointly by the STM and its technology partner, SAP, the application was designed to provide STM riders with exclusive, personalized offers based on their profiles and the preferences that they to choose to indicate. STM has partnered with companies in other areas of transportation, events, and local businesses to create these offers. It divided an extensive network of more than a hundred partners into 12 preference areas. Customers receive geolocated offers based on wherever they happen to be, making the offers all the more useful. The STM reward program offers its participants instant gratification without having to collect points.

STM wants to implement more measures to strengthen customer loyalty by increasing the appeal of public transit. With this in mind, the company has adopted a relationship marketing approach that focuses more on people, their needs, their expectations, and their preferences. The transportation company created an application that has train schedules and streamlines the whole payment process by adding train fare and train passes to the mobile app as a stored value. It created a "Thank You" loyalty program, which incorporates all of the offers, benefits, and discounts already offered to STM clients, including offers for families, partner discounts, and the Maestro status. By offering riders discounts, privileges, and leisure-time activities, the STM aims to encourage its clients to travel more often by bus or metro.

STM management also felt that even if they made commuting easier for customers, many people simply didn't want to ride the trains. One problem was that they needed basic information about when to ride. It is frustrating not to be able to get on the train. Through analyzing ridership data, it is possible to see how people are flowing through the system and predict when the trains will be full. It becomes possible to say that the 7:30 is crowded but the 7:42 usually has seats, and it runs faster than the 7:30 because not as many people board and get off. This is an example of coupling current context, such as location and time of day, with information about previous behaviors, such as the time a person would normally take the train. With these three pieces of data and information on general passenger travel times, STM can create a customized recommendation for its passengers.

The third thing STM's management decided was to work with local retailers to make real-time offers. Suppose they know an individual gets off the train at the Place de Armes station, where there is a La Boulange bakery. STM can send the passenger a real-time offer for a croissant when he gets off the 7:30 A.M. train or an offer for a loaf of bread when he departs the 5:30 P.M. train. This right-time commerce experience works out for everybody. The baker wants to bring in foot traffic, and the train station can help do that. It's good for the train system, because it provides another reason for customers to ride the train. Customers only receive the coupons if they ride the train. It is a way to increase ridership without increasing costs because the bakery gives the bread discount—a win-win for everybody. Offering time-based and category-based promotions is the first step. Over time the goal is for the system to learn more about the riders and to provide more targeted interest-based offerings.

STM has also talked about integrating with other transportation options. Say a passenger needs a taxi when she gets off the train. It's not a difficult scenario to arrange. It's possible to alert the cab company that the train is running 10 minutes late so the driver doesn't have to sit and idle for 10 minutes. STM provides a great example of how companies can leverage context, big data analytics, and partnerships to deliver a right-time commerce experience.

RTEs Change B2B Commerce

Most people think of commerce in terms of consumer retail, but for the purpose of this chapter it encompasses much more. Business-to-business commerce is also being impacted by mobile-enabling workflows and new options for gathering information and bringing products to market, such as big data marketplaces, SaaS, and social media monitoring.

Consumer mobility has changed our outlook on what we should design for a business application. Many enterprise systems that were defined for the PC were difficult to use and are impossible to use on a mobile device. Applications and services weren't always intuitive. In a right-time experience world, the design principle is that many activities often will be completed on a mobile device.

Programmers are building simpler processes. Since the user may have a phone or a tablet that does not have a keyboard, programmers are redesigning the application to get to the heart of what we need to do right away. If we are placing an order, if we are checking inventory, if we are trying to find information about a product, it should be easier and faster to do on a phone or a tablet than on an existing corporate system. It's direct-touch-to-task access instead of multiple clicks of navigation.

Companies that embrace these new technologies are improving existing business processes and developing new ones. In this case, I'm discussing the processes that specifically relate to making a sale. These are examples of commerce-related right-time experiences from an employee's perspective.

It may be as simple as establishing that inventory is available or as complex as explaining the value of a surgical robot. Salespeople need to know when they can get an order shipped. They should be able to input an order directly into a system and have it flow to all affected departments—warehouse, shipping, manufacturing, purchasing, accounting, customer service—without anyone needing to print six copies for distribution. Every employee who needs access to this information should be able to enter data and access data on a mobile device from any location.

Companies are using these technologies to improve processes such as order entry and fulfillment. Leaders are mobile-enabling applications to improve the speed with which products, services, and processes can be moved through the supply chain. They are embracing mobile, big data, and analytics to make sure the right employees, agents, and sources have the right information so they can answer customers' and prospects' questions.

A right-time experience could involve a business routing a service technician to the right place on an emergency service call. It will know a technician is working down the street (location) and can deal with a crisis nearby right away (skill set). Through the sensor data, such as connected RFID tags (Internet of Things), a manager will know if the right part is on the truck, so she will know which truck to send. The business can route its trucks more effectively.

Eliminating Paper

Many organizations struggle with sales tools and associated printed material, such as price books, spec sheets, product documentation, and PowerPoint presentations. These documents constantly have to be updated with the right information. With a sales force of any size— employees or agents—these updates become costly to print and ship. Also, some percentage of the sales team doesn't want to carry them around, anyway. It is inefficient and wasteful. In some industries, such as pharmaceuticals, there could be legal consequences if salespeople use outdated content. Government agencies, such as the Food and Drug Administration, have created regulations that mandate certain industries to always be presenting customers with the most up-to-date knowledge.

We can make this process more effective by giving a salesperson a tablet and creating electronic sales content. If we install the right software in the tablet, we can send that content to the tablet automatically. The next time the salesperson is at a Wi-Fi hotspot, the content uploads. Or, say we operate in a regulated environment; we can set rules that say whenever someone tries to access the drug information or a price sheet, he needs to obtain the latest version. He can't use the one on his machine.

One example of this is Eaton's Power Source application, which is a catalog application for a tablet. Eaton, a $22 billion power management company with its operational headquarters in a Cleveland, Ohio, suburb, has approximately 102,000 employees and sells products to customers in more than 175 countries. It sells thousands of power distribution, power quality, industrial automation, and power control products plus products in the automotive, industrial, and aerospace industries.

Eaton has taken many of its individual catalogs and integrated them all into one application it calls Power Source.[10] The Power Source application offers 15,000 documents of product literature so salespeople no longer have to carry product catalogs. This allows engineers and designers to search for products and specifications from over 200,000 that have been placed into one application. Employees can search for goods by product line, prototype, or application requirements.

All the data the salesperson needs is resident in the application, which means he doesn't always have to be connected to the Internet. The app offers product images, technical specifications, pricing, and product lead times. It also contains a competitive product cross-reference guide so that prospects can look at over 240,000 products from Eaton's competitors and compare them to Eaton products. This allows Eaton's sales representative to find an Eaton product match for most competitors' products.

The app automatically updates weekly so that users always have the most current list of products, news, and information. They can find thousands of detailed documents at the touch of a button. They can also see 3-D models of parts to visualize them from any angle. This makes it easier for prospects and sales teams to make selections more effectively.

The app offers training and product videos because the salesperson may not always be up to date on what has changed in a product, why it's important, and how it should be presented. Mobile apps don't have to be lightweight. Power Source is a full-functioning app that the sales representatives can use to configure even complicated products. Imagine the paper saved and the efficiency improved by having all the information available in a 7- to 10-inch tablet. Not to mention how being able to email any piece of that information to a client on the spot helps to improve sales.

Salespeople can show the product in action or move around the part on a tablet to see what it looks like from all sides. A surgical products company can show a video of its robot performing parts of the operation, which, as the Intuitive Surgical experience demonstrates, helps its salespeople to sell much more effectively.

Intuitive Surgical sells robots to surgeons, not the easiest sales story because few surgeons want to replace themselves with robots. In fact, Integrated Surgical's robots don't replace surgeons. They augment their skills, and surgeons become more efficient with the robots. But how do you convince a surgeon?

Chris Simmonds, senior director of marketing services at Intuitive Surgical, has embraced tablets to enhance the sales experience by providing richer content, such as videos of the robots in action. Today, 85 percent of the company's sales staff is participating in a bring-your-own-device tablet program. Intuitive Surgical first used tablets to replace paper binders. Simmonds says they've created a new tablet application that replaces sales binders, which cost $60,000 apiece. With approximately 850 sales personnel, this will equate to jaw-dropping savings over time because it's cheaper and easier to update and maintain the content digitally.[11] The application also provides richer sales tools by integrating video. If necessary, a salesperson can provide a video product demonstration as the surgeon walks down the hall. The video is much more engaging and comprehensible than a flipchart at the physician's desk, and a tablet is much more portable and flexible than a laptop.

From these examples, we can see that it is possible to reach the point where salespeople always have the most up-to-date information. They are within regulatory compliance, because they have the current information. The business can also save money on printing and salespeople can be more efficient because they don't have to incorporate the new collateral every time something changes. The further step that makes this interesting is that we can make the content more engaging and possibly interactive. Instead of using a sheet of paper, information could be presented in a video and 3-D rendering of the product, the parts, and so on. We can change commerce with the right information in a better format at the point of need. But what the Power Source app shows us is that you also need to be able to deliver action within a business process. Replacing paper is one thing, but you'll start to see the benefit and ROI of a process when the user can take an action, such as configuring a product and sending a customized quote in real time.

After Eliminating Paper, Add Context

FedEx and UPS used the concept of speed and location to build competitive advantage in the transportation industry. These companies pioneered the use of GPS-based route optimization and hand-held mobile devices many years ago. At that time, they used customized hardware and software, and it was expensive. Today, companies have the opportunity to use consumer mobile devices with rugged cases and off-the-shelf software. Companies with equipment and staff that move around can mobile-enable workflows to route employees around more effectively than in the past. With access to context such as GPS, weather, road construction, and current traffic conditions, a company's drivers can save time and money. UPS has saved millions of dollars by mapping more effective routes, which pays for the software to optimize the routes. But UPS and FedEx aren't the only companies that are advancing their business with mobile and context.

Del-Air in Sanford, Florida, provides an example of using mobile's unique attributes to improve its sales and service speed and accuracy. It's the state's largest heating, air-conditioning, and electrical company. The company implemented Xora to automate the collection of worker and customer information in the field and its transfer back to managers in the home office. Xora offers a suite of configurable mobile apps and a web-based management application that helps mobile businesses and their field employees work smarter and faster. Del-Air's 600 field technicians use their mobile phones to clock in and out at the beginning and end of each day.

They also use Xora to record start and stop times for various projects and the status of each job. Xora integrates multiple dimensions of context and multiple functions into the workflow—location, time tracking, photo capture, and signature capture—to make a work experience more seamless. Instead of a separate timekeeping app, mileage log, and job dispatch application, all of these are accessible in one screen. The technicians send the real-time data captured in the field to the Xora management application, where Del-Air supervisors can view web-based maps and reports easily. Here's an example of the sequence a technician might follow:

- Click to record the start of shift.
- Enter miles.
- View the jobs icon for assignments for the day, a summary, and directions to worksite.
- View key appointment details: location, time, and so on.
- Start job to record time.
- Prompt for first action.
- Take picture of installation for records.
- Collect customer contact preference.
- Activate warranty by scanning barcode.

According to John Rucker, Del-Air's CIO, "In the first year we saved more than $350,000 from implementing Xora, and that's based only on the automated time cards capability. Add another $30,000 we expect to save by reducing data entry with the scheduled exports feature, and the cost of the solution more than pays for itself."[12] Historical trend information also improved the accuracy of job costing.

This is one of the real wins for any organization—redesigning a product, a service, or an application so people can put it to use right out of the box. Right-time experiences are intuitive. Users understand what they need to do next, and they can find any information they need easily. Many technology critics have said that the move to mobile requires simple applications with limited features. I take issue with that. A business can create or purchase rich and compelling mobile applications. The challenge is to ensure you go to the heart of the task at hand. What will people do with the application? How are they most likely to take advantage of this smaller format's connectivity, portability, and context? These are the questions that you have to answer to build a compelling right-time experience. Once you've answered these questions, your organization can decide if it should build an application to meet that need or purchase an SaaS application or a solution that combines an app with a web-based management platform.

This was obviously an ambitious process and involved foresight. But many businesses can learn from Del Air's experience and start by using mobile to minimize or eliminate a paper-based process.

Increase Efficiencies and Improve Company Data

There were things that we used to wait to do until we were back at the office, until we were back at home, until we had a larger device with a bigger screen, a keyboard, and a good Internet connection. Now we can accomplish many of those critical tasks on a smartphone or a tablet, or we can access information while on the go that we couldn't obtain before. In fact, one of my customers said that success for their mobile initiative would be when the user was sitting at a desk with a laptop and still selected the mobile device to complete a transaction. To him, this meant that both mobile experience and functionality were on par with or better than the PC-based experience.

Let's look at an example of how mobile can help improve efficiencies and profit without selling additional products. Amtrak provides an example of an organization that created efficiencies by extending and improving a process with mobile technology. Amtrak operates more than 300 trains a day, serving over 500 destinations throughout the United States and Canada over 21,200 miles of track. The company carried 31.6 million business and leisure passengers in fiscal year 2013.[13] However, the company's ticketing process had changed little since the nineteenth century. Customers could make reservations online, but ticketing technology had stopped there. Customers were still issued paper tickets.

"The absence of technology onboard our trains created a lot of inconvenience for customers, and inhibited both the streamlining of back-office processes and the adoption of some safety recommendations," says Tony Flynn, senior director of mobile systems at Amtrak.

One key limitation was the lack of real-time communication between reservation systems and onboard conductors. This slowed the exchange of critical information, like passenger manifests. On the train, conductors had to collect, validate, and sort tickets—a time-consuming and imprecise process—then ship them to a central scanning facility in Texas. Revenue reconciliation took 3 to 10 days from the time of a train's arrival at its destination. Consequently, Amtrak did not know exactly who rode a train or what type of ticket they purchased until the ticket data was entered into the central system days later. In addition, Amtrak lost revenue when it had empty seats from customers who did not travel and that it did not know it could fill.

For customers, paper-based ticketing was inconvenient and sometimes costly. The company required passengers to obtain paper tickets prior to boarding. Once issued, these became value-based documents. If a customer lost one, she had to buy another, pay a $75 fee, and go through a lengthy reimbursement process for the lost ticket. This was the same process the airlines used prior to eTicketing, but "not surprisingly, this caused a great deal of customer dissatisfaction," says Deborah Stone-Wulf, chief of sales distribution and customer service.[14]

The paper-based process also made last-minute purchases or reservation changes difficult. In remote areas of the United States, many of Amtrak's stations are unstaffed, with no way to generate tickets at the station. Customers in these regions had to buy tickets onboard, an uncertain and time-consuming process that took conductors up to four minutes per transaction.

Amtrak had tried to implement an electronic ticketing solution in the 1990s, when the airlines started to switch over. "We had a vision and the solution had to meet the mobility needs of our trains and customers, but wireless technology at that time wasn't mature enough to be able to bet your business on it," says Ghada Ijam, Amtrak's chief relationship officer.[15] With passengers getting on and off trains at multiple stops along a route, and in the absence of gate control, rail travel has more unique requirements than air travel. "Unlike an airline where you can check in passengers at fully staffed gates, trains don't have that environment," Ijam points out. "A mobile solution was really the only way to go."

Amtrak chose AT&T to provide a mobile applications development platform, devices, wireless networking, and mobile device management. The solution puts smartphones into conductors' hands; these connect to back-office reservation and accounting systems. Conductors simply scan passenger tickets on board, and customers have more flexible self-serve ticketing capabilities. For Amtrak, access to real-time information improves onboard operations, safety, inventory management, revenue realization, and workflow.

The solution required Amtrak to build 72 back-end systems to prepare for mobile. To make sure it was on the right track for user acceptance, Amtrak obtained input from the conductors who are responsible for train operations. "We wanted to make sure we were hitting the mark with the actual usability of the device, and that our conductors would not be intimidated by the technology," says Tony Flynn. From screen design to application features, the conductors' feedback was central in shaping the system.

With input from the users, training conductors on the customized application took less than half the time Amtrak expected it to take, and the conductors handled it themselves. "They took right to it," says Stone-Wulf. "It was intuitive, easy, and exactly what they needed." Now Amtrak gives a smartphone to all its conductors, and they connect in near-real time with Amtrak's database. Conductors input and receive passenger ticket and train information directly on their devices.

To address security and management concerns, Amtrak used the MobileIron Connected Cloud from AT&T, which provides mobile device management. "It keeps an inventory of all the devices and gives control and visibility into who's doing what—who can access the application and what version they have. It also reports unauthorized activity," says Ijam. If a phone is lost or stolen, Amtrak can lock it down or remotely wipe its contents.

Amtrak began pilot testing its eTicketing solution on one route in August 2011. It rolled out eTicketing nationwide with about 2,000 active smartphones a year later. According to Stone-Wulf, eTicketing has revolutionized Amtrak's business. "Whether it's how the customer is able to buy and receive a ticket, our revenue management approach, or safety and security, this was transformative," she says. For passengers, eTicketing is flexible, convenient, and quick, eliminating station wait lines and the uncertainty and hassle of purchasing tickets onboard. They can print tickets at home, or even present reservations directly on their own mobile devices.

"With electronic ticketing, customers can change a ticket in the cab on the way to the station and walk right onto the train without skipping a beat," says Stone-Wulf. "They can be five minutes away from the station with ten minutes to go before departure, and they've now got plenty of time." Because tickets are no longer "value documents," a customer who loses one can simply print another. Near real-time connectivity between Amtrak's back-end systems and conductors on trains dramatically increases the company's oversight of passengers, products, and services, improving information quality, safety, and revenue.

Conductors now have the same real-time passenger manifest as the reservation system. As reservations are fulfilled, changed, added, or canceled, the electronic manifest is updated accordingly. When you know exactly how many seats are available, you can improve inventory management and revenues. "If you buy a ticket and don't show up, as soon as that train has left, we know that you're not onboard and we can now sell that seat down the line," says Matt Hardison, chief marketing and sales officer at Amtrak. With better data and reduced ticket shipping costs, the company has realized cost savings and incremental revenue benefits of tens of millions of dollars annually.

The system provides other benefits. In case of an emergency, Amtrak now knows exactly who is on the train. The solution frees conductors to focus more on train and trip operations. They can now enter maintenance requests on the way to the next station so service crews can respond quickly. "The device knows what train you're on and what cars are assigned to that train," says Hardison. "With touch screen dropdowns, you can identify the type of problem, press a button, and it's sent directly to the work management system. When the train comes in, somebody's already got the details." Last-minute reservation alerts enable conductors to make accommodations for any special needs of incoming passengers, like making sure the train stops at the right place to board through a wheelchair-accessible location.[16]

By moving an existing process to mobile, Amtrak has substantially reduced manual processes and costs. Customers appreciate the flexibility and ease of not having to wait in line to buy a ticket, and Amtrak now has real-time information on the number of people on a train versus the number of tickets sold, so it can better control its inventory of empty seats.

Amtrak provides one example of how a business can speed up workflows simply by mobile-enabling a part of the existing process. Let's review what the process might look like in a different industry.

One of my clients is a global pharmaceutical company that has also used mobile to improve efficiencies and profits. For years, the pharmaceutical company's sales representatives had dropped off drug samples at hospitals and medical offices. To account for the drugs, the reps had to type in the samples' 16-digit tracking numbers or write them on forms. Often they would not do this on the spot. For the most part, sales representatives were batch-processing sales and sample orders, which sometimes meant they forgot samples because they didn't have a number at hand. Sometimes they entered the wrong number, but normally the samples were logged well after they'd been delivered. It was administrative chaos.

The pharmaceutical company gave each rep an iPad with a built-in camera. The reps now take a photograph of the product's 16-digit code, it goes into the system automatically, and the system bills the hospital or doctor immediately. Administrative chaos is reduced to order. But more significantly, the company shaved 45 days off of its receivables. All of this was possible only because the firm gave its reps a device with a camera and updated their process to connect that data directly into the company's inventory, accounting, and billing systems. Better data, faster time to billing, and a better experience for the employees—a win-win all around for the company.

The Role of Big Data in Commerce

We've seen how something as simple as eliminating paper can change the sales process. But a company can create even more powerful and transformative apps when we combine mobility with big data. What is big data's role in commerce? Before big data, many real-time decisions and promotions couldn't happen because the executive responsible for a decision didn't have the opportunity to collect and analyze all the data in near-real time. Without this, the manager often lacked the basic insights and comments to make an informed decision. Now it's possible to collect all the data (or several magnitudes more data than earlier) and turn it into knowledge. An employee on the go can send a request back to headquarters for information. A company with the right big data foundation can rapidly analyze a set of data and deliver the information that is useful to the employee.

Leading companies are building right-time experiences that improve customer care, offer creative pricing strategies, and guide particular behaviors.

Big Data Adds Better Information to Speed

Let's take a look at a real-world example of how accessing data on the go can make a difference in commerce. Hilti, headquartered in Liechtenstein, provides technology to the global construction industry. It has around 21,000 employees in more than 120 countries around the world. It markets tools and equipment for heavy construction, metal work, mining, electrical, interior finishing, plumbing, heating, and air-conditioning trades. In the past, Hilti had the raw data it needed—approximately 33 million records—but it used to take hours to analyze it. Now it can take seconds.

Today, a Hilti employee with his laptop out in the field can run a query on what is going on with a customer, what's going on with the products, and so on. If a customer or prospect asks him a question, the employee can run a query and provide the customer with the answer before he leaves the site. When it took three hours, he'd have to return to the office to get the answer.

Now you can sit in your car in front of the customer's office and get access to the data you need on your smartphone or tablet. This real-time access to information fundamentally changes the way enterprises do business. This is the power of big data—being able to get information, basically almost at the point of need, by tapping into all of your relevant customer information and available third-party info.

Add Big Data and Indoor Location to Improve Sales

In 1998, Sam Walton said, "People think we got big by putting big stores in small towns; we got big by replacing inventory with information."[17] Walmart handles more than a million customer transactions each hour and imports those into databases estimated to contain more than 2.5 petabytes of data. "There's big data and there's Walmart big data," says Ravi Raj, vice president for mobile and social products at @WalmartLabs, the company's new media innovations headquarters. "Every week we release half a dozen features."[18] Increasingly, Walmart is marrying its big data with mobile to create new and compelling experiences.

The company now offers a single application that provides different features based on whether the customer is in the store or at home. The contextual-based application operates as a running shopping list, recommendation engine, and weekly ad circular. List generation is enhanced with features such as a barcode scanner, predictive type, and a running tab that adds up all the items on a list.

To make the application location-aware, Walmart created a geo-fence to enclose all of its retail locations. As a shopper enters a store, the application automatically shifts to in-store mode. It makes the list easily accessible and can help the shopper locate items in the store. Walmart is using data from its transactions, website transaction data, and other data sources to create an improved shopping list for its customers. The mobile application has a recommendation feature, so if a consumer finds one item, the app will recommend what merchandise will complement it.

"I want to focus on something much more tangible—people, hundreds of millions of people, and how mobile is helping them save money so they live better," says Gibu Thomas, global head of mobile at Walmart. "The smartphone has touched so many parts of our lives that we no longer think of it as a device, as much as part of our hand."[19]

Thomas adds, "By leveraging big data, we are also developing predictive capabilities to automatically generate a shopping list for our customers based on what they and others purchase each week."[20] For example, if a Walmart application user was in the electronics aisle searching for a video game under $20, she could use a voice feature to tell the application her request, prompting the application to generate a list of the bestselling games in that particular store that meet the requested budget requirements.

Another way to think about big data is as an engine that collects acres of data and starts to learn over time. A business can begin to anticipate customers' needs by tracking their responses and acting accordingly. It can approach them with a right-time offer, and if enough people don't like the offer, the company will know that the offer it presented doesn't work for the type of customers it has. Or, if it works, the company can start to learn the characteristics of the customers who clicked on it.

One of the really interesting things happening in commerce is that it has been based mainly on demographics: female, Hispanic, 18 to 34, married, two children, and more. While traditional demographics are interesting and certainly useful, we are moving into indicators that are interest-based or behavior-based. Big data allows companies to learn what some of those dimensions may be for individual consumers.

Summary

To sum up, connectivity, portability, and context are the three elements that make commerce different in both B2C and B2B commerce. Businesses can use mobile, big data, social, and cloud computing to reach consumers and employees wherever they are. Mobile provides retailers the ability to reach prospects at the point of decision and to present individualized offers. Mobile, big data, and the associated analytics give organizations insights into consumer behavior that were simply impossible in the past. With this information, companies, both B2C and B2B, can be more efficient, offer more attractive products and services, and be more profitable than ever before.

What many businesses want to do in mobile is connect with people at that real-time moment, but it is most successful when you have a dialogue with prospects in which they feel you have their best interest at heart. You understand something about them, their needs, and their situation, and you want to make life easier for them. You also want to sell a product or a service, of course, but the process becomes much less stressful for everyone when the situation is one of the prospect buying rather than the salesman selling.

Creating these commerce experiences creates an ongoing dialogue that helps consumers to proactively engage and buy. Right-time experiences are not just about driving a one-time sale. They utilize context, big data, and mobile as a delivery mechanism to drive engagement and new personalized commerce experiences. These can be anything from the connected fitting room to buying products on your phone to delivering the ability to complete a B2B transaction on a mobile device. But regardless of which solution we're discussing, right-time experiences are different because they are contextual.

Notes

1. www.forbes.com/sites/altheachang/2013/01/07/ebay-mobile-car-sales/.
2. www.mmaglobal.com/files/casestudies/priceline_final.pdf.
3. http://techcrunch.com/2014/01/16/shopkick-starts-100-store-ibeacon-trial-for-american-eagle-outfitters-the-biggest-apparel-rollout-yet/.
4. www.youtube.com/watch?v=fGaVFRzTTP4.
5. Ibid.
6. Information gathered from a booth tour and demos at the Accenture booth at Mobile World Congress in February 2014.
7. www.progressive.com/auto/snapshot-how-it-works/.

8. www.progressive.com/auto/snapshot-common-questions/.
9. www.stm.info/en/press/press-releases/2013/the-stm-launches-a-one-of-a-kind-application-to-thank-its-clients.
10. Video of Eaton Power Source Application and functions: http://vimeo.com/51456764.
11. Chris Simmond's presentation at the Tabtimes event, February 20, 2013, http://events.tabtimes.com/tabletstrategywest/speakers/.
12. www.xora.com/case-studies/del-air/.
13. www.amtrak.com/ccurl/355/968/Amtrak-National-Fact-Sheet-FY2012.pdf.
14. "Wireless eTicketing Transforms Rail Travel at Amtrak," April 4, 2013, http://yourbusiness.att.com/transform/images/uploads/stories/4.4.13_AMTRAK_FINAL.pdf.
15. At the request of AT&T and Amtrak the quote from the case study has been updated with the name of the current executive in charge of customer relations, Ghada Ijam, Amtrak's chief relationship officer. "Wireless eTicketing Transforms Rail Travel at Amtrak," April 4, 2013, http://yourbusiness.att.com/transform/images/uploads/stories/4.4.13_AMTRAK_FINAL.pdf.
16. "Wireless eTicketing Transforms Rail Travel at Amtrak," April 4, 2013, http://yourbusiness.att.com/transform/images/uploads/stories/4.4.13_AMTRAK_FINAL.pdf.
17. As quoted in Walmart's Annual Report 1999, http://media.corporate-ir.net/media_files/irol/11/112761/ARs/1999_annualreport.pdf.
18. Claire Cain Miller and Stephanie Clifford, "To Catch Up, Walmart Moves to Amazon Turf," *New York Times*, October 20, 2013, p. 1.
19. See more at www.ecommercetimes.com/story/78109.html#sthash.e7RRrJFm.dpuf.
20. Cadie Thompson, "Wal-Mart Puts Its Faith in Big Data for Mobile Strategy," May 22, 2013, http://www.cnbc.com/id/100759264.

PART

III

HOW TO PREPARE FOR CHANGE

As we saw in Part I, the future is here. Technology today enables changes in behavior. We can participate in instant communication and commerce from almost anywhere to almost anywhere. It's feasible to create new business processes—the right experience at the right time and in the right place—that were never possible in the past. Technology that permits new behavior and new possibilities is disrupting existing business models. Start-ups and disrupters have challenged established business practices and created new market dynamics. Part II demonstrated the value of right-time experiences in communications, care, and commerce. The issue now is, what can an organization's leaders do to capitalize on this brave new world?

Business executives must update their organizational strategies in a world of continually evolving technologies, ensure that their organizations continue to look ahead, and use technologies to improve internal performance and rewrite business processes (Chapter 7). They need to build a technical plan (Chapters 8 and 9), and they have to engage and empower employees and advocates (Chapter 10).

But the first challenge is, how to start?

Evolve to Right-Time Experiences in Three Phases

I've talked about how mobile, big data, and cloud computing are altering the business landscape. To thrive—or simply survive—in this new terrain, enterprises need a business process and technology transformation strategy. Different companies in different industries need to understand how these technologies can provide new business opportunities. We frequently call this "the art of the possible." Senior management should be saying to themselves, "What business processes do we need to change? How do we provide the right information at the right time for our customers, employees, partners, stakeholders? These are different from the experiences we offer today because of behavioral and technology changes within the market. If we don't capitalize on the options that are available to use today, someone else will, and we'll find ourselves in a profitless desert."

Leaders need to plan for a range of scenarios, abandoning assumptions about where competition and risk could come from. In many ways, business leaders need to be fearless and look beyond long-established models. Organizations will also need to keep their employees' skills up-to-date and routinely evaluate the potential benefits of emerging technologies and the risks they may pose.

One of the biggest challenges that organizations face today is that technologies provide the opportunity and the need to change our business processes. For example, the move to mobile isn't simply about taking your existing business applications and moving them to a smaller screen. Mobile-enabling means you have to modify certain applications, or portions of the applications, to operate over mobile devices. This changes areas such as data display, navigation, and overall functions. To truly take advantage of mobile, a business must actually change its workflows and business processes.

There are many books that address the changes social networking enables, so I won't focus on that in this book. For a viewpoint on how to deal with the evolution of social business, I recommend reviewing books from Charlene Li and Brian Solis. In this chapter, what I discuss is the process of how a business should approach mobile enablement. I chose to focus on mobile enablement versus big data for two reasons. First, it potentially requires touching every application and process within the company. Second, the technologies to mobile-enable the business, while still new, have evolved to a point where businesses can build strategies to support the transition. I'll note that there are many ways to mobile-enable a company, and no single method is the right answer for all companies. However, there are several basic areas that every firm should consider as it embarks on this journey. Of course, big data and analytics are also part of this. I discuss more about the strategy and technical considerations for big data in Chapter 9.

The plan itself has three parts to make all this happen: the business process plan, the technology plan, and the employee roll-out/engagement plan. I discuss the technology and employees in the chapters ahead, but now let's consider the two areas of the business process plan, which include mobile enablement and the associated business process prioritization and reengineering.

Define a Mobile-Enablement Strategy

Disruptive technologies mean entirely new products and services can emerge overnight. You can either fight the tide or ride the wave. Riding the wave will require an organization to create business-model innovations to capture some of that value. While pricing is one business model innovation, mobile enablement of applications, services, and workflows often helps a business find new and innovative ways of delivering services.

Companies recognize that it is impossible to achieve the full benefit of mobility until existing workflows and applications are available on mobile devices. Merely mobile-enabling today's processes, however, isn't enough to create sustainable business value. It's just the first step. An organization must take advantage of the unique attributes that mobile and Internet of Things devices provide, such as location, communications, presence, and sensor data to transform processes.

While business managers may be acquiring cloud services for apps related to human resources, customer relationship management, and marketing, they require IT involvement to create connections between cloud applications and corporate data. Before IT embarks upon creating technical plans, however, the business unit leads should work with IT to identify what metrics are most important and indicate success.

It's a truism that a business can't be successful unless it has a plan. It's certainly true when it comes to mobile-enabling a company's business processes. In 2013, many companies were crafting mobile-enablement strategies, yet only 57 percent of the companies Lopez Research surveyed in Q1/2014 had a defined a mobile strategy. Without a mobile strategy, however, companies won't achieve maximum benefits from their mobile applications development efforts and won't have the proper foundation for delivering right-time experiences. What should companies without a strategy be considering?

Define the Business Requirements

Businesses need a mobile strategy that is aligned with the overall business strategy; otherwise, it will fail to provide value to the organization. The strategy identifies crucial business goals that need to be given highest priority and how mobile-enabling applications and services will help the business achieve its goals.

All businesses want to grow sales and profits, but during any one year a company normally has a set of specific goals and key performance indicators that it's trying to achieve—increase gross margins, reduce customer support calls, improve the sales-lead-to-close ratio. Once we have satisfied the needs, we can focus on some of the desires— the nice-to-haves versus the must-haves. The possible goals are endless.

Define What Should Be Mobile-Enabled

The first component of a mobile strategy plan is defining what applications, services, and workflows should be mobile-enabled. While one could argue that every business process can benefit from mobile access, some workflows benefit more than others. The business process transformation aspect has to do with understanding what your employees or customers need to do while they are on the go. It's understanding what apps or services they need to use as well as what aspects they *want* to use on the phone or tablet.

It's also about understanding how those experiences differ from those on a computer. In the mobile world, we want more direct access to content and tasks because it can be hard to browse on a small screen. Or we may be using the mobile device to find some specific information, such as the inventory of part #ML-6523, the flight status of Singapore Airlines Flight 304, or a company's address and phone number.

One of the biggest challenges with mobile-enabling an application is building one that people will use. If IT builds it and no one uses it, it's a failure. While analytics is essential to understanding what went wrong, you want to minimize issues at the outset.

IT should work directly with the line-of-business (LOB) managers to understand how to prioritize these applications and what features need to be in the applications. One early mistake that companies made was to build new mobile apps and services with minimal user input. As companies redesign their applications to be mobile-ready and to provide right-time experiences, IT and the apps team should define who'll be using the app and work with the users to determine what the app needs to be.

One way to do this is to purchase the mobile version of these applications, if they are available, from the software vendor. If the software vendor doesn't offer a mobile version, the business can get started by selecting a portion of the application to mobile-enable. For example, a company may choose to mobile-enable product lead-time-to-completion and current inventory availability so its sales and supply chain managers can answer questions when they are away from their desks. A business might get started by offering a micro-application, such as list price and discount rates. It might purchase a mobile version of its existing applications or an SaaS app, if available. However, the company will most likely also build workbench apps that take information from multiple applications and data sources. This is often called creating composite apps that connect to back-end systems. These composite apps will help a person complete a workflow on a mobile device and are richer than micro-apps. There are numerous technical challenges in accomplishing this task. But before you can address any of those, the business needs to focus on what needs to be mobile-enabled and how business processes should be changed to incorporate context, access across multiple devices, and the ability to analyze data more effectively.

In order to do this, IT must work with LOB leaders to define what needs to be mobile-enabled. The internal IT or apps team will either build a custom application or hire an outside technical team to do it. The Ottawa Hospital provides an example of this. The hospital replaced paper but also took the process a step farther. It built a custom in-house app called the Clinical Mobile App. The app facilitates three major aspects of physicians' daily workflows: accessing patients' clinical information, viewing clinical images such as X-rays and CT scans, and ordering clinical tests and prescriptions. With a tablet and the app, the doctors have a complete record of all the patients and can immediately start to diagnose and treat them. The hospital estimates its doctors save approximately two hours a day in their clinical care activities by using the application instead of shuttling between meetings and a PC to gather patient information.

This example highlights that real-time data capture and access, such as updating customer records and processing sales transactions, are a logical place to begin a mobile deployment. In many cases, mobile-enabling these processes can deliver immediate return in investment, such as in the case of Ottawa Hospital. By mobile-enabling the systems that employees already access at their desktops, companies can shorten sales cycles, improve data quality, and enhance customer satisfaction.

Prioritize the Apps and Workflows

Given that a business may have hundreds or thousands of applications to mobile-enable over time, it should prioritize its development efforts based on business goals. Once IT and the apps team have defined the target audience for various apps—customers, employees, partners, or some combination of stakeholders—and worked with the business leaders to prioritize the apps, the business needs to evaluate what assets it has in-house. This includes employees, partners, and technology assets.

IT should determine whether its staff has the necessary skills available to analyze, design, and deploy mobile solutions. Mobile strategy requires skill in everything from wireless networking to mobile application development. It is not uncommon for organizations to have ample internal resources available for personal computer software design, but many companies lack personnel with skills in mobile areas such as app development.

Reevaluate Early and Often   The concept that a business should routinely reevaluate its strategic plans is hardly a revelation. The challenge for any strategic plan, especially in the mobile area, is to create a dynamic plan that is constantly updated. In fact, the challenge for many organizations is first to define a mobile strategy. Five years was the normal length for long-term IT strategy planning in previous technology waves. In the Q1/2014 "Lopez Research Enterprise Mobility Benchmark," 45% of IT leaders said they anticipate updating the company's mobile strategy every two years. Given the rapid change in mobile, I believe a business should reevaluate its strategy annually.

Understand the Risks and Accept Certain Risks   Business leaders must keep their organizational strategies updated in the face of continually evolving technologies, ensure that their organizations continue to look ahead, and use technologies to improve internal performance despite the risks. One risk companies normally focus on is loss of devices, such as smartphones, that have valuable information on them. Another risk could be that as more data gets uploaded into the cloud services, like Dropbox, we need to ensure that these services are secure and meet compliance regulations. A third risk is that the new technology services might not be as reliable in the early stages. For example, enterprise email cloud services, like Google Apps and Mail, can experience outages for hours.

One question a business must ask itself is what type of outages are acceptable. Can the business live without its human resources application for a few hours? Most likely that answer is yes. Can it live without email for a day? Most businesses would say no, but this is debatable. Can a financial trading house live without its trading platform for several hours? No. Moving to the new world requires businesses to develop a risk plan *and* be willing to tolerate a certain amount of risk. I can't stress enough that this undertaking does have risks, but indecision has even higher risks. For example, the longer you take to mobile-enable your business, the more likely it is that your employees will mobile-enable themselves. This puts corporate data at even greater risk because you don't have insight into what is being used.

The second dimension is that we might want to build an experience that is different depending on the features of a device. For example, an employee might want to review a document on her smartphone but not edit it. She might want to view and edit on a tablet. Just because the devices are small, we can't make the mistake of thinking people only want to do quick-and-easy things with them. An employee might access the latest sales statistics on his tablet. But if the numbers are bad or unexpected, he might want to drill down and create queries on the fly. Even though tablets are not laptops, owners frequently want to use them as if they were. We need to understand the use cases and prioritize the apps and workflows associated with these use cases. As part of our overall strategic plan, we need to think of these devices as evolving to become the devices that will eventually run all aspects of our business.

We also need what I call an open device strategy. People think the device strategy is hard, when it is actually simple. Devices come and go pretty quickly. We can't necessarily certify every device, because they are outdated within six months. We need to build a technology plan that assumes the organization will be able to secure and support multiple device types and multiple operating systems.

In summary, once we decide what we need to do, we need the technical underpinnings to do it, which are security and management tools, application development tools, and content management tools. This is where the enterprise mobility management (EMM) software that I discuss in Chapter 8 comes into play. It will help a business manage and secure devices, operating systems, and applications. We also need a mobile application development strategy and a set of development tools to go with it.

And we need all of this just to get started. Sure, businesses have rolled out mobile applications before defining a process and a technical strategy. However, many businesses have wasted both time and money doing so. If you are starting today or if you are broadening your efforts, it makes sense to lay the proper foundation.

Update Systems to Embrace New Technologies

As I have been arguing, the move to right-time experiences is a shift that touches every aspect of an organization. It requires changes in how an enterprise structures its daily workflows and the systems that run the business. It requires the organization to update existing systems and adopt new technologies. It also requires a management plan that brings employees into alignment with the new vision and with market realities and requirements.

As companies grapple with how to address this seismic shift in business, many executive leaders believe a technology transition is the first step. Technology is a critical piece of this transformation, but it isn't the first thing the businesses should focus on. Again, a company must define what exactly it is trying to do before it can select the most appropriate technology to accomplish its goals. I suggested earlier in the book that right-time experiences require businesses to operate in a different fashion than they have in the past. If this is the case, many of the business processes we have today for serving our customers and for delivering information to our employees and partners are faulty or broken or won't translate easily into the new world.

An organization's first priority, therefore, is to rebuild its business processes to function effectively in a mobile world. But what exactly does it mean to function effectively in a mobile world, and why is it important? The first difference between the former world and the mobile world is that computing in itself has changed. It's no longer confined to a single destination, such as an office desk. Nor does it involve a single device, such as a desktop or laptop computer. And it takes more than adding mobile devices such as smartphones and tablets to the list of devices the company's systems support (although this is necessary).

Computing is now about connecting a wide variety of objects that have sensors and that connect to the Internet. I've already discussed how there are now sensors in wind turbines and parking spots. In fact, the very nature of computing is changing to become more natural and intuitive. Intel calls this "perceptual computing," which it defines as adding senses to the computer's brain to make computing more intuitive. We have touch today, but this refers to the concept of making touch, voice, and gestures a more natural, intuitive, and immersive life-like experience. This means future applications must be device-aware, sensory-aware, location-aware, and network-aware to offer right-time experiences.

How to Be Device- and Sensory-Aware   It isn't simply that a business is trying to get its apps to work on a four- or five-inch screen. Work in the new mobile-plus-cloud-computing world is about being able to do business on whatever device the user has. People expect they'll be able to use their applications and services on multiple devices and that they'll be able to pick up a workflow as they move from one device to another. Consumers want to use multiple devices for the same task and assume they'll be able to start a transaction on one device and complete it on another. This means applications must embrace the concept of data persistence across sessions. For example, it could be that our customer wants to begin the check-out process on a smartphone and end it on a PC. It could be that a knowledge worker begins editing a file on a tablet but wants to complete it on a laptop. The list of possible situations goes on and on.

If people are using multiple devices to access systems, it's critical that any application or service they use can automatically update and synchronize information across devices. Cloud storage created the expectation that your data isn't tied to a physical device such as a PC or a physical place such as an office or your home. When we combine cloud storage concepts with portable connected mobile devices, the expectation has become that all services and data should be easily accessible from wherever the user may be.

For example, Evernote.com is an application that allows users to collect information from anywhere—video, audio, text—into a single place. The information can be in multiple forms, from text notes to web pages to files to snapshots. Evernote offers applications that run on your PC, your tablet, and your smartphone. With Evernote, all of your notes, web clips, files, and images are available on every device and computer you use. It automatically synchronizes these files across all of your devices so they each have the same information. In a business context, it is possible to invite individual coworkers to one or more "Business Notebooks," and the content you've shared automatically appears in their Evernote account for collaboration, or you can publish your content for the entire company to see.

Dropbox.com and Box.com are two other examples of applications that allow you to store documents, update files, and automatically synchronize this data across multiple devices. This type of availability on multiple devices and automatic synchronization across devices has become expected in consumer services but has yet to be built into a majority of enterprise applications and services. Anyone building mobile versions of enterprise applications should be creating applications that can run on and synchronize data across a variety of devices, including personal computers, smartphones, and tablets. As I pointed out earlier, this is challenging because the operating systems—Google's Android, Apple's iOS, Microsoft's Windows, and more—are different for different platforms.

Being device-aware also means that applications and services should be able to recognize what types of sensors or functions are available within the device. This is the beginning of what Intel calls perceptual computing. It means a business must consider not just screen size but also the type of data-input mechanisms and the type of sensors that exist within these devices. The software industry and corporations building custom apps are just beginning to build applications with touch. There are over 15 sensors in the average smartphone today that can provide information on everything from location to motion. Most companies are currently designing only for location, but there is a wealth of opportunity to employ other sensors within the device to make experiences more engaging. Consumer applications, particularly gaming, have begun to tap into data from these additional sensors, but few enterprise applications have done so.

One element of redesigning existing processes to be right-time experiences is building the best navigation for the task at hand. Touch is available in PCs and smartphones, and voice recognition was gaining traction in 2013. Depending on the situation, it might make the most sense to use a keyboard to enter information, touch a screen to select fields, or speak to the device to search for something.

Gestures such as hand movements, eye tracking, shakes, and nods will become part of a normal set of navigation parameters. I discussed Google Glass in Chapter 4. In their most basic form, devices are being built to listen and respond to our voices. For example, Motorola's Moto X smartphone has a microphone that is always listening for commands, and certain Samsung's smartphones offer eye tracking. Smartphones and other devices will begin to continuously monitor the environment by integrating data from cameras, microphones, and other sensors and react intelligently to changes.

Intel's perceptual computing is an effort to give better control with gesture and voice. Today's gestures have to be broad and sweeping; tomorrow's will be smaller. We'll have 3-D cameras in smartphones, tablets, and personal computers. Imagine how this could change retail businesses such as eBay. I could take a 3-D image of anything I wanted to sell. Voice recognition software will also become much more natural. We'll be able to say things like, "I'd like Chinese food tonight," and our device will know our location, find the Yelp recommendations, search through recommendations from our social network connections, and display a list virtually immediately. For another example, we can ask our device, "Will I need an umbrella today?" and receive a trustworthy forecast.

While this might sound and look silly in 2014, it has huge implications for the change we could see in future services. Imagine applications that can use gesture and voice to free the user's hands. Manufacturing, surgery, and numerous other fields can benefit from hands-free and heads-up displays of information. Automakers are already offering voice recognition and heads-up displays in new cars.

Businesses must be careful not to dismiss the potential benefits of technology that looks ridiculous or is clunky today. Technology is moving rapidly, and what might appear silly today could be amazing (and popular) within 6 to 12 months. Companies must define which navigation methods will be most appropriate for the various uses of their applications as they redesign them to work on the next generation of mobile, wearable devices, and PCs. Managers in their respective fields will become leaders by trying to envision imaginative new ways these technologies could be used to improve existing business processes.

How to Be Network-Aware   Wireless networks are becoming more pervasive, but a business can't design its applications with the expectation that its customers and employees will always be connected to the network. This means information technology must design applications that can store data when the user loses connectivity. Our business process must have the ability to be connected only part of the time. Even if we are connected 100 percent of the time, businesses must take network quality issues into consideration when designing apps. As people move around, the mobile device frequently shifts between high-speed 4G and 3G networks to lower-speed 2G networks. If an application isn't designed with this in mind, it might crater as users roam about with their devices.

Some applications, such as voice and video, are very sensitive to delays in the delivery of the service (technically called *latency*). If the network is congested, like a highway at rush hour, video or audio data doesn't arrive promptly. Consumers and employees simply won't use an application that performs poorly.

IT must also have systems in place that can define what problem a user is experiencing. Companies need monitoring software that gives its support staff clear answers about where problems lie and how to fix them. For example, when a user calls with an issue, the business must have software that can tell if it's a telecom network issue, a device issue, or an application issue. It's important to have service management to take the complexity out of mobile support.

Companies also haven't planned for the new connectivity demands. In the old PC world, businesses purchased remote access plans that allowed employees to connect to the Internet when they were away from the office. Today, employees are using a variety of smart devices, but most of the connectivity plans associated with these solutions don't offer any connectivity for roaming workers. Mobile and the Internet of Things will require a company to modify its network connectivity and security models. Businesses must also prepare for a massive increase in data and the need to process at least some of this data in real time. In the 2014 Cisco VNI index, Cisco predicts global mobile IP traffic will reach an annual run rate of 190 exabytes in 2018, up from less than 18 exabytes in 2013. The report also notes that IP video will represent 79 percent of all traffic.[1] To support this diverse device landscape and roaming mobile workers, a CIO's mobile strategy should support a range of wireless connectivity options, including WLAN, Bluetooth, and 3G and 4G connections.

How to Be Location-Aware   Over the past three years, many consumer applications have started to tap into location data available to their smartphones and tablets, but most business applications have not. The notable exception is in the transportation and field service industries, where software that defines the optimal route for vehicles to drive or the workflow for service calls has been available for years. Even in retail, the industry segment that discusses location the most, location services are fairly crude. The store might know I'm nearby or that I've entered the building. However, it doesn't know precisely where I am and it doesn't know why I'm there. The key to unlocking value for consumers and employees is to understand context from the data—not only where you are but what are you doing.

Location is one of the first elements of context that businesses should build into their processes because it can be used to automate processes and trigger timely communications. In business services, location can be used to automate time card tracking, understand how long a service repair person remains at a client site, or provide an alert to a salesperson that multiple customers are within a mile of their next meeting. In consumer services, it can tell users if friends are nearby or if there are places they might want to visit based on previous destinations.

Right-time experiences use the location of both people and things to improve workflow and engagement. As businesses rebuild their applications, they should consider how location information could change the flow of an application or service. For example, a company could rewrite its application so that an employee who's roaming on a data network in a foreign country can download the latest training videos only when she is on a Wi-Fi network. Or it could say that the employee or consumer can't have access to certain financial data when he is visiting a foreign country. This would require IT to design an application that collects location information, analyzes it, and acts on it in real time or near-real time. It's important that the business and IT define which applications would benefit from location and how location data could change the workflow.

Location isn't just for people. It's for assets as well. I can use Tiles to track my keys or iCloud to track a lost iPhone. An oil and gas company can track equipment moving in and out of mining areas, as well as track employees and other personnel working in potentially dangerous areas to ensure their safety. Location will be a critical component of most right-time experiences.

Make It Easy to Use

In addition to the aspects listed above, right-time experiences will differ because they are easier for customers and employees to use. We've been talking about better user experience for years. What's different now? Customers have apps that delight them. They may have started simple, but many of these applications offer a rich list of functions and manage to please users. Consider airline apps. People can select seats, obtain a boarding pass on their phone, purchase future trips, and review what they've done. Not only has this improved life for air travelers, it's also improving life for the airlines.

So there are no excuses any more. We can't hide behind "Oh, that's just a simple consumer app" or "That's just a gaming app" or "We could do that if we didn't have to integrate it with our legacy software systems." First of all, these apps aren't simple. Many are fairly complex. Second, many of these applications are connecting to legacy back-end systems such as enterprise resource planning (ERP), supply chain management (SCM), and financials.

Even in the category of consumer apps, it's not a slam-dunk for organizations to build something compelling. Many mobile apps are downloaded, but getting continued engagement is another matter altogether. A Localytics report states that only 34 percent of apps are opened 11 or more times per year.[2] A business has to provide a compelling reason for consumers to download its mobile application. The application must be easy to use and provide features that deliver value and create engagement. Regardless of the type of company, user experience is one of the more difficult items to master.

Customers and employees have different expectations today. They don't want to take multiple steps to have an experience. They want frictionless transactions and engagement. After all, one of a company's goals in offering right-time experiences is not only that it is providing the right information/offer/alert at the right time, but also that it's making it easier to consume this information.

Business processes must also change in terms of the user experience. We often describe the user experience as the graphical interface on a device or application, but a good user experience requires more than making something pretty. A right-time experience is about efficiently serving up the right information at the point of need. It's about making the processes and workflow fast and intuitive. If our processes were broken or archaic, we got around the roadblock in the PC world by what was called Sneakernet: We walked down the hall and asked someone to make it work. This isn't so easy when someone is trying to use an app at 3 A.M. when the help desk is closed. It also fundamentally breaks down when the user is working with another person in a customer care scenario.

The user doesn't expect to navigate five screens to get the answer to a question in one app and then another five screens to get a different piece of information in a second application. This is what we did in the PC world. An employee would surf through multiple screens in a procurement application to find the right item number (SKU) for a product. The user would then go to the supply chain management system to see if it was in stock. If it was out of stock, the user might have to go to a third system and sift through several screens of data to find a substitute product and then alert the customer of the change. If the customer accepted a change in the product, the employee would then go back to either the same system or a new system to order the product. In the new mobile world, systems must be interconnected.

These workflows should match how people actually work, live, and play. The user, whether a customer or an employee, expects to get the answer to a question within several clicks. While users don't want an app to be ugly or featureless, they want it to be simple and to assist in information discovery or completing a transaction. The world has moved to a nearly instant gratification society. Sadly, few business IT systems have yet to follow this path. Thus, the biggest potential for success or failure in creating a right-time experience is getting the flow right. Easier use is a function of the user understanding what needs to be done next and how to do it. It's also a function of redesigning the process with the outcome in mind. Instead of thinking of the application as a monolithic entity, a business should look at the application as a set of vignettes. Right now my user wants to fill out a form. Later, the user may need to do research on product features.

Create Portable Business Services

As I mentioned with the Evernote and Box.com examples, mobility and cloud computing will change how applications and processes are constructed. Instead of business services being locked to the device or to the business location, employees will be able to securely access corporate services on multiple devices (e.g., a smartphone or a connected screen such as a tablet or TV) and from multiple locations (e.g., hotel, home, coffee shop, or a client's office). While devices will be intelligent, the availability of virtualization and cloud computing means decoupling software from hardware and from a physical location will be possible. One thing that makes this possible is that SaaS applications permit employees to connect to applications over the Internet instead of establishing a secure connection back into corporate headquarters. Because the connection isn't going directly back into the headquarters, intruders are less likely to gain access to the entire corporate network.

Data security is still paramount regardless of whether the application resides in the cloud or at the corporate headquarters. Since an employee can access potentially sensitive data on any number of devices and from a variety of locations, a business must have multiple ways to verify that the person accessing the data or the application is in fact an employee and is authorized to do so. To do this, employees will have to use several methods of authentication to prove they are who they say they are. For example, employees may log in with a username and password but be asked to type in a code that is sent to them via an SMS text message on their smartphone.

Identity solutions—the ability to validate employee identity and thwart unauthorized access—will become critical. Identity solutions should provide single sign-on, which means users have to enter their security information only once to gain access to multiple applications. When possible, solutions should also provide federated identity management (FIM), which is an arrangement that can be made among multiple enterprises that lets subscribers use the same identification data to obtain access to the networks of all enterprises in the group.

Federated identity is more common among business-to-consumer services where authorization messages among partners in an FIM system can be transmitted using security assertion markup language (SAML) or a similar extensible markup language (XML) standard that allows a user to log on once for affiliated but separate websites or networks. We've started to see business-to-consumer services use social identity integration, such as a Facebook user name and password, as one way to sign into a service without creating a specific password for the website. For example, if you want to shop at Amazon. com, you can use your Facebook ID to log in. MGM Grand is also letting its guests use their Facebook credentials to log into the hotel's wireless Internet service.

Going forward all organizations will have to update their identity solutions to support authenticating people who will use multiple devices and to support new IoT devices that will connect to systems. These upgraded identity systems have to walk the fine line of usability and security. I expect we'll see many new solutions over the next three years in this space.

Evolve to a Mobile-Enabled RTE Business

As mentioned in Chapter 2, businesses won't become RTE providers overnight. Organizations need a phased approach to what otherwise can become a hopelessly complex undertaking. Each phase offers the organization new capabilities and benefits, and over the next three to five years, I foresee enterprises evolving to right-time experiences in three phases:

1. **Extending** existing business processes. Extend is the easiest phase. It takes what we have today (or parts of what we have today) and makes these bite-sized pieces of applications and services available on mobile devices. It could be that we embrace cloud computing, EMM, and SaaS. Or it could be that we offer access to a subset of a workflow in a micro-app. The extend phase in mobile means an employee can have access to data in places he would not have had access before. I call these efficiency/productivity gains.

2. **Enhancing** existing processes. Enhance is where we start looking at what we can do differently in a mobile, cloud computing, and big data world. We want to push beyond efficiencies and seek ways to improve a business process (or processes) through mobile enablement and introducing big data and analytics. What new data or functions can we access? This is where context such as location, camera, and sensor data comes into play. We not only extend our existing business processes but start to change them to take into account all the new data we can generate and turn into knowledge.

3. **Transforming** the business with new processes. When we are comfortable with first extending and then enhancing our processes, we start to look for ways to transform our products and services to give more consumers, employees, and partners right-time experiences through mobile, big data, and analytics to change the business and create competitive advantage. The third phase transforms the business when a company uses connected devices to deliver new workflows and new products and services it couldn't create economically in the past.

Let's review an example of how these three phases could occur in retail. In the past, companies sent retailers printed cardboard with photographs and examples of how to create the display. Today, they can send a video to tablets that demonstrates how to set up the display in various combinations. Instead of certifying in a form that the display is complete, the retailer can upload a photograph of it in place. Or the staff can create a new design and upload that to management. Replacing paper is an example of extending a process, video is enhancing the process, and uploading the store's own design is a mix of enhancing and transforming the process. Figure 7.1 highlights several examples of what the three phases may look like in different verticals.

Where you begin to implement right-time experiences will depend on several factors: available IT resources, the time needed to develop the right-time experiences, and the required return on investment per project. Business leaders must consider the available IT resources and understand the amount of time and money involved in executing a right-time experience strategy. Most organizations won't have enough available IT and financial resources to redesign and mobile-enable all of the necessary business processes overnight.

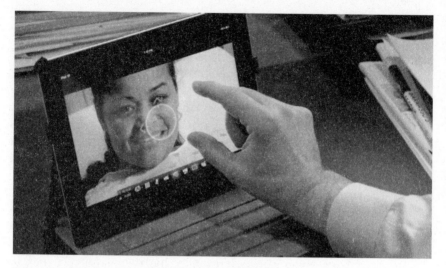

Figure 7.1   Examples of the Three Phases of Evolving to RTEs

This is one of the reasons that companies must approach designing right-time experiences in phases. The phases will also help businesses define what works well and what might need to be changed to have the best chance of success. To begin, a business should identify the specific goals the company is trying to accomplish, the level of maturity of its current mobile management and development strategy, and what resources it will take to get to the next level.

Phase 1

Phase 1 is about creating efficiencies that save costs or gain productivity or both. These moves may start to improve revenue, but mostly because the organization is more efficient. Efficiencies save money or save time. For example, customer care efficiencies normally focus on improving the post-sales experience and resolving problems. Sales efficiency is doing something faster or cheaper. It is typically doing something that you've done before more effectively.

An example of this could be a building inspector who can use a tablet or smartphone instead of a clipboard to record his findings. Salespeople can record their customer visits. Train conductors can electronically punch rider tickets. Anyone who has to capture data in the field is probably a good candidate for a smartphone or a tablet and an appropriate application. In the consumer domain, it could be the taxi passenger having the picture and profile of her driver before the cab arrives to pick her up. If you have access to data wherever you are, you can act on it wherever you are. You can log information immediately. An example is a nurse at a patient's bedside noting the vital statistics on a tablet instead of writing it down to have someone type it into the computer later—or worse, leaving only the paper record.

We see this happening in construction with checklists, in retail with work schedule charts and work plans, and in doctors' waiting rooms where patients fill out a form about their health and current insurance. A medical provider can buy or build an app and put it in a tablet as long as it has the proper patient record security. The patient enters the information once or updates it on subsequent visits. It makes it easier for the office to capture the data accurately, and accuracy is a big deal for many organizations. United Airlines, American Airlines, and Delta eliminated the thick binders of FAA charts pilots had to carry, eliminating some weight (always a concern for an aircraft) and making it easy for the agency (and the airlines) to distribute updated information.

Paper replacement is the low-hanging fruit. What other items might be part of Phase 1? These may be workflow enhancers such as work orders, purchase orders, or travel, vacation, and expense approvals. All of these speed up the process of getting something done. They are efficiency gains but also delight employees, who hate administrative tasks. In the retail world, these could be things such as mobile coupons and point of sale. In the sales world, price books are obvious candidates, but CRM dashboards would also be good for this type of first phase of extending the business process. These are quick hits that managers can use to prove the value quickly. They make a workflow or process more efficient, which in turn improves productivity.

Phase 2

In Phase 2, companies push beyond efficiencies and seek ways to improve a business process through mobile enablement and introducing big data and analytics. In this phase, companies begin to redesign applications and workflows to take advantage of contextual elements such as location, sensor data, and time of day. Mobile devices give employees real-time access to data in back-office systems to improve decision making and customer service at the point of need.

Applications and business processes that can be improved through mobile's unique attributes—such as location, image capture, and voice-enablement—are a good place to start. Leveraging technologies inherent to mobile, such as location-based services and geofencing, can provide application access to employees within a virtual boundary in a physical geography.

I've described some of the efficiencies with mobile in reducing paper, cost, and duplicate effort. Many of those are efficiency plays. So what are the things that help us move beyond efficiencies? It is the concept of integrating new sources into our business process. While a retailer may be able to deliver a mobile coupon to somebody that is more efficient, the retailer wants to go one step further and turn that coupon into a transformative experience. This is where the connected fitting room that Kohl's offers or the ability to shop at Tesco by scanning QR codes in a train station transforms an existing retail experience.

Capturing context and adapting that context to the current moment will change how we engage with our customers, partners, and employees. For example, if I am having a problem with a cell phone and I call the carrier, the customer service person should know why I'm calling and should already have the solution for my problem to present to me on the call.

In general, managers tend to believe that location must be tied to a specific individual to be valuable. However, the location of multiple people or things in an aggregate can also be valuable. Sense Networks is a New York–based company that applies big science to mobile location data for predictive analytics in advertising. It provides an example of how location can be valuable even if the data is about a group of individuals instead of a specific person. Sense Networks created a service that can look at the GPS signals of all of the cell phones in a city and identify the greatest concentration of phones. How is this relevant?

Imagine you head a taxi company in New York City. This information could tell you where people congregate in Manhattan on a Saturday night at 11 P.M. Are there large clusters in the Meatpacking District or Times Square? Is there a concentration near a specific venue? The service can look at this data over time and figure out how it varies by time of day or day of week. Instead of having taxis wandering aimlessly about the city, the taxi company could use this service to predict where people will be and dispatch taxis to that area. This is an example of how location in the aggregate can be used to improve a business process.

Utility companies can improve service and profits by assigning orders to crews in real time, monitoring the progress of work throughout the day, and redirecting field resources as required. In some cases, a company can buy software as a service that will give them the benefits of a right-time experience without building a custom mobile application. Mobile workflows also change how businesses engage with customers and employees. Businesses will enhance existing processes with location-based services and the geofencing discussed in Chapter 3, a virtual boundary in a physical space.

For another example of using technology to enhance a business process (and provide a right-time experience for both customers and produce managers), consider the Tesco broccoli-cam. Instead of the manager checking the produce display and telling the employees to refill the empty broccoli bins, a video camera pointed at the produce uses video analytics to tell if a bin is empty, and if so, it sends an alert to the produce manager's mobile device. The broccoli bins are always full and customers are delighted. Tesco inventory turns over faster and employees are more efficient than in the prevideo and premobile days.

We're also seeing early examples of how sensor data can change business processes. Last year, scientists at MIT created a sensor that has the ability to detect the ripeness of produce. Now a grocer can keep track of fruits and vegetables and sell them before they spoil. The sensor works by detecting levels of ethylene, a gas produced by ripening fruits and vegetables.

One good example of a company pushing beyond efficiencies to seek ways to improve a business process through mobile enablement and introducing big data and analytics is Coca-Cola.

As I discussed in Chapter 1, previously a delivery person followed a route, checked the vending machines, refilled them as needed, collected the cash, and drove on to the next machine. Today, machines connected to the Internet can report sales, inventory, and service issues in real time, which dramatically improves service levels at substantially reduced operating costs.

But knowing when a machine needs more Coke or Aquapure or Barq's is only the beginning. Coke said it planned to roll out tens of thousands of machines that accept smartphone payments and track user purchases to offer an occasional discount or free drink. Coke spent a year testing 200 machines in Austin, Texas. It's currently testing

Google Wallet and NFC, but other options could emerge. The new machines make it relatively simple for the company to offer a loyalty program. Thousands of "loyalty-equipped" vending machines will allow people to use their My Coke Rewards cards to earn points and redeem points for free drinks. It also means the company can change prices virtually immediately. It would be possible, for example, to raise prices during a heat wave, then drop them when the weather changes.

The "show car" of Coca-Cola vending machines displays custom content—videos, games, and TV commercials—on a 46-inch touch screen. Coke typically places these in high-traffic sites at colleges, malls, airports, and amusement parks, where they create an immediate connection with teens, says the company. Dan Avenick, Coca-Cola Refreshment's director of vending strategy, says, "These machines accept several forms of payment, deliver customized messages and offers, and remain in-stock and fully-operational due to real-time data transmission and management. We are driving innovation in the industry and differentiating Coca-Cola vending to both delight our consumers and generate profitable growth for our company."[3]

In Phase 2, the process itself isn't always new. Phases 1 and 2, extending and improving business processes, usually affect the same process, and it's a matter of improving or adding enhancements to the process. For example, Amtrak's conductors still have to record passenger tickets, but it's far easier and the process for understanding if a passenger has boarded the train is greatly improved. In other areas, such as field service, we can see the same phased process occurring. Service technicians have done planned maintenance on equipment—steam engines, locomotives, turbines, automobiles, office equipment—as long as machinery has existed. Today, these industries can have access to data that tells the company when to do it and what needs to be done.

I've already discussed how extending the business processes in retail could include mobile coupons, inventory availability on handhelds, and mobile point-of-sale. Retailers have been able to do much of this for years, but even in the mobile domain, there are new ways of making this more efficient. Enhancing would equal leveraging geofencing and the push notifications as you enter the store. If a person is standing five feet in front of the supermarket's cold cereal display and Kellogg's wants to send him a coupon for Crunchy Nut, sending it 10 minutes later isn't good enough. Delivering a relevant real-time experience requires a business to perform analytics on large volumes of data and respond in real time. This is no small task.

The process improvement is that a marketer can communicate exactly when the person enters the store instead of sending her a generic email at 4 A.M. or printing out a coupon at the register for Crunchy Nut, which is triggered because she bought General Mills' Cinnamon Toast Crunch. You extend a process by making something like a coupon digital. You enhance a process by taking a static print catalogue or magazine and making it interactive by creating apps and QR codes that link to videos, the web, or some other content that can be displayed on a phone.

Phase 3

The potential of mobile enablement is far greater than simply improving what a business does today. The real value occurs when a company uses connected devices to do things that were not possible in the past. Soon, "connected" will apply not just to our devices, but also to the buildings we work in, the vehicles we drive, and the machines we use. Location, voice navigation, and image capture have already enabled the first wave of simple yet transformative experiences, such as real-time parking availability, voice search within corporate applications, and mobile check deposits.

In a Phase 3 example, a new process enables shippers to reroute a package on the fly. For example, UPS allows customers to reroute packages from their home, office, or another location. It sounds easy, but it's complicated to accomplish, and it requires precise knowledge of where everything is and exactly how long it takes to get something from one place to another. Adding sensors to report vibration, motion, and temperature to tell shippers their packages' condition throughout the journey also transforms the business.

Southwest Airlines Cargo offers a service called Cargo Companion, which the press release describes as "a comprehensive asset tracking service, providing customers with complete visibility regarding the location and environmental status of high-value and time/temperature-sensitive items."[4] It is designed for freight forwarders, couriers, perishable commodity shippers, and shippers of time-critical and high-value items.

The service features wireless asset tracking devices that monitor the location, shock, light, temperature, pressure, and humidity of cargo during transit. It has tracking by air waybill capabilities that enable customers to track the status of their cargo on swacargo.com.

Finally, it prompts email alerts that inform customers when their shipment crosses predefined checkpoints and arrives at its destination, or if potential issues arise during transit. The service gives customers "a new level of visibility regarding the status of their cargo," says Wally Devereaux, director of cargo sales and marketing for Southwest Airlines. "The information provided by this service will enhance the customer experience and improve operational efficiencies and minimize the impact of delays within the supply chain."[5]

The real value of mobile-enabling occurs when a company uses connected devices to deliver new workflows and products that it couldn't create in the past. For example, Orlando Health is transforming patient care by allowing a neurologist to examine a patient remotely from any location using a tablet, like an iPad, that can control a camera at the patient's bedside (see Figure 7.2).

Coca-Cola is also using mobile and big data to transform its business. Within the supermarket/convenience store environment, Coca-Cola Enterprises made changes to its business processes. It tested a custom application that uses a mobile device's camera. Delivery people in the field can take an image of the aisle they are restocking and send the photo to headquarters.[6] The goal is for it to link to an analytics program that can analyze the store's sales in real time and compare the figure with past orders and past sales by seasonality, weather, local events, and anything else that would affect

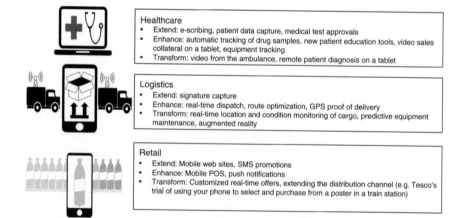

Figure 7.2   Polycom RealPresence Video Enables Remote Diagnosis on Mobile Devices

Source: Polycom, Inc.

consumer purchases. This data would feed back into the application and suggest how much the retailer should be ordering and the product mix. Ideally, a delivery arrives just before the store is out of stock, improving inventory turn and reducing customer frustration.

I've talked about how companies like Groupama and Progressive are transforming customer care in the insurance industry. I've described how Tesco has used mobile to take retail to new places and how Walmart is using big data to understand its customers. Google Glass and a new wave of connected devices will enable new ways to collect and access data. We are at the beginning of the mobile and big data wave. We have yet to see many transformative experiences, but you can work on creating them today.

In Phase 3, many businesses will use analytics tools to integrate existing transactional data with current contextual data to create predictive and prescriptive services. Phase 3 right-time experiences focus on assessing and responding to intent with the best information for a series of potential scenarios. While predictive and prescriptive services sound very sci-fi, businesses can start to reap the benefits of mobile today with very simple changes.

Summary

To recap briefly, a business must define a mobile-enablement strategy in order to create right-time experiences. The strategy starts by defining business goals and mapping what apps and business processes need to be mobile-enabled to achieve these goals. Over time, businesses will need to mobile-enable a majority of the apps and services. This will require IT and LOB managers to work together on prioritizing business workflows and applications.

While a business is going through this exercise, it's important to realize that we want to evolve our business processes to take advantage of new contextual data sources and data processing techniques. This means a business must rethink business processes and consider how these processes will evolve. Generally, a company will go through three phases to transform business processes, which means it doesn't have to do it overnight. This phased approach is important because many senior executives can be overwhelmed by the thought of rapidly transforming the business, its processes, and its applications.

In the three phases, Phase 1 involves taking what we have today and moving into a more distributed mobile-plus-cloud-computing world so our employees, customers, and partners can access data and services from anywhere. Phase 2 is looking at all the new types of data sources I talked about in earlier chapters and thinking about how to incorporate these sources into business processes to make them better. And Phase 3—a bit difficult to describe—is thinking about what the organization should be doing in a new way and creating a fundamentally new process or business model that didn't exist before. These new processes and business models will offer a more advanced version of right-time experiences to stakeholders. These could be adaptive, predictive, or prescriptive services.

Phase 3 is the most difficult stage to navigate. Yet it also includes the series of changes that will produce the largest long-term impact on the business. Phase 3 creates the strategies that can make or break a company. While these strategies may be empowered by technology, they are really the manifestation of ideas on how the world should work. At times, these ideas seem outlandish and fundamentally counter to the existing worldview. In the late 1990s, it was crazy to think that digital music would replace records. Saehan's MPMan and Diamond's RIO led the challenge in 1998. However, leading the challenge isn't enough. You also have to have the right technology, the right timing, and the right ecosystem. Apple proved this in 2001 when it released the iPod.

The questions senior managers must ask themselves are, "What would we do if we started from scratch today? How would we build something? How would we price it and market it?" Even if the company doesn't build that item or service, it's important to understand the art of the possible. At the very least, this exercise will highlight the types of threats the company might experience in the future.

Notes

1. www.cisco.com/c/en/us/solutions/service-provider/visual-networking-index-vni/index.html#~forecast.
2. www.localytics.com/blog/2013/localytics-app-user-retention-data/.
3. "Digital Technology Drives Coca-Cola Refreshment's Vending Innovation," Vending Marketwatch.com, March 23, 2012, http://www.vendingmarketwatch.com.
4. http://www.swacargo.com/swacargo/about-PressReleases-20120717.shtml.
5. "Southwest Airlines Introduces New Cargo Companion Product," July 17, 2012, www.swacargo.com/swacargo/about-PressReleases-20120717.shtml.
6. Phone interview with Esat Sezer, Senior VP and CIO at Coca-Cola Enterprises, June 26, 2013.

Understanding the Components of the Technical Plan: Mobility

What's Part of the Plan?

Business leaders have long focused on operating metrics, such as margin improvement, marketing campaign effectiveness, and time to close. Technology has become a critical component of improving these metrics. It's no longer like electricity, which simply keeps the business operational. It's the foundation for executing new and creative strategies. As I noted in the last chapter, IT and business managers should define a methodology for selecting the appropriate processes and applications to enable mobile. These teams must also define what old and new data sources these processes can access and where that data lives.

To support this, IT should craft a technical plan that supports securing, managing, and developing applications for the new computing landscape that is cloud- and mobile-enabled. It starts with supporting smartphones, tablets, PCs, and the new convertible 2-in-1 computers. However, the Internet of Things will require us to expand our current thinking to include a wide range of connected devices with sensors, such as machinery, medical equipment, and building climate control systems. While there are numerous technical challenges a company must address, a technical enablement strategy should include at least the following three areas:

1. **Enterprise mobility management solutions.** Security and management tools are commonplace for PCs, and we need a similar set of solutions for the new connected devices (including IoT

devices). This is software that helps to secure and manage devices, distribute and manage applications, and track the telecom and support expenses associated with mobility. It will also define who has access to what data, when, and where.

2. **Application development strategy.** This is the technical strategy that outlines the "what," "when," and "how" of developing mobile apps. It will answer questions such as which development approaches the company will use (e.g., native application, mobile web app development, or hybrid). It will define what operating systems (e.g., Apple iOS, Android) and device types (tablets, smartphones, TVs, autos, etc.) the company will support. It will match the development tools to the type of operating system and development approaches the company has selected. This also includes the option to use responsive website design and build HTML-5 applications. It defines the executive management and LOB stakeholders who will participate in the design process to make the applications a success. Finally, app strategies should be designed with the assumption that they will be updated frequently. Rather than every year, updates could happen as often as every several weeks.

3. **Big data and analytics strategy.** This strategy supports contextual services. It starts by evaluating the types of data a business will collect and the types of questions the company needs answered. The technology team will then evaluate how different big data storage, processing, and analytics tools can be used to meet the various requirements of different departments and different types of data. There isn't one perfect method for storing and analyzing all types of data. Different methods will be better suited to certain types of problems. IT must spend time mapping the right tools to the right problem in order to have successful big data projects.

As executives support and fund new technology initiatives, it's important to understand the challenges that IT and development teams will face. This chapter will focus on the first two parts of the technical plan, enterprise mobility management and the application development strategy. Both of these are closely related to mobile. I will focus on describing the key issues and terms that business leaders should know in order to build a successful strategy in conjunction with your IT team. This is not meant as a definitive technical guide for how to deploy a mobile strategy, but it will highlight what the basic elements of a mobile strategy should include. I'll tackle the third part of the technical plan, big data, in the next chapter.

Enterprise Mobility Management

IT leaders have accepted that employees are bringing their own computing devices—smartphones, tablets, and more—into the office. It started as a groundswell from the rank and file, and management also expects IT to support the latest new gizmos. CIOs and CFOs are now worried that these new devices will create compliance and security issues for the company—and with good reason. Security breaches are at an all-time high in general, and mobile provides just another opportunity for malicious parties to infiltrate your business and steal your data.

As a result of these threats, a new category of software vendors emerged to provide management and security solutions for mobile devices. IT, realizing it could not ignore the issue, originally took a heavy-handed approach to mobile management that was reminiscent of what corporations built for PCs. While no set of solutions can guarantee a company's devices and data are 100 percent secure, IT began to look for tools that would secure devices. Product vendors responded with a variety of solutions that were meant to lock down the mobile devices.

Historically, as more employees brought their personal gadgets into the workplace, IT executives first tried to put software on them to secure the devices themselves. This first wave of management software was called mobile device management (MDM) and focused on managing device-level features. This was the first wave of enterprise mobility management (EMM).

While many employees at first thought this was okay, eventually there was a backlash against using this software. The security software changed the user experience by requiring security measures, such as long passwords. Mobile device management software could also wipe all the data off a device. As a result, employees often didn't want to report a unit as stolen because they were afraid that IT would wipe it and delete all of their personal data, such as contacts, photos, and videos. In other cases, employees became concerned that the company could monitor whatever they did on their personal phones and tablets. In the end, many users were reluctant to use the solution, and the IT department didn't get the security it had hoped to ensure.

In the early days (2010–2013), it was also challenging to buy a solution that provided everything IT needed. Companies needed a solution that could provide device management, application management, content management, security, and expense management. Most organizations thought they simply needed security and device management. In the beginning, there were separate tools for mobile device management, content management, security, and expense management.

IT only understood after they had installed mobile device management that they also needed application and content management. Companies require mobile application management to manage applications at a deeper level than MDM provided. Mobile application management solutions provide the ability to control the provisioning, updating, and removal of mobile applications. These solutions provide a way for employees to discuss and download corporate and sanctioned third-party apps from what is called an enterprise application catalog. Think of this as iTunes or Google Play for custom and off-the-shelf enterprise applications. It also enables IT to monitor application performance and usage and remotely wipe data from managed applications.

IT was perhaps a bit overzealous in its use of mobile device management and mobile application management. IT continued to annoy users by blocking access to popular applications like Facebook. Additionally, IT used this software to block useful business applications that they deemed insecure, such as Box.com and Dropbox.

Many companies didn't purchase a solution while they waited for a chaotic landscape to settle. Recognizing that IT didn't want to buy 15 different products from as many different vendors, product vendors responded by building more functions into a single product suite. Larger companies also acquired smaller companies to fill out existing portfolios. This more comprehensive set of management tools is called EMM software and will provide the foundation for mobilizing your workforce.

These tools are designed to address the IT department's security concerns and the employee privacy concerns. They separate corporate information from private information on a personal device. They also enable IT to fully control a corporate-owned mobile device. There are several different technical approaches to achieving this separation today but the goal of securing just the corporate data is the same across vendors and solutions. Over time, these tools will look

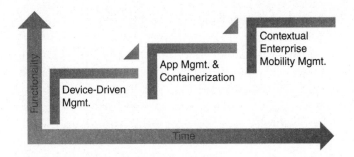

Figure 8.1   Three Phases of Enterprise Mobile Management

transparent to the user. The market continues to evolve almost monthly as vendors acquire companies, add new features, or fold.

In 2013, PC management and mobile device management were separate. Established PC and security management vendors, however, expect to unify PC, security, and mobile management software to make it easier for IT to manage and secure a diverse and ever-changing set of devices. Over time, IT should be looking for this unification, or at least the integration between mobile and PC management and security solutions. Mobile management will evolve from device management to content and data management, which we call contextual management. It will manage and secure data based on elements of context, such as user, job function, device type, location, and content type (see Figure 8.1). Effectively, the market will evolve to defining a security profile based on the user and the content, not just the device and the application.

The latest software provides a choice of approaches for protecting content while empowering employees to do their jobs from any location. IT should purchase enterprise mobility management as a way to distribute, manage, and secure information on both employee-owned and corporate-owned mobile devices. These solutions can help CIOs to secure corporate data unobtrusively while maintaining employee privacy and device usability. So, an enterprise mobility management strategy will provide the foundation of the technical plan to support right-time experiences in a business-to-employee situation.

What's in Enterprise Mobility Management?   If enterprise mobile management is critical, then it's important to select the right solution. Such a management solution should include the following:

- **Mobile device management.** Mobile device management software secures, monitors, manages, and supports mobile devices for both company-owned and employee-owned devices. It manages the data and configuration settings for all types of mobile devices and monitors the health of the device. Mobile device management also includes basic over-the-air distribution of applications and provides the foundation of a security strategy. It offers basic security features such as password enforcement, remote locking of the device, device tracking, and removal of the data on the device if it's lost or stolen.
- **Mobile security.** This could be considered part of device management or its own entity. Device management is just one level of the security and solution. CIOs need a comprehensive mobile-security solution that provides multiple layers of protection. The first layer is protecting the device and its data, which also includes the data on removable storage (SD and micro-SD) cards. The second layer is the data as it moves through the network, which is typically some type of secure communications channel. The third layer is protecting access to the corporate network by preventing any device that appears to have been tampered with or doesn't have the proper security software on it from accessing the corporate networking, which is called quarantining. The fourth and fifth layers are securing the application, the content, or both within the application if necessary. These last two layers were typically considered part of mobile application management but also cross into the domain of security solutions. Mobile device management vendors have updated their solutions to support many of these features, and security vendors now offer mobile solutions that support centrally defined and distributed security policies, device and removable media encryption, and two-factor authentication such as biometrics. A mobile application management solution focuses on securing the application while mobile security solutions can provide device-level security.
- **Mobile applications management.** Basic applications management provides application delivery, version management, performance management, and analytics such as crash log reporting and usage data. It helps IT define user and group access control, securing applications with app wrapping or containerization. Mobile analytics helps the application development

team understand if the application is operating properly and what could be improved. It also provides analytics to monitor how employees and customers are using the application. This data can help the app team understand if the application is working the way they thought it would and if anyone is even using it.

Mobile applications management offers version management, which means IT can make sure users always have the most up-to-date software. Early mobile pioneers were using consumer applications stores like Apple's iTunes and Google Play to deploy enterprise applications. This works if the company is distributing apps to its customers, but it is awkward at best for internal company applications. The latest mobile app management tools provide custom enterprise app catalogs where employees can log in and download apps just as they would on a consumer app store. This offers the benefit of a centralized location for employees to find applications and for IT to manage the software licensing for these applications. It also eases security concerns because employees will be downloading their applications from a trusted and secure location.

Specialized vendors have emerged to offer mobile application management software, but mobile device management software and security vendors now offer at least basic application management. Instead of using the native email and browser that comes with a particular phone, IT may chose optional services that can include secure email clients and secure browsers. With mobile device management software, a company is able to keep all email, browsing, and application access within a secure container on the device. In addition, it will enable secure data sharing between any app that has been secured by the management vendor's software as well as app-level encryption independent of the device used.

- **Secure content management.** While content management was considered a separate set of products in 2014, it is quickly being integrated into the overall EMM suite. Increasingly, companies are looking for ways to securely distribute key pieces of content, such as price lists, spreadsheets, and presentations, to mobile devices. A business needs intuitive mobile solutions that allow employees to access, update, and share business content without sacrificing enterprise security and control. It's unrealistic to expect a company to move all of its corporate documents into one repository just to support mobile access. This means a company needs a mobile content management system that's able to link directly to other content management systems, such as Microsoft SharePoint, shared network drives, and others. New cloud-based document storage and document-sharing solutions with various levels of security, such as Citrix Sharefile and Box.com, have emerged as one way to solve this problem. This is a rapidly evolving area, and the IT department should stay abreast of developments.

Some other key features a company should look for include the ability to support multiple types of content, including office documents, PDFs, images, video, and audio files. A business should be able to safely store content for offline review and editing and automatically receive new versions of updated documents. The employee should also be able to search for content across all sites—cloud and on-premise—and folders.

- **Mobile Service Management (MSM).** This is the mobile form of IT Service Management (ITSM). ITSM is a widely deployed best practice framework to align IT and the business, structuring IT services across people, process, and technology in order to deliver a series of IT services at the level of quality commensurate with what the business will fund. Mobile Service Management focuses specifically on mobile devices, apps, and services across multiple roles in the IT service delivery chain. MSM empowers IT operations to deliver, monitor, alert, repair, and optimize mobile services and apps to ensure high quality of service while minimizing downtime. MSM empowers support teams with remote diagnostics to quickly resolve mobile issues and enables mobile user self-service for lower cost of support. MSM empowers IT management with visibility and analytics to make more informed decisions and optimize service delivery.

Enterprise mobility management is critical to mobile-enable apps but isn't required for building consumer applications. Business-to-consumer apps require security vulnerability testing and compliance testing with consumer app stores. At least a portion of the management for consumer applications is provided by the consumer app store vendor, such as Apple's iTunes and Google's Play Store. This doesn't mean, however, that you can abdicate all responsibility for security. The company still needs to secure B2C transactions. A company should still rigorously test its application's code for security vulnerabilities, for both business and consumer applications. Consumer mobile application security will start with an extension and adaptation of your existing online security solutions. Detailed strategies for consumer solutions are outside the scope of this book. A few good references for this are *Hacking Exposed Mobile Security Secrets & Solutions, Android Security Cookbook,* and *Mobile Device Security for Dummies.*[1]

Four Questions to Evaluate Mobile Management

There are numerous types of mobility management vendors and several deployment models, including on-premise, cloud, and hybrid deployments. With such a complex landscape, how do we decide which solution is right for our company? The technology team, which is composed of both IT and business leaders, should define what types of data will be accessed, assess the risk profile of that data, and evaluate the available technology solutions based on the needs of the application and content. If an EMM project is stalled, it's important to reevaluate the solutions frequently, as most vendors offer new product versions every three to six months. Both business and IT leaders should ask the following four questions as the company evaluates how to support its mobile workers:

1. **What percentage of our employees will be bring-your-own-device-light (email and calendar only), full BYOD (access to corporate apps), or corporate-owned-personally-enabled (COPE)?** There isn't a one-size-fits-all approach to supporting devices. It's also rare that a company will support only corporate-owned devices or only BYOD devices. While many CIOs are supporting BYOD, many other business and IT leaders are purchasing smartphones and (increasingly) tablets for their employees. CIOs must define a management strategy that supports BYOD-light, full BYOD, and COPE. IT and HR must also devise a global strategy that meets the security and privacy regulations of different countries.

2. **How will we manage the entire application life cycle?** Today's enterprise mobility management must go beyond what mobile device management has been. Whatever solution a business

deploys must offer a scalable way to get apps and content onto devices securely, one that doesn't alienate employees. It must also be easy for the end customer to access and update apps.

3. **What level of security do we require?** CIOs should define what apps will be accessed on mobile devices, what kind of data will be stored on the device, and what regulations the business is required to support. For example, a health-care company may choose a solution that does not allow any patient personal health data to be copied to a mobile device. While a company might choose lighter security constraints, it is important that the vendor it selects offers a rich portfolio of security solutions in case the customer's needs change.

4. **Do we want to support enterprise mobile management in-house, hosted, or both?** Mobile management solutions are critical to the business's operational health and security, but many firms don't have the IT resources required to evaluate, install, and manage enterprise mobile management. IT should assess its available resources and decide if it should deploy enterprise mobile management on-premises or in the cloud. In some cases, CIOs may wish to use hosted solutions in geographies where IT staff are limited but on-premise solutions at larger locations.

Building Mobile-First Applications

Mobile first is an interesting term that has spread within the industry over the past several years. It came into existence to discuss the mental shift application designers must make when designing apps for both consumers and employees. It also described the mental shift that business managers must make when redesigning workflows and business processes to work in a mobile and cloud computing–based world.

Mobile first can be a polarizing term for organizations. It implies that everything we've built in the past must be thrown out and or recreated. It also implies that we are only designing for mobile devices. This isn't the essence of what mobile first is or what the transition is that businesses face today.

In reality, mobile first is about designing applications and services to provide the right information and user experience for the device they are using at that time. Experience doesn't equate to prettiness and touch navigation. Experience is about having access to the right functions on the right devices. It's about providing easy access to the right information. It's a right-time experience. Brian Katz, director and head of mobility engineering at Sanofi and author of the blog, "A Screw Loose," says, "Mobile First does not mean Mobile Only. It means we start from a mobile perspective but use Responsive design to match the app to the screen/device."[2]

It doesn't mean we redo all of our applications to work on smartphones. It does mean that we have to figure out what parts of what applications should be available on any given device. It also means we need to reimagine how our apps and services will evolve in the future. In the consumer world, this can be easier because many of the applications are new and don't need to access a corporate back-end system, such as material resources planning or corporate financials. In the enterprise world, it's harder because we have systems that may have been built more than a decade ago. We still need to use these systems or some portion of these systems. Perhaps *mobile ready* would've been an easier term for enterprises to deal with. Natalie Lambert, director of integrated product marketing at Citrix, says, "But in the user's mind, it isn't about mobile first. It's about *me first.*" She calls it the era of user-centric IT.[3] Whatever we call it, we need to redesign at least part of our processes.

Companies across all industries have begun to build mobile apps. But many of these companies are using concepts that worked in the PC era. Leaders in the space, such as Coca-Cola Enterprises and Tesco, are designing with mobile in mind. These companies are redesigning applications and services to be contextually aware and adaptive. In the majority of cases, we've seen mobile-first applications being built for consumers, not for an enterprise's employees. Employee applications are just starting to get off the ground due to the security concerns I discussed in the EMM section and difficulty connecting to corporate systems.

There are also extreme differences in how a company builds applications for its customers versus its employees. For example, Nike had brilliant, sexy apps for its customers long before it offered mobile applications to its employees. Art King, formerly the mobility lead in global architecture for Nike Inc. and currently the director of enterprise services and technologies at Spidercloud Wireless, provided an interesting perspective on enterprise challenges with mobile apps. In our interview, he told me, "Enterprise IT faces a number of challenges when moving to mobile. There are a significant amount of minor business applications whose business owners don't have budget or can't prioritize a necessary mobile evolution of even parts of the application."[4]

He also said, "This creates a very long tail of applications that are blockers to getting to the end state of having your full office in your hand that many IT strategists are seeking. Enterprise app projects that do not receive sufficient budget, for whatever reason, to create the expected consumer-grade user experience of intuitive, simple, and attractive apps—without this, enterprise apps may be sidelined by adoption failure."

In many cases, companies that serve consumers hired outside consultants to build mobile-first or at least mobile-friendly applications. In the consumer world, the first generation of mobile applications that companies built were micro-apps that performed one of two functions flawlessly. Some of these applications remained micro-applications, but most application developers built additional functionality based on consumer reviews and requests.

Consumer applications are upgraded frequently. These upgrades may be spurred by user feedback, a change in the version of an operating system, or a change in design tools. Consumer applications are rarely considered finished. Iterative design is normal for consumer applications. In fact, there's even the concept of a disposable app in the consumer application world. Examples of these include marketing apps that are built to support a specific event, such as the Super Bowl XLVII Official NFL Game Program app and Lady Gaga's mobile application for her album *ARTPOP*.

This new generation of app development is particularly challenging for enterprise IT application design. The entire process is different. Once the management and security foundation for mobility has been defined, a business begins to offer access to corporate data, such as expense management and customer relationship management. Once employees get a taste of accessing any corporate data on devices, they quickly want access to everything. Given their experience with consumer applications, employees expect their corporate applications to be easy to use and constantly evolving.

Enterprise application design teams are accustomed to building software that was updated annually. In fact, the pace of change breaks most software design cycles. Consumer mobile applications may be built in weeks and can be updated as frequently as every few months. Consumer apps become feature-rich apps through iterative design.

Many of these concepts of rapid and iterative design haven't translated at all into the enterprise mobile application market. Enterprise designers want to build applications that are feature-rich right out of the gate. Since the app development team is writing applications that run the business, the team expects to write mobile applications that will last many years. This isn't necessarily an unrealistic expectation. Most of a company's existing enterprise applications portfolio took years to customize and deploy. In enterprise IT, it could take up to six months or more to get an application updated.

Times have changed. It's not that a company doesn't need robust applications. However, a company needs applications that can adapt to a rapidly changing technology and business environment. This means the manner in which we design and update enterprise applications must also change.

The concept of agile design isn't new. It started in the early 2000s. Agile design is described by many as software development methods that focus on iterative and incremental development. It promotes flexible planning, evolutionary development and delivery, and demands rapid and flexible response to change.

Mobile and cloud computing have created an environment of agile design on steroids. In the cloud, consumer applications from Facebook and Google are updated every few weeks. And it's not just consumer applications that are using these principles. Even business cloud applications, such as Salesforce.com and Successfactors.com, have regular and frequent updates. In the first wave of consumer app development, programmers had to change the pace of development to meet the ever-changing shifts in devices and operating systems. The same must be true for enterprise applications if we are to provide right-time experiences that deliver the right information to the right device at the right moment.

People adopted mobile applications because they were easy to use and solved a need or desire. Consumers continue to use an application if the company fixes issues quickly and adds new features that users request. This dynamic has already changed how applications are built for consumers, and it will set the tone for the approach to designing applications for a company's employees.

Sencha, a developer of frameworks that enable developers to build cross-platform mobile and web applications, claims an application development team must provide three items: universality, great design, and compliance.

In the white paper entitled "Application Development Strategies for a Multi-Device World," Sencha said, "The application must provide a consistent user experience regardless of device, and all features and functions must work the same way across device types, in any context." For great design, the company said, "Functionality alone is no longer enough; a business app needs to be visually engaging and work as smoothly and intuitively as consumer apps."[5]

Finally, mobile apps and services must also meet internal policies for security, privacy, and regulatory compliance.

Let's discuss the choices that a company's application development and IT teams must make to deliver mobile-ready applications.

The Choice of Features   The question developers should ask themselves as they build employee-facing applications is simple: What functions or workflows do employees need or want to use on a mobile device? What single function would allow employees to get the job done faster or easier or both? You should be working with your IT and apps designers to define what you need and how you would prioritize your needs. One way to start is by dedicating one or more members from each group to act as a liaison to IT.

For customers and prospects, the questions are, What information or service do consumers need to get to the next logical action? Are they trying to research a specific product or service, find a location, or purchase a product? Are they exploring or are they trying to accomplish a specific goal? For both employees and consumers, app design is about more than just shrinking a webpage or an application.

The mobile application design represents the new era of application design. What's in the new era? First, the post-PC application landscape will offer fewer features within an application, especially in the apps' early stages.

Fewer features doesn't mean the application is inferior. It simply means it has fewer extraneous features. Think of it as "the right features" rather than every feature. While it may be nice to have 500 functions within an application, enterprise applications are frequently cluttered, clunky, and unusable. New applications won't be designed to support every use case. Developers will start with micro-apps for both consumer and enterprise audiences but should expect to grow these into richer mobile applications. In some cases, applications were designed with obsolescence in mind, such as a catalog application for the Christmas holiday.

Today's enterprise software is expected to last 5 to 10 years because it runs our business. Applications should be built with iteration in mind. Many new mobile applications will also be designed with a shorter lifespan in mind to support a specific LOB goal. For example, marketing could launch an app to support a product launch, sales could request a special catalog for the Christmas season, and field service could build an application to support construction for one project. These should have specific ROI metrics, such as number of downloads and uses in the area of marketing or time saved in areas such as accuracy of status reporting. Being a mobile-first or mobile-ready company requires new thinking around the design of both the applications and the business processes to support mobile.

Look for the Quick Wins   We've entered an era where customers are no longer silent about their wants and desires. Consumers, whether employees or customers, expect to be part of the process. They want to give feedback and they want to be heard. They have invaluable insights and suggestions. This means that a mobile app development strategy is about more than just the tools. It is also about the process of gathering requests and feedback on applications. It's the LOB manager's job to ensure that the app team knows what the group needs. It's also the team's job to be part of the process of designing, testing, and recommending changes. For consumer apps, the apps team should also offer several ways to collect feedback, including in-app submission of feedback, a link to rate the app in the app store, and web-site feedback forms.

Sometimes, IT will look to build the perfect app, which can take too long and often leads to disappointing results. Instead, IT and business unit leaders should start small by defining a few lightweight apps that can be built and deployed quickly as well as changed quickly if necessary. IT should work closely with different business units to define what apps will deliver value while meeting the criteria of short development cycles. A short enterprise design cycle could be 90 days and a refresh of the application could be within 60 days of launch. Jessica Bartley, IS Security Manager of Telephone and Data Systems, summed up the opportunity perfectly during our fireside chat at the 2014 M6 conference. When I asked her to provide advice for enterprise app development, she said, "Done is better than perfect." [6] In the 2013 Anypresence Mobile Readiness Study, roughly a third of the companies interviewed reported releasing updates or enhancements once a month or more frequently.[7] Once IT has a few successes under its belt, the team will require additional funding for larger mobility initiatives. Business unit leaders and the CFO need to prepare.

Apps need to be built in a few months, not take six months or a year. They shouldn't start as the magnum opus of a company. Delivering the next masterpiece will take too long. An app should be useful and function well. While a company doesn't need to build everything into the app at the outset, it does need to make sure that everything it has built works flawlessly. For both consumer and enterprise apps, the company should list what features it plans to build next and solicit feedback.

The Choice of Development Methods   The fragmented mobile landscape has put IT shops in a bind as they try to figure out the best way to mobilize apps and processes for the widest range of devices without reinventing the wheel every six months. As in the early days of web applications, a thin (mobile web) versus thick (native device apps) argument has ensued. What are your options? A company's IT team will need to select from the following development options:

- **Native apps.** Building native apps means you write your app using the programming language and interface for a specific operating system and device, such as Apple's iOS or Google's Android. This normally delivers the best performance, but it requires a different version for each operating system. IT may also spend more money developing the app because it has to be built and maintained in each operating system. It also means that you need app developers who understand how to write in each language.
- **Web apps and websites.** Most new devices have a web browser. Companies can now build web apps that have a mobile "look and feel." The pros of this approach are that it's far easier and cheaper to find web developers than it is to find native app developers. It also only requires the company to build an application once. The downside is that a web app still doesn't have all the features a native app would. Web apps support most devices, but they often cannot access mobile device features, such as a camera or contact list. A complementary and additional approach to web apps is also creating a responsive web design. Whatis.com defines *responsive design* as an approach to web page creation that makes

use of flexible layouts, flexible images, and cascading style sheet media queries. The goal of responsive design is to build web pages that detect the visitor's screen size and orientation and change the layout accordingly.[8]

- **Hybrid apps.** This option is a compromise between native and web development. You write in industry-standard web programming languages, such as HTML5 and JavaScript, then package in a natively installable format for app store distribution. This allows application developers to reuse a large portion of code they've developed to build apps that can run on several operating systems, saving money and time.

I've found the discussion of development methods to be very philosophical within organizations. Developers appear to have very strong preferences for "the best way" to do things. Some swear by native and some swear by HTML5. The opinions also change over time. While many started by believing HTML5 web apps were the best solution for all problems in 2011, the tide appears to be shifting back toward native apps. In the Q4/2013 Appcelerator survey of 6,698 executives (fielded by IDC), the company reported that "the number of developers reporting to be 'very interested' in developing apps with HTML5 slipped to 56 percent, the lowest percentage in the brief history of the specification. Correlating this slip, almost half of those with experience building apps in HTML5 report a neutral or negative experience."[9]

In truth, developing a strategy for mobile devices is not an either/or choice. Although some people swear by one method, some by another, there's no single perfect implementation choice for all applications. A company will most likely build a combination of native, hybrid, and web apps. The choice of the development method should be based on the type of experience that the company is trying to create, the connectivity requirements, and cost. Native apps have full access to device features (e.g., accelerometers, camera, etc.) and the benefits of local processing, persistence, and integration with other native apps such as contacts and calendar.

However, mobile web development provides multiplatform support, a large pool of developers, and rapid deployment cycles. The latest advancements in HTML5 also bridge some of the gaps between native and mobile development by providing support for a small amount of local storage, web-structured query language (SQL) databases, and geolocation. In fact, the difference isn't that stark, as most native apps have user interface elements that incorporate web technologies taken from HTML5. If a firm needs access to specific device features, such as the camera and the contact list, it can only gain access to these functions if the application is native. If the app is sensitive to intermittent connectivity, the app design team should evaluate building a native application so the user can work offline and store data on the device.

Design Method Should Match Application Requirements   The challenge for app developers is to understand the trade-offs between the various approaches and to make a selection based on the specific applications requirements. In order to do this, the application development team must partner closely with the various lines of business to understand the worker's true requirements. If this doesn't happen, you'll end up with apps that are technically brilliant but lack the usability and functionality your employees need. While I've discussed what this choice of development models means for employees, the same set of concerns arise for building B2C apps. You have to understand what the consumer wants and select the development method that is best suited to create that experience.

A business should build a functionality map for each app and workflow that it needs to design. The app team should then map these functions to the appropriate development method. For example, a social networking app will most likely be a native application in the near term because it requires access to a device's contact list, camera, and GPS. Facebook discovered this the hard way. It released its mobile application in HTML but later decided to build a set of native applications to improve performance. Meanwhile, an app that just looks up inventory and doesn't require access to the device's other features could be a simple web app.

Cost Is Also Part of an Application   I've discussed the challenge IT faces in using the right tool for the job—not just selecting one method, but picking the right method for the application. The challenge for business managers is to balance the cost of building an application to the required functionality. The technology team doesn't have the budget for mobile-enabling every application in the company. They'll work with the CFO to fund applications that everyone in the company uses but will consult with the department heads for LOB applications.

If you are a marketer who is looking to build a best-in-class brand experience, you may want a native application. However, this native application may cost you hundreds of thousands of dollars. Do you have that kind of budget for a single app? How many apps will you need, and how will you fund both the initial design and any ongoing updates? Many marketing teams have headed to design agencies to build applications. This has two potential issues. The first is that it can be expensive, although it may be necessary if the company doesn't have its own design talent. The second is that the company needs to be able to update the app and must plan for this eventuality.

Many companies don't have the internal skill to build native apps and don't want to pay consultants to build and maintain apps. In this case, a cross-platform design toolkit is often a very technically suitable and cost-effective measure for building a certain set of enterprise apps. In other cases, a company may choose to start mobile-enabling apps by using the web team to design HTML5-based apps.

The Choice of Tools   Once the team has mapped out what the company wants to build and how it wants to build it, IT needs to select development tools. Given that IT must support multiple operating systems, app development teams should review several areas. First, what languages must be supported, and does the team have the necessary skills in-house? In the past, IT could use a wide variety of development tools, but businesses looking to support multiple systems such as Android and iOS must develop fluency in Java and Objective C. This means the choice of the tools is at least partially defined by what development method is selected. There are several types of mobile application development platforms to choose from:

- **Native app development platforms.** These allow you to develop for a single specific operating system, such as Windows Phone, BlackBerry, Android, or iOS. For example, developers of iOS apps frequently use Xcode and Objective C while they use Java for Android apps.
- **Web toolkits.** These tools allow you to design web apps that run on almost any operating system. While the presentation can look good, there can be drawbacks, such as slower performance, inability to use the app when disconnected, and a lack of a native look and feel.

- **Hybrid apps development platforms.** These are sometimes called mobile application development platforms (MADP) and will often include tools that support native and web app development. The idea is this is the one-stop toolkit for building cross-platform mobile apps. The challenge with this is that these tools tend to have proprietary features the developers have to learn how to use. The upside is the components allow the developer to use similar coding conventions across all platforms, which vastly increases the quality and speed of development. At the same time, it reduces the cost of maintenance when updating multiple platforms. While it may not be perfect, and it may be difficult to train IT staff on a specific solution, many businesses will find this approach to be the easiest for the long run. It should also offer runtime client application program interfaces (APIs) designed to enhance security, governance, and usability. Remember, you have to connect to the back-end systems, which is why you need APIs.

IT's strategy should define how apps will integrate with back-end systems. A business will need to connect to systems that may or may not be mobile-enabled. Mobile-optimized middleware serves as a gateway between applications, back-end systems, and cloud-based services. This set of connective tools could be purchased as standalone software or could be purchased as an SaaS service, which is frequently called Mobile Back-End as a Service (MBaaS). What tools a firm selects will be based on whether it wants prepackaged mobile apps, support for a wide range of operating systems, and offline data collection and how quickly it wants to embrace the mobile web. The following are several considerations the business leaders and app team should discuss:

- **Usability.** It goes without saying that usability is critical. As I said in the last chapter, usability is more than just the graphical user interface, although this is important as well. The design will fail if there are too many buttons and icons or if they are too close together. The button has to be big enough for an adult finger. When working with a mobile interface, you have a limited amount of space, and some designers add too many buttons or icons. Another consideration is the size of the human fingertip. If the buttons or icons are too small, users could make errors with selecting the wrong one. If in doubt, test your layouts and get feedback.

- **Consistency.** Another issue is consistency of workflow. App designers should try to design a user experience that remains the same on all platforms. Of course, there may be some differences based on the device function. But if the experience changes too much between devices, you'll confuse and annoy your users.

- **Life cycle.** A business should think of its processes and apps as living organisms that change and evolve over time. This means that companies need to build a design life cycle. IBM's MobileFirst initiative provides an example of what should be included in the app design life cycle. It includes tools to support application design, testing, deployment, and analytics (see Figure 8.2).

- **Instrumentation.** I've already discussed design and development. Instrumentation means the business can analyze that application's performance and usage. It's surprising how few companies do this today. It's important to build analytics into your applications at the design phase. Without it, you run the risk of building apps but not understanding how or if they're being used and if you are getting an ROI. We can do this after the fact with mobile app management tools, but it's easier to incorporate the analytics at the front end of the process.

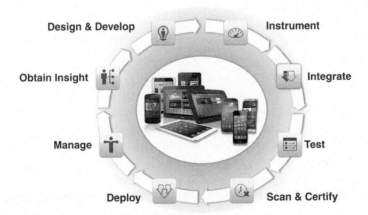

Figure 8.2   IBM's View of the Mobile Application Development Life Cycle

Source: IBM.

- **Integration.** This means building links to data in systems that may or may not be mobile-enabled. These are frequently called transactional systems or systems of record. Examples of the types of data in these systems include inventory availability, pricing, financials, sales figures, and the list goes on.
- **Application testing.** Poor performance and user interfaces kill usability. Testing is a critical part of PC application design processes but even more critical in mobile application design. Various platforms behave differently. An application may run well on one operating system but poorly on another, so it's important to test the app on each operating system and on the web to see how the features and functions change. IBM calls this scanning and certifying the application. I believe this is part of app testing and means the app developers should test for vulnerabilities in the code before they release it. Different operating systems also have different vulnerabilities, and companies need to keep this in mind when they are developing for the various environments.

Don't Forget App Analytics   The IBM lifecycle example mentions the concept of obtaining insight, which I believe is particularly important for delivering right-time experiences. It should be part of every application's life cycle. It's unlikely that any company creates an application or service right the first time. Even if the developer nails it, the end customer's needs will change over time. Obtaining insight is about understanding what's working and providing feedback for future enhancements.

Analytics provides a crucial role in this. It improves applications and experiences by understanding the device, what the person is doing, where he's doing it, and much more. This knowledge can help company management understand if what has been built works the way they thought it would. If the firm built a game, it wants to know how people are using the game. Are users playing all the way to the end? How difficult is it for players to work through the game's different levels? Game designers think about these questions and build analytics into their services.

People who build enterprise software and consumer-facing services must do the same. Companies need to collect data on how well the experience works for users. As we move into a new era of rebuilding and purchasing new applications and services, we have an opportunity to avail ourselves of the contextual information to make a better product that works more effectively for the person using it.

How Much Does It Cost?

One roadblock companies must overcome is the investment for mobile apps. Cost is a difficult thing to nail down in mobile. As you can see, numerous choices impact the cost of mobile-enabling a business. To get a handle on what it would cost an organization, let's look at the main components of the mobile technical plan, which include enterprise mobile management, development tools and platforms, developers, and back-end integration expense.

Many organizations believe BYOD is cheap or free because the employee owns the device. Nothing could be further from the truth. According to Good Technology, the annual mobile cost of ownership per user is $1,900. This includes not only device and carrier costs but also infrastructure, software, support, and many other costs. Those who have tracked and measured these costs are surprised at how much it exceeds their initial estimates. Good Technology created a calculator where a business can type in its actual figures for various costs, such as labor and telecom expense, to calculate their annual TCO (which can be found at www.good.com/mco). Once a business has a picture of the full costs, it's clear that IT should purchase some form of mobile services management to help the organization minimize labor burdens.

As noted above, EMM is one set of technologies that IT should invest in and in some cases includes mobile service management. The cost of enterprise mobile management has dropped considerably over the past two years while the functionality has increased. Businesses should budget between $1 and $5 per user, per month for basic enterprise mobile management. The cost varies for adding mobile application management, content management, and services management. For business-to-consumer applications, businesses don't need enterprise mobile management, but they will be testing the apps and distributing them through the consumer app stores.

Mobile app development, including back-end integration, is one of the hardest mobility costs to model. It may be that a company outsources this task to a systems integrator or app design firm. Alternatively, a company can evaluate and deploy enterprise-grade

MADPs that offer connectors to common apps such as SAP, Oracle, Microsoft, and others. Even with a platform, the company may still need integration assistance. MBaaS providers offer another alternative, but I believe this category will eventually become part of the mobile application development platforms. Today's MADPs will eventually evolve into *enterprise mobile application platforms* that offer development tools and middleware for back-end system integration. The cost of the platform today ranges from open source tools that are free to platforms that cost hundreds of thousands of dollars.

According to the Anypresence's Mobile Readiness benchmark, the cost for building an application isn't cheap. In the survey, "more than half of respondents indicated the average cost of initial development for a typical mobile application (including environment setup, mobile service development, SDK and UI development, testing, deployment, and project management) was estimated to be more than $50,000 for a single app. Roughly 25 percent put the price tag at $100,000 or greater per app." If IT needs to mobile-enable hundreds of apps across the company, it's no small task from a design or a budgeting perspective.[10]

Mobile enablement, however, isn't a luxury, a frill the business can afford to ignore. It's a necessity. We can't control that or deny its reality. So we have to find the funds to make it happen. What we can control is the building of a solution that provides the company with flexibility but also scalability. We can minimize the throw-away investments.

Benjamin Robbins is the founder of Palador, a mobile application consultancy in Seattle, Washington, that specializes in enterprise application development. He believes there are several steps to estimating the cost of an application that include more than just the cost of the tools. While app estimation is usually a technical exercise, business leaders should be aware of the moving parts that affect budget. Many business leaders often misjudge the complexity of "just needing it to do this one thing." Much of an application's cost is in connecting to other systems. As a business leader, a few simple questions you can ask to understand an app's complexity are:

- Is the data in our control or in a third-party application?
- Is the user interface simple or fancy?
- Is the app trying to do one action or many actions?

Once you grasp those high-level questions, you are ready to jump into a discussion of the more detailed nature of app estimation. Robbins provides the following as a method of determining the cost of building applications.

Palador's Application Cost Estimate Framework

Robbins says, "There is no magic involved in app cost estimation. There is, however, a bit of an art to it. Before we get to the more fuzzy nature of estimating, we can first look quantitatively at the app we want to build. The first step in estimating the cost of an application is the ability to articulate what it is we are trying to build. In years past, this involved a time-consuming and process-laden herculean effort. In the light and nimble world of mobility, there is a much easier approach."[11]

Mock-Up

The first thing you or your app development team should do is draw a picture (a mock-up or wireframe) of each screen or scenario you envision for the app. It doesn't have to be pretty, perfect, or precise. It can be physical or digital. It can even be on the back of a napkin. The key is to not get hung up on form or format but just to work in whatever medium you are comfortable with. I prefer a whiteboard, but you may like Visio, your tablet, or the old-fashioned pen and paper.

Drawing a picture accomplishes several things. First, it gets the team over the blank-page dilemma that many people struggle with. Second, there is nothing like being able to physically, albeit in a limited fashion, interact with your design. This will point out holes quicker than any written explanation. Lastly, a mock-up allows you to quickly communicate your idea with others.

Use Cases

Once you have fleshed out your general design, it is time to put that design into verbal form. This task may seem daunting at first, but it really isn't so bad. Your goal isn't to articulate an app; rather, it is to articulate an experience from the user perspective—use cases in technical-speak.

Use cases should contain the following:

- Name—usually a description of what the goal is
- Actor/persona—the role within the org that is using the app
- Description—a few sentences about what actions the user takes
- Desired result—the end result that the user will experience

These use cases are not just for the app team's benefit. You as business managers need to help develop relevant use cases for your team. Development and testing should be oriented around these use cases to support the end users. By doing so, the app team will not only create an app but also assure that they're thinking of how the app will work from the user's perspective. This is important for developers and testers, who by nature think of technology before users. By thinking of the end user's experience, they will build an app that will keep users coming back for more.

App Codification

Once your use cases are done, the app development team can begin to break down the constituent requirements into four primary buckets:

1. General structure
2. User interface
3. Data/integration points
4. Reporting/analytics

General Structure Every app requires a basic structure to be set up in order for it to function. Essentially, the app needs a container to hold it. This includes both a programmatic and a data structure. A small percentage of hours is needed to set this container up. For simple apps, it is probably on the order of 5 percent of the total time. For complex apps, it can be closer to 10 percent of the time.

User Interface User interface is relatively straightforward in that you can usually break it down screen by screen. Those with simple elements such as text boxes and drop-downs will require relatively few hours to develop. Those with dynamic changes and interactions that are not standard will take longer. For simple elements on the page, it will take four to eight hours per element. Complex user interface functionality can take anywhere from 24 to 40 hours.

Data/Integration Points   Most apps will need to create and access data. Data is often located in many places. This data can be local to the app, local to the network, on a private cloud, on public Internet, or in another system altogether. In general, the more control the company has of the data, the cheaper it will be to integrate it into an app. The further the data moves away from your network control, the more challenging it will be to coordinate integration. Data that the app keeps to itself will take relatively little time to develop. Simple data interactions take from 8 to 16 hours to implement, while complex integration with third-party systems can take up to two weeks or more, depending on how well documented and responsive the other vendor is.

Reporting/Analytics   Many apps have reporting and analytic functions built into the app. These can be broken down by function and can take from 8 hours for simple reports to 24 hours for more complex functions. Reporting is one area where people frequently underestimate the total time taken to display the data. Make sure you break each function down into its simplest component part to estimate correctly.

Project Management

Projects cannot happen without some basic oversight. Project management should, at a minimum, be a line item on your project budget. There are often many details for which you need a resource to coordinate communications. Integration points often prove troublesome, and a project manager is an effective way to chase down the details. Often a project's budget and timeline status must be communicated to management. Development resources should not do this, as their time is too valuable and they are better suited for technical tasks.

We can boil down project management requirements to a quick-and-dirty estimate of how communication-heavy the project will be. Does management expect detailed progress reports? Does the project have many integration points that will take research and coordination? If the project is light on the project management requirements, you can estimate 10 to 15 percent of the total development hours. If you recognize that there will be many communication tasks for this effort, it is better to estimate 15 to 20 percent of the total development hours as project management hours.

Testing

Testing is a function that is never truly done; there is always more you could test. There is no such thing as too much testing. This, however, is not a practical approach on any project. At some point, you need to stop testing and say the product is good enough. Testing estimation is similar to project management estimation. If your project has many points of integration, then you are more susceptible to breakage. Complex report options or analytics will also cause an increase in testing hours.

At a minimum, your testing hours should be a third of your development hours. More complex applications can expect to see this figure reach 50 percent of development hours.

Deployment

One item that managers often overlook is the amount of time it takes to deploy the app. Even simple deployments to app stores take time. Complexity and control often determine deployment time. The more complex an app—meaning databases, web services, integration points—and less control the organization has over the final deployment environment, the more time will be required. Simple apps can take 10 percent of development hours to deploy, while more complex apps can approach 15 percent or more.

Buffering

One important thing to remember when it comes to app estimation is that most people underestimate the amount of time it will take to implement an app. Only the most cautious personalities estimate correctly or overestimate the time required. Unless you have an overly pessimistic approach to life, it is safe to assume that you need to buffer your estimates by 25 to 40 percent. This may make your conclusion unappealing even if realistic, but ask yourself, how often does a project ever run perfectly and according to plan? The more complex an app, the more you should buffer. If your app is just a few simple screens with no integration, you can expect to be on the low end of the buffer estimate—but you should still assume the worst.

Final Thoughts

Robbins wrapped up the discussion of the framework by saying, "It is important to perform app estimation to get a sense of how much time and money a given project is going to cost. As with anything, your ability to estimate this will improve with practice and knowledge of your team. Most of all, remember that this is an art rather than an exact science."

He also brought up a great point about the difference between defining budgets for consumer applications versus enterprise applications. He said, "These estimation techniques will get you in the ballpark and allow you to set some reasonable expectations. Don't be discouraged by the numbers app estimation produces. We have been conditioned to think of apps as $0.99 disposable things. But the cost to create these seemingly simple things is anything but cheap. This is one reason we find that most independent app developers are not making any money in the consumer market."

Summary

The workforce is mobile, and consumers are mobile. With the right technical foundation, companies can achieve workforce productivity gains, enable real-time decision making, and improve customer service.

A technical enablement strategy should include enterprise mobility management solutions, an application development strategy, and a big data and analytics strategy. Enterprise mobile management software secures, monitors, manages, and supports mobile devices for both company- and employee-owned devices.

The technology team should define what types of data will be accessed, assess that data's risk, and evaluate the available technology solutions based on the application's needs and content.

We need not redo all of our applications to work on smartphones, but we do have to figure out what parts of what applications should be available on any given device. In addition, we need a technical application development strategy. Businesses should be open to supporting multiple types of development tools.

A mobile app development strategy is more than tools. It includes gathering requests and feedback on applications. The LOB manager must ensure that the app team knows what the group needs and must be part of the process of designing, testing, and recommending changes.

An application's cost involves more than the cost of the tools. It also includes an app's usability, consistency, life cycle, testing, and more. One framework for estimating cost involves a mock-up of each screen or scenario, use cases, codification, general structure, user interface, data integration, reporting/analytics, and more.

Hopefully this has provided you with a sense of what a huge undertaking mobile-enabling the business actually is. It's a critical step in any company's journey and a difficult one. It offers peril and opportunity. The mobile landscape is highly dynamic. Unless we have a working crystal ball, no one can predict where we will be in five years. The key to success is creating a strategy at the outset; executing the strategy in small, rapid phases; and reevaluating that strategy frequently.

Now I'm going to discuss an equally challenging topic, the role of big data in your organization.

Notes

1. *Hacking Exposed Mobile Security Secrets & Solutions by Neil Bergman*, Publication Date: July 9, 2013 | ISBN-10: 0071817018 | ISBN-13: 978-0071817011 | Edition: 1; *Android Security Cookbook*, by Keith Makan, Packt Publishing (December 23, 2013), and Scott Alexander-Bown, ASIN: B00HL2GODC. *Mobile Device Security For Dummies*, by Richard Campagna, Publication Date: August 9, 2011 | ISBN-10: 0470927534 | ISBN-13: 978-0470927533 | Edition: 1.
2. Phone interview with Brian Katz on April 3, 2014.
3. http://www.forbes.com/sites/netapp/2014/06/19/cio-user-centric-it/.
4. Phone and email interview with Art King on March 26, 2014.
5. Sencha whitepaper, "Application Development Strategies for a Multi-Device World," page 3.
6. On-stage interview at the www.m6mobiltyxchange.com conference on May 14, 2014.
7. Anypresence white paper on "The State of Enterprise Mobile Readiness," www.anypresence.com/Mobile_Readiness_Report_2013.php.
8. http://whatis.techtarget.com/definition/responsive-design.
9. Appcelerator Q4/2013 Trends Report, www.appcelerator.com.s3.amazonaws.com/pdf/q4-2013-devsurvey.pdf.
10. Anypresence white paper on "The State of Enterprise Mobile Readiness," www.anypresence.com/Mobile_Readiness_Report_2013.php.
11. Several interviews with Benjamin Robbins of Palador in March 2014. He designed the framework listed to help his clients understand what it costs to build a mobile application.

CHAPTER 9

Understanding the Components of the Technical Plan: Big Data

How Big Data Helps Deliver Better Outcomes

In the beginning of the book, I discussed the changes in the volume and types of data companies now have access to. This new unstructured data represents a powerful untapped resource. With the joy of more data has come the pain of finding solutions that can turn this tsunami of data into useful information. In this chapter, I discuss how big data and the four *V*s (volume, variety, velocity, and veracity) are changing the types of tools that IT and line-of-business managers have access to for gathering insight.

IBM and others have coined a fifth *V*, for value (see Figure 9.1). I'll discuss each of the *V*s in further detail in a moment. Similar to the last chapter, the following pages will provide a basic outline of the opportunities, challenges, and things business leaders must understand to effectively work with their technology teams and, most importantly, extract value from big data efforts.

Let's take a moment to define *big data* in its broadest terms. Edd Dumbill, principal analyst for O'Reilly Radar and author of *Planning for Big Data*, defines big data as "data that exceeds the processing capacity of conventional database systems. The data is too big, moves too fast, or doesn't fit the structures of your database architectures. To gain value from this data, you must choose an alternative way to process it."[1] Basically, big data doesn't fit nicely into the traditional storage and processing systems. Once we are able to store and process it effectively, however, we must also find other tools that help us discover the patterns and insights from all the data.

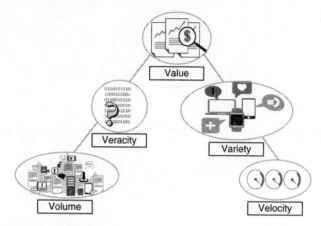

Figure 9.1   The 5 Vs of Big Data

Technology is wonderful, but no company has the money to purchase technology just for technology's sake. There always has to be a return on investment. In some cases, ROI is easy to prove. It shows up as dollars and cents that are saved as a result of installing technology. In other cases, the return isn't quantifiable as hard-dollar savings, but it's still evident. In the case of Memorial Sloan Kettering that I discussed in Chapter 5, big data helps save lives with better cancer treatment plans.

Let's begin with a discussion of some of the opportunities big data can provide.

The Business Case for Big Data

Analyzing data is not new, nor is the challenge of coping with large volumes of data. What is new is technology that can integrate and analyze large data streams that vary in structure. This allows businesses to think about challenges and opportunities in different ways. Industries such as financial services, retail, and telecommunications have been working with large volumes of data for years, with many challenges and at great expense. These industries were also early adopters of today's big data solutions and can provide us with insight on the power of using big data.

Amdocs, a provider of software solutions for the service provider industry, headquartered in Israel, describes the difference in big data as a move from understanding the past to predicting and acting on the potential future. "Business intelligence was a scripted set of questions. We wanted to understand what exactly happened in the business and why did it happen," says Avia Dadon of Amdocs' CTO office. "Big data analytics is more advanced. Companies will use the analysis to characterize data/information that is predictive in nature. It's not just what happened and why did it happen, but also what is likely to happen next. It's also prescriptive in what we should do about it. Companies, especially market leading service providers, are using big data analytics to define what actions and corrective measures the business should take in order to exploit the predictions, which the analyses have dictated."[2]

Dadon describes the importance of real-time (what I call right-time) actions requiring subsecond response times versus other use cases, where response times could be minutes or even hours. In working with service providers, Amdocs identified a dozen use cases across six functional groups with service providers where big data and analytics could be used to drive business value. These include right-time cross-selling and upselling, proactive customer care, multi-channel customer care opportunities, and more.

Amdocs then worked with data from communications service providers to define which of these use cases provided the best revenue or cost savings. This is the practical application concept of driving business value and outcomes, not just insight. It's no surprise that having the right data when a customer calls a communications service provider can lead to better support. It also has the potential to unlock new services revenue for the telecommunications and cable provider.

By understanding what the consumer has used in the past and what other consumers like her have used, service providers have the opportunity to deliver targeted offers either online or through the contact center. These use real-time analytics to produce highly targeted product and service recommendations. While the success rate of the targeted upsell sales varies, the rate of success is far greater with targeted offers than with generic offers.

If you multiply that additional spend by millions of customers, the revenue dollars add up fast. Not only that—once you have built a big data and analytics foundation, you can use it across multiple departments. According to the Amdocs study, proactive care is also high on the list of right-time experiences that operators want to provide. What does proactive care look like? Amdocs provides an example of how it is possible to eliminate a call from a potentially dissatisfied customer.

Assume Mary has three out of 10 numbers defined on her "Friends and Family" telephone plan. Assume further that Mary is at the end of her billing cycle and is approaching the point where she will be charged for overuse. Proactive care identifies the situation—Mary is underutilizing her rate plan—and recommends an action plan. Proactive care automatically triggers an email to Mary recommending she add more numbers to her Friends and Family plan. Mary updates the numbers on her plan, and as a result, her phone bill is right in line with what it's been in the past. Finally, in an ideal world, Mary tells all her friends about how her service provider helped her avoid overages.

Dadon describes a right-time action as one that could alert a customer that he has used 95 percent of his data plan. This could occur days or hours before the user has to take action. A real-time experience understands, at the time a customer is calling the contact center, if she is experiencing a poor-quality connection and why.

This isn't just theory. Sprint was plagued with customer experience problems that drove excessive calls into its contact center in 2008. It performed a root-cause analysis to define what problems, such as dropped calls and billing errors, caused a majority of the contact center calls. By minimizing the top problems discovered in that study, Sprint reduced its customer care costs from $3.7 billion a year in 2008 to $2 billion per year in 2012.[3] Imagine what a company can do if it can save $1.7 billion from improved customer experience. Granted, Sprint didn't have the same big data solutions that we have today, but the concept is the same. The company may have been able to react even more quickly to market changes with the modern big data and analytics solutions.

Insurance companies have had large volumes of customer and actuarial data for years. Companies such as MetLife are now using big data to create a 360-degree view of their customers. This isn't a new concept. MetLife had wanted to develop this solution for almost a decade. The technologies finally caught up to help it accomplish its goal.

To do this, MetLife had to bring together 60 different teams and 70 separate administrative systems, claims systems, and other data sources. This was no small task. It also highlights that projects are only successful if there is a business commitment and resources across the company, not just within IT. The company had to select a solution that could meet complex federal and state regulatory requirements imposed on the annuity and individual and group insurance products that MetLife sells.

MetLife wasn't going to rip out legacy systems anytime soon. It needed a solution that could bridge the old and the new world. The company chose one of the newer big data technologies, a NoSQL database called MongoDB, because it could collect the existing structured data but also work with less structured information without the same level of time-consuming database mapping.

Gary Hoberman, MetLife's senior VP and CIO of regional application development, said, "Any other database wouldn't allow us to view customers as a single record without caring about structure at all. With Mongo, we can bring a group policy and an individual policy together without any [data] normalization, and we use a Web services layer and the application to render the best view of that data."[4]

MetLife worked with an outside agency to create an interface that looks like Facebook's wall. It unifies all of the touchpoints into a single customer profile that lists products owned, contact center interactions, Internet logins, and in-person interactions. The new experience, called The Wall, was rolled out to 200 U.S.-based call center and claims administration researchers in April 2013. Currently, The Wall handles 45 million agreements with 140 million transactions.[5] MetLife is assessing the ROI, but it believes the new 360-degree customer experience is creating shorter hold times, better call-resolution measures, and higher Net Promoter Scores.

At the time of this writing, The Wall was still in beta mode. Right now, it doesn't support updating legacy systems of record, which will be key to maintaining clean and consistent records in the future. One challenge of this process is obviously eliminating dirty data and making sure that all of the records associated with a customer are indeed that customer's data. Hoberman says one way the company is addressing this issue is by having the agent ask the customer to verify information, such as existing services, when she is speaking to the customer.

The system is a prime example of using data to create a right-time experience. It also highlights that businesses can use the integration of big data and mobile as an opportunity to redesign business processes. As MetLife designed The Wall, it was able to change a customer service process from 40 clicks to just one click. In other cases, it simply makes it easier for the reps to see the information they already had by consolidating from 15 different screens to a set of more manageable screens.

Walmart also provides a great example of using both mobility and big data to drive ROI. Overall, 50 percent of Walmart's customers have smartphones and 50 percent of Walmart.com's traffic is driven by mobile.[6]

Gibu Thomas, Walmart's senior vice president of mobile, digital, and global e-commerce, believes mobile applications provide the opportunity to deliver the output of big data to customers while they are in the process of shopping. "Our goal is to create shopping tools that become second nature to the customer, providing assistance with every part of the retail experience from pre-store planning to in-store shopping and decision making to checking out. By leveraging big data, we are also developing predictive capabilities to automatically generate a shopping list for our customers based on what they and others purchase each week."[7]

Walmart has a targeting team within @WalmartLabs that uses big data to try to improve product selection on the web and with mobile in the store. It takes in almost every clickable action on Walmart.com, what individuals buy online and in stores, trends on Twitter, local weather deviations, and other local external events, such as the San Francisco Giants winning the World Series. The company uses big data and predictive analytics to intelligently tease out meaningful patterns so millions of Walmart.com customers have a shopping experience that is individually personalized.[8]

The company discovered through big data analytics that app users make two more trips per month to Walmart than shoppers that don't use the company's mobile app. Highly engaged mobile app users make four more trips per month. The data also revealed that highly engaged app users spend 77 percent more than other shoppers.[9] Clearly, Walmart's using big data and mobile to create a right-time experience that improves the commerce experience while driving additional sales.

These are just three examples of how businesses can drive return on investment using big data. There are many more.

The Challenge of Big Data

We have always had data; that's nothing new. We have also always had a problem making any use of the data. As senior executives have long complained, we're drowning in data when what we need is information.

Advances in computing, such as social networks and imaging technologies, are generating large volumes of raw data. It is purely mathematical; more people than ever before are using computers.

There are also more connected devices than ever. It's a number that continues to grow as people use several computing devices such as tablets and smartphones. More connected devices are coming online as we embed sensors in cars, phones, airplanes, and manufacturing equipment that emits data. Because computing—both general business and personal—has been around for a few decades now, more historical data exists than ever. Twenty-five years ago, only "information workers" and the systems that supported them were generating data. Now, billions of people all over the world have mobile devices, social networks, and connected gizmos that are part of the data creation mix. We have industrial equipment, household appliances, and just about anything with a sensor and connectivity creating a new stream of data.

There is far more data than our current systems can turn into actionable information. In fact, this problem existed before big data and has now become even more pressing. In the past, the technology team and managers set up constraints to keep data processing manageable. They said, in effect, "We need to know exactly the question we are trying to ask, and we need to be very clear about the sample set we use so we know we generate the most accurate results from the data we have." They were very careful about the inputs and very specific about what the outputs needed to be. (Remember GIGO—garbage in, garbage out?) They were specific about creating the right questions to achieve a certain output, and the process took time. If the branch offices sent all their sales data from around the country to one place (a data warehouse), the IT department could use analytics software to ask predefined questions and obtain answers within a range that could span a day to a week.

Unfortunately, by the time the answers arrived, they might be useless. There is a time value aspect to information. Moreover, the systems could only take in data in a certain way and of a certain type. If the data a business collected wasn't in the proper structure, such as rows and columns, the business software system had trouble making sense of it. The IT department had to spend time taking data that didn't fit into the existing database structure and reformatting it to fit before it could manipulate it. The process was time-consuming, expensive, and inflexible.

Moreover, an executive could not easily ask additional or ad-hoc questions. For example, if the first analytics structure a company created was designed to ask three questions, IT would have to recode the system to add a fourth question. The fourth question went onto the IT project list, and it could take months (no exaggeration) before it rose to the top of the list. Management could only have answers to its three questions in whatever format the machine spit them out. If you wanted a pretty visualization or a dashboard, IT had to create this or buy a set of software to do this for you. Once executive dashboards existed—computer displays showing results from several different sources—executives frequently wanted more information, but there was no easy way to meet their ever-evolving requirements. And too often the dashboards weren't very pretty or user friendly.

So, while we have long had data and almost from the beginning were drowning in it, we had poor tools to extract information from the volumes of data we collected, and then quickly extract some insight from that data. Some brilliant Internet engineers thought about this and said, "We need a better way to process data." If I am Google or Yahoo!, trying to index every piece of information in the world, I need a way to effectively and efficiently process search requests. If I am Facebook, I need a way to help several hundred million users find who they might want to know about or to be friends with.

Some great minds devised ways to make collecting, storing, and querying data easier for people: big data processing and platforms. I'll discuss these more in a moment. While not a panacea, these tools do allow more flexibility and better data manipulation than in the past. What was really revolutionary was that the new tools, with less preprocessing than the past, could take in various types of data. It could be email, video, audio, photo. If it's text, audio, video, or whatever, the technology team now has options for a collection of tools that will engage with all of it. There is also an opportunity for end users to have access to all of the data to process and analyze. Users can ask questions based on a broader base of data and it is easier to change their questions whenever they want. In some cases, answers that took hours to obtain now take minutes. Recall the case of Hilti, discussed in Chapter 6, where the company went from hours to minutes to process 33 million records. Other cases, such as interpreting video data, are faster but still require businesses to have sharp programming skills.

Evan Quinn, a software developer, product manager, and now industry analyst, points out that marketing professionals realize that there are multiple data points available about their customers.[10] Maybe if they could combine much of this data, they could reduce the guesswork involved in understanding what these customers like and don't like. With the right tools operating on the data, perhaps they could begin to predict how consumers might react to new pricing or new offerings. Law enforcement could have the ability to combine crime data with location-based data, weather data, and perhaps store hours to enable the police to predict where and when crime hot spots might arise and deploy staff and resources more effectively. Medical teams could combine loosely related research data with disease treatment data and do a far better job coming up with treatment plans.

All the data pouring into big data processing platforms, indeed, enables us to start to ask new questions, or ask old questions in new ways, or even learn how to solve problems in ways never before considered or that we weren't even aware were problems. But three things have stood in our way:

1. Most of the operational computer systems designed for businesses were not originally designed to handle the increase in volume, velocity, and variety of data (storage). In addition, and more important, they were not able to handle the far more complex queries we need to ask of this data to come up with answers to unique questions.

2. The business intelligence/analytics tools assumed a rather arithmetic or simple statistical set of uses (for example, total revenue, average spend per customer, seasonal variations), versus the far more statistically sophisticated and even predictive tools that can be applied to big data.

3. Very few people have the skills to understand the data, the business or human endeavor context, and the statistics that might work. Moreover, we have to be able to share all these answers with people who can use the answers. They, too, might ask new, pertinent questions, and thus participate in the feedback loop of fresh insight—and value.

Fortunately, the ability to process big data, to turn a chaotic mass of raw material into useful, actionable information, changed the game fundamentally because three things came together:

1. We developed incredible speed we didn't have before. A Google search for "big data" a moment ago found about 846,000,000 results in 0.34 seconds.

2. We were able to access lots of data, not just a little segment of all the data we have. Theoretically, an organization can analyze all its data and in any format, whether structured, from a database, or less structured, from machine logs, web logs, social sites, documents, multimedia, and so on.

3. We were able to process big data on relatively inexpensive hardware. We didn't need a room-sized Cray supercomputer, although there are some highly sophisticated Cray computers being used for big data—and they are no longer room-sized. We also have the option of using racks of ordinary servers for at least some of these tasks. In some cases, we can buy the resource as a service in the cloud (which I'll discuss in a moment).

These changes mean we don't have to know all of our questions up front. We could change our questions. We could start with one set of questions and, if they aren't working, try a different set. Because the analysis is fast and the system can work with anything, we don't have to throw out data. In the old method, organizations routinely did not include data because they couldn't store it and had already defined the questions' parameters, so they saved the data that addressed only those questions. If they decided those were the wrong questions, data on which to base new results might not be necessary.

Let's begin with a discussion on some of the opportunities big data can provide.

Making Big Data Useful

In a March 2013 report, "Big Data: What's Your Plan," McKinsey says any big data plan requires three core elements: (1) data, (2) analytical models, and (3) tools. This is a simple yet effective way to describe the challenge.[11] I discuss each of these in further detail throughout the chapter.

We need to collect and integrate pertinent data across the organization. We aren't—or at least we shouldn't be—living in a world where departments don't talk to each other. But somehow corporate data continues to remain on islands, effectively isolated within a single department such as finance, marketing, or human resources. This has probably been the case since organizations established separate departments, and very little has changed. However, a business can't design right-time experiences on an isolated island. These experiences require the participation of multiple departments and information flowing freely across the organization. Building new ways to store and analyze data provides us with an opportunity to fix this problem.

In this new world, every department and nearly every role—marketing, accounting, manufacturing, human resources—will want access to this data and will want a way to turn this data into insights that allow them to make informed decisions. For example, marketing might need access to financial data to understand how pricing changes can affect sales and profitability. The data alone is useless, as are the answers if they require a PhD in math to understand them.

Companies need to provide responses in a format that real people can understand, not just data scientists. This means data needs to be translated into what the knowledge means for a manager or an employee. Ideally, a response would offer ranked suggestions of what next actions a person might take. This is referred to as *prescriptive analytics*. The next evolution of this is *predictive analytics*, where the data starts to predict potential outcomes based on the facts available.

In the beginning, however, it's most important to simply be able to have access to information in a way that it can be understood. "Sales are down" isn't enough information. "Sales are down in Kansas" also isn't enough. The report needs to provide plausible reasons *why* sales are down in Kansas. It could be that the company changed the product mix in Kansas, a new competitor entered the market, or simply that a freak blizzard prevented people from shopping during the sales period.

Big Data and the 4 Vs

At this point, you might be asking how big data changes our systems and what all the fuss is about. I've discussed several of the big data opportunities, and clearly there are many I haven't discussed yet. There are at least four main issues that any business will face as it tries to build a technical plan that supports big data.

These include the amount of information (volume), type of information (variety), and speed of turning this information (velocity) into something meaningful at a reasonable expense (cost). Ensuring high quality of information (veracity) has always been a challenge. In some ways, big data makes this more difficult by increasing the volume of information that must be processed. It makes it easier in other ways because it's easier to spot trends and anomalies in information. I'll come back to this point later.

Let's begin by discussing the challenges with volume and how it relates to the current technology solutions. Data is often stored in a database, which is a method for storing and organizing data. A database management system (DBMS) is software designed to create and manage electronic databases. A data warehouse is a central repository of data, which is created by integrating data from one or more disparate sources. Data warehouses store historical data and sometimes the most current data. Companies have traditionally used analytics packages, such as SAS and Teradata, for creating trending reports, and analyzing historical data to improve products, sales, and customer service.

Until now, a majority of data had been stored in some form of relational database management system (RDBMS) from companies such as Oracle, IBM, and Microsoft. It's called *relational* because data is stored in relations, such as tables with rows representing items and columns representing different attributes of those items. A *database* is a set of data that has a regular structure and that is organized in such a way that a computer can easily find the desired information. Data normally went through major processing before it was stored. Data analysts cleaned up the data to improve its accuracy. The analysts also defined schema for the data, which is a blueprint of how a database is organized. While this was very useful for building databases for transactional systems, it was also a time-consuming process that limited the data being stored and the type of inquiries that could be made based on the data.

Why do you care about the history of databases? Good question. Relational databases have been a predominant choice for information storage in new databases since Oracle and DB2 introduced commercial relational databases in the 1980s. But many things have changed since the 1980s. While applications and interfaces have changed tremendously over the past 30 years, the underlying methods for storing and managing our data haven't changed that much. Unfortunately, big data breaks traditional systems.

What makes big data different? Part of it is in fact size. It can be huge, such as the human genome and 3-D video, which makes it expensive to store in a traditional database architecture. It can require subsecond processing, such as millions of Internet packets per millisecond that need to be analyzed for network quality and security threats or financial trading. This means it needs to be processed as it's happening, instead of stored and processed in a batch every hour, night, or week. It can be unstructured and fast moving, such as social networking traffic. Big data often involves frequently changing data sources, which means it's difficult to keep up with all the data structures. It turns out that big data analytics was a good usage for parallel data processing, which splits processing into threads to take advantage of multiple processors, and then joins the results back together.

Employee and customer expectations have also changed. If a person hits a web page or clicks on something in a mobile application, the user expects an immediate response. In effect, people expect information to be immediately available, and they expect to have access to it whenever they need or want it. While they wouldn't phrase it this way, people expect to have access to all types of data and have that data integrated regardless of what systems it comes from and where the data currently lives. If I'm a customer on the phone, I expect the agent to know who I am, why I'm calling, and the answer to my question. This answer may be in three or more different systems, but I expect them to act as one to provide me the experience I need.

If we go back to our original discussion of databases 101, we can see where the trouble begins. The process of cleaning and creating a data schema represents the first issue with supporting big data. Traditional relational databases have difficulty supporting the variety and volume of data. A business might want to add new sources (variety) of data to its analysis, such as sensor data, social data, and third-party data like government statistics. Traditional databases also have difficulty gathering data that is flowing into the system so quickly and in large volume. It's like trying to funnel Niagara Falls through a straw. This issue is called a problem with data ingestion.

The second issue is that we need to augment and advance today's business intelligence, which typically looks backward. It looks at previous data at a point in time. These reports are still valuable, but our requirements will be different as the business moves forward.

Business is moving faster and faster, which means we need information and insights faster. People want access to information and insight in near-real time or real time. A week or a day may not be fast enough. We may need to know something this hour or this moment. I pointed out earlier that in the past we had to design our databases in a specific way so they could answer certain questions (for example, how sales have changed in the past week). This need for speed moves us from historical reporting to stream processing. True, we can process information in real time with traditional tools. However, we can't process it effectively if the data is too great or not in the right format. It's also difficult to integrate and analyze multiple types of data at the same time.

In a conventional business intelligence architecture, the data is presumed to be stored in a repository (such as a relational database or, on a larger scale, a data warehouse). The organization asks questions, called *queries*, based on that data. Stream processing is different; it extracts knowledge from a continuous and rapid steam of real-time data. Instead of collecting and storing the data first, which creates a significant delay, we run analytics against the data as it becomes available to the organization. Another term you might hear is *complex event processing*, which is a method of tracking and analyzing what is going on in terms of business process and workflow in real time, and then deriving conclusions about what is happening and taking appropriate action. One could think of complex event processing as a kind of big data for business process, rather than purely data.

At the end of the day, what we need is a set of solutions that support both store and analyze functions (data at rest) and analyze data on the fly (data in motion).

All of this is beyond the simple reports, dashboards, and queries that were the essence of business intelligence of the past. Yes, there are more advanced business intelligence software solutions that help data analysts understand the business, but these tools aren't generally available or usable for managers and employees throughout the company. Thus, big data existed in pockets, like IT and engineering, who had the special resources to make big data work. The goal of big data solutions now, however, is for it to make it easier for the technology team to get data out to the end users who need it, at the time they need it and in a format that is useful.

Most dashboards built for line-of-business executives in areas such as finance, sales, marketing, and operations show the organization's recent results. But executives need cross-functional views of key performance indicators (KPIs) from various departments in order to make good decisions. We also want to use this data to provide insight to more people within the organization. Most important, we want to access and analyze new sources of information and immediately incorporate this new insight into our decision making.

Given the wide range of data that exists today, we can ask questions that we could never have answered before and never could have imagined. In 2006, it was nearly impossible to understand our customers' perceptions and product experience in real time. Today, social networks provide a real-time window into a customer's world. Every day, more than 4.75 billion content items are shared on Facebook (including status updates, wall posts, photos, videos, and comments), with more than 4.5 billion "likes," and more than 10 billion messages sent. Unfortunately, our existing data warehouse systems were not designed for this variety and volume of data, nor were our analytics systems.

With traditional tools, it is difficult to ask or change questions based on this type of data. We might have deleted part of the data that would answer the question as part of the cleaning process or because we simply didn't store all of the data. We may have to rebuild a database with new structure and reload the data to support asking new questions. This takes time and possibly money if new storage is required.

Today, business executives need to ask questions, get answers, and modify questions based on the current and changing situation. We will need to constantly be asking questions, refining questions, and throwing out questions to understand the shifting market. Most of our existing systems are woefully inadequate to support this need.

Big Data Platforms to the Rescue

Several years ago, companies debated what cloud computing was and what type of architecture was best suited for the workflows and applications that they were placing in the cloud. It was a rapidly changing market with many unknowns.

Within five years, the industry had defined the use cases and a set of technologies that would satisfy these use cases, such as unpredictable growth applications, disaster recovery, and application test environments. The market also defined at least three deployment models: public, private, and hybrid.

Fast-forward to today. Big data is going through the same evolutionary path. Product vendors are delivering a set of software and hardware solutions that are loosely defined as "big data platforms." Big data platforms include technologies to help you acquire, organize, and analyze data. They look promising and are evolving rapidly. They combine open-source technologies and enterprise-grade solutions.

Like cloud computing, the big data platform market also offers a mixture of in-house and hosted models for all or portions of the big data platform. They don't necessarily include an advanced analytics and visualization package, which you may get from vendors like SAS, IBM, SAP, or specialized visualization vendors like Tableau and Roambi.

What has changed the most between big data platforms and what we do today is that we've built new types of databases and query tools to support storing and analyzing massive volumes of data. As a result, many technologists refer to big data platforms by the name of the database or data store they are using. You may hear your IT team discussing solutions such as Hadoop, MongoDB, Cassandra, and more. For simplicity's sake, you don't need to know everything these technologies entail, and you don't need to know specifically why one solution may be better than another. I mention these so you'll know what they are when the term gets thrown around in a meeting.

Big Data Platforms and Traditional Databases Are Complementary

While I'm on the subject of selecting the right tool for the job, I'd like to make an important clarification. I've mentioned numerous times that existing systems can't handle big data. This does not mean that we are throwing out everything from the past. It would be a mistake to think that everything we've spent years building is useless and needs to be replaced because of big data. Far from it.

In fact, we need our existing data warehouses and our existing reports to keep the business running. New database tools, like NoSQL and NewSQL, are more likely to complement, rather than replace, your current storage and processing platform. These are part of an emerging set of solutions called big data platforms, which include all of the hardware and database software that you'd need to store and process data.

Together, such complementary approaches can help boost your company's overall ability to understand and respond to changes in the marketplace. As we move ahead, certain aspects of data warehousing and analytics will continue as they always have, with daily, weekly, and monthly reports. We still have data that has already been structured for analysis or is easy to structure (for example, accounting figures). We still have data that's of a reasonable size and data that doesn't require on-the-fly analysis. All of these are still suited for our existing tools. We want to use the new tools to collect, analyze, and merge unwieldy big data with the data we've already organized into a structure.

Big data platforms are simply one set of tools that help make the organization more efficient, more responsive, more profitable. A business may continue to run its financial reporting on a monthly basis and provide management with daily sales reports. However, an organization might use new big data platforms, such as a Hadoop platform (note that many people may say Hadoop but are actually discussing the platform that contains several open-source technologies such as HDFS, Hbase, Hive, etc.) because it can help a company calculate results on large volumes of data more efficiently. It can turn a day's worth of processing into less than an hour.

In other cases, a task may need to be completed very fast or in real time. For example, marketing and customer service might need analytics that allow the company to sell or service a customer in real time or near-real time. For these tasks, we can use a big data platform to process large volumes of unstructured raw material at lightning speed. A business must become more proficient at what it currently does while adding new ways to store and process the wide variety of data that exists and that can advance the organization.

The Right Tool for the Job

We still need to support business as usual, and we need to build solutions that can meet tomorrow's demands. Furthermore, many IT budgets are shrinking. The average IT budget declined 5 to 10 percent by the end of 2013, according to the Lopez Research annual IT benchmark. The chaos of new technologies, declining budgets, and the changing pace of business has IT leaders pulling their hair out.

As you can see, it is a confusing landscape for your IT team to navigate. There are numerous debates about what technology is better. The truth is very similar to what we discussed in mobile. There is no one solution that solves all problems. Your IT team will need to pick the best tools for the applications.

Each of these solutions offers pros and cons. Like building mobile applications, the choice of a big data and analytics solution should depend on what the company is trying to accomplish. This may mean that a company will select different tools for different applications. For example, MongoDB is well suited for dynamic queries. MongoDB's native support for geospatial indexing makes it easy for organizations to leverage location-based data, enabling new features and an increasingly personalized user experience.

Telecom providers that are looking at correlating network quality issues with customer care issues in real time may use complex event/data stream processing. In another situation, a company might collect data that changes only occasionally but where the version is important. An example of this type of query would be for customer relationship management and content management system reporting. A database solution, such as CouchDB, may work better for this situation, whereas a database like Riak might be better for rapidly changing data.

Social networking companies use graph databases like Neo4j to uncover the relationships and connections between individuals. Storm is a stream processing and continuous computation solution that Twitter acquired to process a stream's new data and update databases in real time. It allows Twitter to do things like post into browsers what topics people are talking about on Twitter. The browsers will have a real-time view on what the trending topics are as they happen.

Clearly, all of these types of applications are different and require different characteristics from a big data platform. An organization can use any number of tools, but management should only select a set of tools once it knows the jobs it needs to perform. It's also likely that over time you'll need to select more than one platform to support the entirety of your data needs. Shorthand: Don't expect that IT can just walk out and buy a big data solution off the shelf or turn it on like SaaS service. Even if the company plans to purchase a hosted big data infrastructure service, it must define its data analytics needs before selecting a service. Speaking of host big data services, let's look at how the trend of cloud computing is impacting the options for acquiring big data infrastructure.

Build versus Buy

Businesses have adopted cloud computing for updating, expanding, and replacing existing data centers. The hardware and software required to effectively manage big data is another large investment for many organizations. Cloud providers, such as Amazon, Qubole, and others, have responded to this opportunity by providing cloud services for various parts of the big data platform or the entire big data platform as a service. Some of these are forms of infrastructure outsourcing. If you are looking to outsource these services, you'll need a combination of the storage, processing, data extract/repository, query processing, business intelligence, and analytics tools, as well as the visualization. Finding all of these options in one platform is difficult today, but this will continue to evolve.

A study by Accenture, "Where to Deploy Your Hadoop Cluster," provides useful insight on the models, the technical considerations, and the return on investment. Accenture states that enterprises have four options for deploying Hadoop:[12]

1. **On-premises full custom:** Businesses purchase commodity hardware, install the software, and operate it themselves, giving them full control of the Hadoop cluster.
2. **Hadoop appliance:** This preconfigured Hadoop cluster allows businesses to bypass detailed technical configuration decisions and jump-start data analysis.
3. **Hadoop hosting:** As with a traditional Internet service provider model, organizations rely on a service provider to deploy and operate Hadoop clusters on their behalf.
4. **Hadoop-as-a-service:** This gives businesses instant access to Hadoop clusters with a pay-per-use consumption model, providing greater business agility.

In the first case, your IT department does everything. In the second case, your IT department skips the hardware installation and focuses on the software stack and the analytics. For Hadoop hosting, your IT team has a dedicated set of hardware and software resources that the service provider manages. This leaves the grunt work to the Hadoop hoster and frees your team up to focus on designing the strategy and the right analytics. The downside of this is that you have to use whatever tools they offer. Finally, there is the service angle. HaaS is a great way to get started when you aren't sure what your overall requirements for an on-premise solution will be. If it works and is cost-effective for your use cases, there's no reason to move from it.

Accenture said organizations must consider five key areas when determining the appropriate deployment model:

1. Price-performance ratio
2. Data privacy
3. Data gravity
4. Data enrichment
5. Productivity of developers and data scientists

Based on the use cases that the firm analyzed, Accenture's study revealed that Hadoop-as-a-service offers a better price–performance ratio. Of course, this could be different based on what your firm is trying to do. Once again, the key is understanding what you are trying to do and mapping the needs back to the various solutions.

Big Data Is About People and Tools

Big data isn't only about technology. It's about people as well. New technologies require new skills within the organization. One new role that has become popular is the data scientist. We've already had business analysts and data analysts. A data scientist is another evolution of these roles. Evan Quinn summed it up best: "A data scientist is like the Swiss Army Knife of big data human resources—part software developer, part data analyst, part business analyst, part statistician— someone who can help bring all of these elements together for a big data solution."[13]

If this sounds like a tall order, you're right. It's a skill set that is part MBA, part mathematician, part technologist, and part designer. It's also an ill-defined role with a job description that can sound like an advertisement to recruit Superman (able to leap tall data sets in a single keystroke). In fact, McKinsey claims, "The United States alone faces a shortage of 140,000 to 190,000 people with analytical expertise and 1.5 million managers and analysts with the skills to understand and make decisions based on the analysis of big data."[14]

Making sense of big data requires technology most companies currently don't have and staff that currently isn't in the building. This is a conundrum, but the success of any business will reside on its ability to navigate this new challenge. And the first phase to navigating the challenge is to build a plan. The plan should include both a technical and a human resources strategy.

Since data scientists are in high demand and aren't hanging around job fairs, a business needs a human resources plan that grows existing talent from within and a strategy to work with talent outside of the organization. The Data Guild, headquartered in Palo Alto, is one of the new types of consulting companies that are forming to address this challenge. By leveraging a network of world-class data scientists and engineers, The Data Guild helps its customers identify the questions that will change their business and define the technologies and approach that will produce actionable findings. They use a multidisciplinary approach, where they bring designers, big data engineers, data scientists, social scientists, and entrepreneurs together into high-performing teams.

David Gutelius, one of the founders of The Data Guild, said, "A company should invest in its people more than it invests in things (technology). The investment in people is where you'll see a return on investment emerge. A company should realize that big data's real promise has less to do with machines and software than it does with people. It takes a certain kind of person [to] work with these new technologies. These people aren't only the data scientists within and organization, but also the entire team that supports the data process from acquisition to insight/decision-making."[15]

Given that we might not be able to acquire data scientists easily, we'll have to train our current employees. To start, these data and business analysts should interview the various roles within a company to define questions the business should ask to produce meaningful business results. Again, the point is not to accumulate data and manipulate it for its own sake, but to capture meaningful data that can be transmuted into knowledge the organization can put to profitable use. Ideally, a business would be able to bring in mentorship from genuine data scientists. Gutelius said, "The mentorship aspect is underappreciated. Frankly it's going to be impossible to grow data scientists organically. Today's business analysts are just a different breed—it's hard for them to completely retool mentally."

Big data technologies are changing rapidly. Many IT executives are getting hung up on what database and file system technologies—such as NoSQL or NewSQL databases—they should buy. In one way, this is a useless exercise because the technology is evolving at a breakneck pace. I asked Gutelius what advice he could provide on how a company should approach the big data, knowing that it will continue to change. Gutelius said, "Data heterogeneity is the rule, not the exception (even though vendors will try to convince you otherwise). A company must build big data processing and analytics solutions that allow for diversity in environments. There are many solutions. A business should allow its data scientists to use whatever solutions or combination of solutions that they want. This is table stakes."

He also noted that "the blanket statement that real-time or near-real time is intrinsically more important than non-real time is wrong. It depends on your business and what creates insight and advantage. Likewise, certain characteristics may be more important depending on the question you are asking." Some of these data characteristics include items such as data scale, complexity, and volatility.

Analytic Models

While the databases and the schema are an essential part of your big data strategy, you also need analytics models to make sense of the vast wealth of data. Evan Stubb, author of *Delivering Business Analytics*, offers several practical guidelines for creating analytical models. A business should use analytics to drive for outcomes, not insight. While insights are interesting, the goal of business analytics is to drive value creation. Stubb writes, "Insight is essential, but it's an intermediary step. The other thing to remember is that what's interesting isn't necessarily valuable."[16]

Analytics models are linked to the question that a business is trying to answer and the outcomes it would like to achieve. A business should iterate and eliminate questions as necessary. One of the sizable challenges with big data, like any other project, is that it's nearly impossible to get it correct right out of the gate. An organization must embrace experimentation to see what works. While a company should build a strategic plan for procuring the right technology, tools, and talent, it should also be experimenting with solutions and questions to help define what works.

"What's lacking in big data is a normative practice for data product experimentation," said Gutelius. "Businesses need rapid-cycle analysis. This means the data team within a company should start with small, quick experiments and scale up as you prove success. A business can't remain married to a technology if it isn't doing the job. IT must be ready to abandon approaches and technologies that aren't showing promise and value." Businesses should invest in results. "A business should realize that the questions they ask will change with more information. The company will learn to ask better questions over time. Understand that the promise of insights from analyzing data that has any scale or complexity comes from iterative experimentation and exploration."

Understand Data Isn't Perfect

Data is frequently inaccurate, incomplete, redundant, or troubled by any number of issues that will make it difficult to analyze for business decisions. This is often called dirty data, and we've had it since the dawn of data collection. Dirty data can consist of mistakes such as incorrect spelling or punctuation, incorrect data associated with a field, incomplete or outdated data, or even data that is duplicated in a database. Names are a classic example of the variations that can happen. A name can be saved in a database in a number of ways. The single name, "Maribel Lopez," could also be stored as "M Lopez," "M. LOPEZ," "M.R. Lopez," and "Maribel R. Lopez."

This means the data analyst team will need to perform what's known as data cleansing or data scrubbing to detect, correct, or remove corrupt or inaccurate data. There are many ways of doing this, including parsing the data for the detection of syntax errors, mapping the data from its given format into the format expected by the appropriate application, and removing duplicates. Analysts can also use statistical methods such as analyzing the values of mean, range, or algorithms to find ones that are unexpected and thus erroneous. Data cleansing is a complicated and time-consuming task, and the methods of doing this warrant a book of their own. Suffice it to say, the presence of large volumes of data only makes data preparation a bigger job.

McKinsey says that big data plans "may highlight a need for the massive reorganization of data architectures over time. . . . In the short term, a lighter solution may be possible for some companies: outsourcing the problem to data specialists who use cloud-based software to unify enough data to attack initial analytics opportunities."[17]

The Data Guild's Gutelius says a business should "assume that you never have the data you need in the form you need it. Assume you will spend most of your time and energy in data acquisition, cleaning, and ingestion. You should assume that part of the most useful data isn't 'inside' the company, and be prepared to combine heterogeneous external data sets with internal ones to create impact." This relates back to my earlier discussion on what is different about right-time experiences in Chapter 3. Right-time experiences require companies to gather, combine, and analyze data that comes from sources within the company as well as outside of the company.

Getting data into the proper format to analyze it has always been a concern, but big data tools make it easier to deal with data variety and experimentation. Two benefits big data solutions provide are the storage capacity to keep large volumes of data and the ability to store data in its original format, which can be structured like a spreadsheet or unstructured like Twitter messages and video. Assuming the company kept a raw source of data, it can go back and redo an analysis if the company structured the data incorrectly for the first one.

What's Your Role?

While you're not responsible for selecting the actual big data platform tools, you do play an important role in helping IT design an effective big data strategy. In my opinion, the first step in this direction is to get people talking about what's available, what's needed, and how it will be funded. The CIO should build a cross-functional team with line-of-business executives to understand what information they'd like access to and build strategies to share this information across groups.

Any big data strategy should begin with defining the business requirements for a solution. One of the great things about big data and analytics is that multiple groups within the organization will be able to benefit from this model. In effect, if you do it right the first time, you'll have an information store and a set of analytics solutions that can be used by more than one department. Walmart provides a great example of this. It consolidated information from 10 different websites into a 250-node Hadoop cluster with over one petabyte of data. It meant that departments across the globe have access to a majority of Walmart's data.[18]

Your IT team will already have a sense of what data the teams are using today. Part of this process will require various groups to work closely with IT to define what the business needs. Your role as a line-of-business manager or executive is to support the IT team by defining business requirements. There are several steps in the process that you should participate in:

- **List and categorize the business problem(s) that big data can solve for your group.** Consider your business goals for the next 12 to 24 months. What types of information would be useful to advancing those goals, and how does it differ from what you have access to today?
- **Define the data sources.** IT's job here is to understand where it's located and how big data solutions will access the data. Your job is to help IT understand what you need access to and if it exists within the company or if you need to acquire additional data sources. There are now numerous big data marketplaces where your business can acquire additional data sources, such

as Infochimps, Windows Azure Marketplace, and Factual, just to name a few. In addition to defining data sources, your team should earmark budget to support third-party data acquisition.

- **Reevaluate your data retention policy.** The cost to store data isn't free, but it's getting cheaper with tools like Hadoop and commodity hardware. Your business now has the option of keeping more data for a longer period of time. Just because you can keep something inexpensively, however, doesn't mean you should. Many data sources lose their value to the organization over time. Is sales data for a product still valuable five years after the firm has discontinued the item? Probably not. You need to reevaluate how long you keep your data.

- **Design the output.** Big data solutions are the foundation for delivering insight to your team so they can do their jobs better. You need to help IT design a solution that provides data in a format that is both usable and useful with minimal end user effort required. This means you have to sit with the IT team and discuss the problems you're facing, the types of computing tools the team will have access to, and what they need to create agility in a process. The solution should offer several components:
  1. The data.
  2. The presentation of the data (often called visualization): Is it charts, graphs, or raw figures?
  3. The various analysis and outputs from the data.
  4. Data exploration: What method should be available for end users to explore the data? What information can the end user analyze deeply versus what should simply be provided as a set of reports?

- **Create a pilot that is focused on an actionable result.** While discovery is a large benefit of big data, it isn't the place you should start. Pick a problem that needs to be addressed, such as "reduce returns by 3 percent" or "decrease credit card fraud by 2 percent."

- **Measure the result and adjust accordingly.** Even with proper planning, your big data solution may not provide actionable insights and results immediately. This is the time to modify existing solutions or try new solutions.

- **Participate in cross-functional teams.** Data silos and data hoarding have been common practices in organizations for years.

The idea is to share information and benefit from new insights that other groups may see in your data.

- **Don't expect the moon, and do expect insights to take time.** Big data has been tagged as the panacea for all of a company's ailments. While better data and insights can help a business, there's no guarantee that a big data platform and analytics will provide you with revolutionary insights. Also, insights are just one piece of the puzzle. The business still has to change processes as a result of this new information.

Summary

To recap, big data is an opportunity and a challenge. It's an opportunity because with it, an organization has the possibility to ask new questions and to ask old questions in new ways. With big data and the appropriate analytics, an organization may be able to solve problems it could never solve before.

Big data is a challenge because older computer systems were not designed to handle the volume, velocity, and variety of the data that is now available to enterprises. It is a challenge because it requires statistically sophisticated tools to be useful. And, not many people understand the data, the business/human requirements, and the statistics necessary.

While the technological details can be overwhelming, the important thing to keep in mind is that the information has to reach and be useful to the people who can apply it. Evan Quinn says that there is a huge misunderstanding in business, one that believes a genius elite data scientist group figures stuff out and tells executives, who then change the world. He notes, "That's a one-in-a-thousand shot."

The real power in big data is giving all these fresh decision capabilities to those who can use them best. Help the marketer price better. Help a salesperson determine whom he should or shouldn't call on. Give the procurement specialist a more optimal approach for understanding when and how to buy supplies and what to buy.

The real power of big data, ultimately, is not about giving a few specialists an edge on everyone else. It's about improving the efficiency, quality, and value of virtually every organization.

Notes

1. http://strata.oreilly.com/2012/01/what-is-big-data.htm.
2. Phone interview on 7/23/13 with Avia Dadon from Amdocs.

3. Sprint 2012 shareholder meeting remarks by CEO Dan Hesse. He stated there was a $1.7B reduction in annual customer service expense during a four-year period, from $3.7B in 2008 to $2B in 2012.

4. www.informationweek.com/software/information-management/metlife-uses-nosql-for-customer-service-breakthrough/d/d-id/1109919?.

5. www.mongodb.com/press/metlife-leapfrogs-insurance-industry-mongodb-powered-big-data-application.

6. http://www.walmartlabs.com/2013/11/.

7. Gibu Thomas, presentation at the Open Mobile Summit on November 12, 2013.

8. www.walmartlabs.com/2012/11/26/targeting-walmartlabs/.

9. Gibu Thomas, presentation on Walmart Experience Track, April 2013.

10. Evan Quinn is the founder of QuinnSight Research and a prolific blogger. http://quinnsight.com. Interview January 15, 2014.

11. www.mckinsey.com/insights/business_technology/big_data_whats_your_plan.

12. www.accenture.com/SiteCollectionDocuments/PDF/Accenture-Technology-Labs-Where-To-Deploy-Your-Hadoop-CLusters-Executive-Summary.pdf, page 2.

13. Telephone and email interview with Evan Quinn on January 20, 2014.

14. "Big Data the Next Frontier for Competition," www.mckinsey.com/features/big_data.

15. Interview with David Gutelius of The Data Guild, October 2013.

16. Evan Stubbs, *Delivering Business Analytics: Practical Guidelines for Best Practices*, p. 37.

17. From McKinsey's "Big Data: What's Your Plan," www.mckinsey.com/insights/business_technology/big_data_whats_your_plan.

18. Stacey Higginbotham interview with Stephen O'Sullivan, senior director of global e-commerce at WalmartLabs, http://gigaom.com/2012/03/23/walmart-labs-is-building-big-data-tools-and-will-then-open-source-them/.

CHAPTER 10

Engage and Empower Employees

I've discussed some of the process changes that are necessary to evolve into an organization that provides customers, employees, partners, and other stakeholders right-time experiences. I've outlined the initial steps to a technical plan. The issues I want to discuss now are the challenges and opportunities new technologies—mobile, big data, and cloud computing—put on the overall organization. These technology and behavioral shifts will change how organizations should operate.

The future of work is here, and it's different than in the past. It's distributed. It's mobile. It's real-time and multimedia. The up-and-coming generation of workers grew up with mobility, cloud services, and social networks. Everywhere you look, technology and IT are at the center of the changing of the future of work. Business and the workplace are no longer tied to a physical location. The future of work is focused on teams and projects.

The office can be anywhere and everywhere the employee goes. Employees can be in different countries. They can work from their homes, the office, or a corporate location. Mobile, social, and video have the power and promise to create a new workplace that is more connected and collaborative than it has ever been.

Technology will change how we recruit, manage, and motivate. It's stating the obvious to note that organizations that can find and keep top talent are apt to gain competitive advantage, improve client satisfaction, and enhance their bottom lines. But the talent has to be engaged and have the right skill set.

In this new world, businesses will need to define what types of new programs and new employee roles will be important. For example, the business needs to evaluate if it should create new groups, such as a Mobile Center of Excellence, or new roles within an organization, such as a chief mobile officer or a data scientist role. A company will also need programs to retain and motivate existing employees.

Companies will also need to retrain at least a portion of their existing workforce on new technologies and tools across all groups. For example, I discussed how marketing and sales needs to create new ways of engaging consumers. Scott Brinkner, Co-founder and CTO at Ion Interactive, Inc., wrote in his blog that "marketing is rapidly becoming one of the most technology dependent functions in business."[1] It was once focused on areas such as creating advertising and performing research surveys. Today it has many new ways of digitally connecting with customers and prospects. Each of these methods comes with its own set of methodologies and tools, which are rapidly evolving. Brinkner went on to note that "a new type of executive is emerging at the center of the transformation: the chief marketing technologist. CMTs are part strategist, part creative director, part technology leader, and part teacher."

The CEO of a major corporation once told me that the worst part of his job was telling formerly productive employees that the organization's needs had grown past the manager's capabilities. As we move into the new world, we must work to actively evolve the organization through its people, processes, and technology. Let's look at how some companies are using technology to solve the skill set issue.

Use Mobile, Social, and Big Data to Recruit

A recent IBM study found that 70 percent of CEOs claim human capital is the single biggest contributor to sustained economic value. While unemployment levels are high, 65 percent of global companies have difficulty finding candidates with the skills their workforces require. The need for hiring the right candidate for the right job at the right place has never been greater.[2] Business leaders can now employ mobile, social, and big data analytics to improve hiring.

Harris Interactive conducted a U.S.-based online survey of 2,100 hiring managers and human resource professionals on behalf of CareerBuilder in 2013. It found that nearly two in five companies (39 percent) use social networking sites to research job candidates, up from 37 percent last year. More than two in five (43 percent) hiring managers who currently research candidates via social media said they have found information that has caused them not to hire a candidate, up 9 percentage points from last year.[3] Clearly, social is changing the hiring landscape. Going forward, business leaders should be looking for ways to use social knowledge to match the right candidates to the right job.

According to Scott Garrett, cofounder of MoBolt, the number of candidates searching for jobs on their mobile devices has tripled since 2011. A SimplyHired survey found that 70 percent of the respondents had searched for jobs on their devices.[4] It's surprising that only 36 percent of Fortune 500 companies examined by iMomentous have a mobile optimized career section, and even fewer (5 percent) had a mobile optimized application process.[5] The result is that as many as two-thirds of all mobile job searchers don't complete the application due to their frustration with awkward formatting. Computing is mobile, and mobile is the primary computing method for a large number of people globally. If you want to hire new talent, you should have a mobile-accessible recruiting process.

Make Recruiting Mobile and Social

MoBolt sells mobile recruiting tools to help companies get a better ROI for their recruiting efforts. The idea is to make the process simpler by eliminating roadblocks. It has eliminated the login creation portion of the mobile application process, which turns away the largest percentage of potential applicants. Job seekers search a company's open positions using a custom interface based on the location and language. They may use one of their social profiles—Facebook, LinkedIn, Dropbox, or Google Docs—to fill out the form. One click submits the completed job application—a right-time experience made even better when the company follows up with an interview.

As MoBolt points out, employee referrals are a company's most valuable source of candidates, and mobile is particularly well suited for employees to reach their social networks and begin the referral process. They can search for jobs, match their friends to jobs via social networking, and refer jobs to their friends with a personalized message or notification about the opportunity and a link to the application. The software tracks these mobile employee referrals to ensure the source is captured and employees get full credit for the candidate.

LinkedIn has also evolved into a resume complement. In fact, some may say that LinkedIn is now a better tool for understanding the breadth and depth of a person's experience. Your LinkedIn profile grows organically each time you include a new skill or accomplishment, share information, or engage in various other types of LinkedIn activities.

Use Big Data to Improve Hiring and Retention

Perhaps more significantly, big data is transforming the way organizations hire, promote, and motivate employees. "Larger companies have a significant edge in terms of access to data from their hiring systems and using predictive analytics, assessment, and behavioral tools to make selections," says Rudy Karsan, the founder of Kenexa, which IBM acquired in 2012.[6] The company sells recruiting and talent management solutions. This access to data has enabled corporations to use sentiment indices to predict the capability, culture, and capacity of individuals as they come into the workforce and the company.

Karsan says that the combination of analytics and insights into human behavior gives organizations better capability to find candidates and better predictors of where their next level of talent will come from—with the ability to predict the success of potential candidates before they walk through the door. Organizations are able to hire individuals who are the best fit for a given job, not only in terms of abilities and skills but also based on culture fit. Firms can use data from performance management solutions and surveys to increase efficiencies, engagement, and productivity, which will positively impact the top and bottom lines. For human resources, the competitive advantage lies in analyzing and using the large amounts of employee-generated big data to enhance productivity, service, innovation, execution, and employer/employee behavior.

One interesting ramification of big data is its effect on workplace myths. For example, employers often avoid hiring candidates with a history of job-hopping or those who have been unemployed for a while. Companies assume that the past is prologue. There's one problem: The data shows that it isn't so. An applicant's work history is not a good predictor of future results.[7]

Another example: Conventional wisdom suggests successful salespeople must have an outgoing personality, be naturally friendly, and get along with everyone. After studying more than 1,000 salespeople in several companies across diverse industries, Kenexa discovered that sales success is more likely to occur when salespeople have emotional courage and persistence—the ability to stay engaged at work and keep trying even when told "no" time after time. Karsan says, "Our data shows salespeople who exhibit these traits consistently are the cream of the crop in their profession."[8]

Using data analytics, organizations are now able to study potential candidates and pinpoint with amazing accuracy those who have the capability to do the job, who have the capacity to learn new skills that may be needed in the future, and who are a good match with the culture of the company. Kenexa calls these—capability, capacity, and culture—the three essential Cs of business success. It believes these three elements are the keys to giving any enterprise a competitive edge, giving employees the meaning they crave in their work, and, as a result, shaping a better society.[9]

Another company that offers predictive analytics and cloud computing to help businesses improve workplace productivity is Evolv. The firm identifies the characteristics of the most qualified, productive employees within an hourly workforce throughout the employee life cycle. By using data-driven methodologies and machine learning, Evolv assists operational and financial executives in making better business decisions.

For example, Harte Hanks provides contact centers to many global brands. The company employs thousands of hourly workers in its global call centers who offer technical and presales support, as well as lead generation and sales. Harte Hanks was looking for a fundamentally different, data-driven approach to hiring, one that could guarantee candidate quality as well as meet the company's hiring and perform-ance targets. The proposed Evolv solution automated candidate screening and ranking to filter out poor candidates and prioritize the best by using big data and analytics. Because of the risk involved in completely changing its hiring strategy, Harte Hanks hedged its bets with a side-by-side comparison between the Evolv solution and its existing process and provider. A data-driven process showed an imme-diate—and continuing—difference between Evolv and non-Evolv hires. For example, the 30-day attrition rate for Evolv hires was 35 percent lower than Harte Hanks's original solutions, and its 90-day attrition was 25 percent lower. It also found that in the first six months, the employees selected from the Evolv approach reported 29 percent fewer missed work hours than those hired through the standard approach. Building on the significant results of implementing the Evolv solution in one location, Harte Hanks engaged Evolv to inform workforce management decisions in all of its domestic call centers.[10]

Social, mobile, and analytics can also make a difference in creating a strategy to hire temporary workers. Headquartered in San Francisco and launched in May 2011, Gigwalk offers an on-demand mobile workforce, connecting businesses large and small to a smartphone army to get work done anywhere. By the end of 2013, there were over 350,000 Gigwalkers in over 6,500 cities across all 50 U.S. states, Puerto Rico, Canada, and the United Kingdom. These consumers use Gigwalk on smartphones to earn money doing store audits, competitive tracking, location inspections, field interviews, site photography, usability testing, and much more. Effectively, this is the concept of crowdsourcing labor that has been made possible by mobile and social.

Through mathematical models, Gigwalk has also discovered that you can use data, such as average response time to a job, as an early indicator of a temporary worker's success. "If you reply within an hour, your success rate for completing a job ends up being about 97 percent," says Gigwalk chief executive officer Bob Bahramipour. "But if it takes longer than five hours, that number drops to 47 percent."[11]

Gigwalk scrutinizes data to find undervalued talent, to find good workers without personal interactions. "We never meet our workers, never interview them, and never look them in the eye," says Bahramipour. After all, interactions cost time and money, and they don't necessarily reveal much. "Selection at temp agencies is a somewhat random process," he says. Gigwalk, by contrast, claims that it knows more about its workers than anyone has ever known about workers.

As an example of creating a workforce virtually instantly, consider Reckitt Benckiser's experience. This multinational consumer goods company (French's, Clearasil, Finish, Air Wick, and Lysol) released a new home product, investing heavily in R&D, new packaging, and retail promotion to drive awareness and sales during the fourth-quarter holidays. Unfortunately, POS sales data showed that sales were not what the company expected. Management needed to learn how shopper behavior was driving sales and how well certain products were displayed and promoted throughout the store. They used Gigwalk to engage 500 people to complete 500 in-store audits, conduct 1,300 shopper interviews, and take 800 photos across the United States in two weeks—reporting their findings by smartphone.

The results: Gigwalk's mobile audit revealed that 54 percent of stores failed to execute special displays. In-aisle consumer interviews established that Benckiser's packaging did not sufficiently communicate the new product's key benefits. Customer interviews also tested package designs with consumers in the field, and the firm selected an improved design. "These audits empower us to see what is happening in a retail partner's store—with very short notice," says L. Baez, consumer and market insights lead at Reckitt Benckiser.[12]

Clearly, the Harte Hanks and the Reckitt Benckiser examples highlight how a data-driven approach can create a right-time experience that works well for both the worker and the business team. It gets the company talent at the point of need. It improves the fit between the worker and the job, and it gives consumers the ability to work when they are available. Social facilitates word-of-mouth marketing for services such as Gigwalk, and mobile is the perfect on-the-go tool for getting the job done.

Use Collaboration Tools to Streamline Hiring and Onboarding

Cloud computing, new collaboration software, and mobile provide tools to enable remote work. The future of work is about hiring and retaining talent wherever they may be. Hence, IT is providing HR with video services that allow them to hire beyond local candidates.

Video interviews allow HR to interview more candidates faster. It eliminates travel expenses and simplifies schedule management. It also makes it easier for the entire team to interview a candidate and quickly meet to discuss their findings. Once a candidate is selected, HR is using video to onboard new employees. Video has become an integral part of hiring and training the best talent.

Employees frequently had to travel to the corporate headquarters for training. Video allows IT to partner with human resources to deliver globally accessible multimedia training to every employee. If recorded, these video trainings deliver a consistent training experience that can be viewed at the employee's convenience on a smartphone, tablet, or PC. Since many organizations have mandatory training requirements, IT can support HR and the chief risk officer with video training and compliance tracking. Finally, video provides an immediate return on investment by saving employee time and travel expenses. Since I'm on the topic of training, let's take a moment to discuss strategies for effectively training your workforce.

Build a Training Plan

U.S. executives at large companies confirm that a skills gap persists for their businesses, with nearly half (46 percent) concerned that they won't have the skills they need in the next one to two years, according to recent Accenture research.[13] The study also found that 51 percent of companies expect to increase investments in training over the next two years, and 35 percent of executives whose companies are facing a skills shortage admitted that they have not invested enough in training in the past.

Accenture's 2013 survey of 400 executives at large U.S. companies assessed hiring, staffing, and training strategies. While nearly three-quarters (72 percent) of executives identified training as one of the top ways for employees to develop new skills, only 52 percent of workers employed by the companies surveyed currently receive company-provided, formal training.

The survey also found that businesses are facing big consequences as a result of not fixing their skills gap. Among companies currently facing or anticipating a skills shortage:

- 66 percent anticipate a loss of business to competitors.
- 64 percent face a loss of revenue.
- 59 percent face eroding customer satisfaction.
- 53 percent say they will face a delay in developing new products or services.

"The mismatch of skills needed and skills available is forcing organizations to rethink everything from how they define jobs to how they mine their organizations for hidden talent to how they recruit and evaluate candidates," says Katherine Lavelle, managing director of Accenture Talent & Organization, North America. "Companies are increasingly looking outside their industries for potential candidates, and they are evaluating broader generalist skill sets and competencies so that they can quickly build on these to develop more specific skills for a job."[14]

In my opinion, this research highlights the need to retrain existing talent. In some areas, such as data scientists, there simply aren't enough prospective employees available. An organization's best bet is to hire one or two employees with the proper skill, if available, and have them assist in developing a training plan for other employees. If this option isn't available, the company should hire an outside firm with the appropriate skill set and have this firm design a training program for the existing workforce.

As executives explore the current skills gap and future needs, they are using new methods to deliver employee training. The Accenture survey found that 42 percent use mobile, 35 percent use social media, 27 percent use massive open online courses (MOOCs), and 13 percent use gamification, which I'll talk about in a moment.

Accenture offers several suggestions for executives who recognize the skills gap:

- **Find a balance** between formal and informal learning. As digital technology blurs the boundaries between formal and informal learning, companies should consider ways to strike a balance between the two and help ensure that they work in tandem. For instance, embedding learning in everyday work—shadowing others, participating in mentorships, or learning from peers through online forums—can help formal online or classroom training become more relevant and more effective.
- **Embrace new ways** to develop skills. Other recent scalable developments are helping training become more relevant, such as social media tools that facilitate collaboration and knowledge sharing, gamification that immerses employees in virtual scenarios, and mobile training delivery that allows learning to take place wherever and whenever an employee happens to be available.
- **Expand your candidate pool.** Given the reported difficulty of finding qualified candidates, companies should consider dropping the notion of finding the "perfect" candidate based on a list of specific skills, education, or experience. Instead, they could look for candidates with more generalist skills—even those outside their industry, in other geographies, or with adjacent or overlapping skill sets—that can be easily developed to perform the job.
- **Screen talent** based on newly emerging data sources. Instead of screening potential candidates based on key words in a resume, exploit new data sources as part of the effort to get fuller and more predictive insights into future performance. For example, emerging websites offer samples of a candidate's work, assessments that gauge a person's cultural fit and motivations, or social media contributions that can reveal their interests.
- **Invest earlier in the talent supply chain.** Leading companies are partnering with colleges and universities to review and revise curricula so relevant skills are acquired as part of their programs. Some companies are even setting up open-access

training programs to ensure that more people have the skills they need in specific regions. Once trained, the first right of employment is with the company that trained the students.[15]

KnowledgeAdvisors, a learning and talent analytics company headquartered in Chicago, markets learning analytics software that helps businesses improve the business impact of learning. The firm's experts help organizations better allocate their human capital investments through practical learning measurement advice that allows for faster, more accurate, data-driven decision making than previous systems. For example, it had a buyer in the health insurance market that needed to reduce employee turnover. The buyer had 30 percent of its employees leave the company each year. The insurance company studied strategies for continuously improving its recruiting process, new hire satisfaction, and associate engagement scores. It then implemented an automated 30-, 60-, and 90-day touch-point evaluation process, which identified flight risks for an early intervention process. These changes enabled the company to reduce its administrative time by more than 70 percent while retaining 93 percent of the flight risks after 90 days.

"The employer gained these benefits because it applied a simple continuous improvement process: Measure the problem, determine potential causes, apply an intervention, and monitor improvement," says John Mattox, director of research for KnowledgeAdvisors. He says that as recently as three years ago, the hardware and software available could not handle either the volume or the velocity of the data. Today, big data and the analytics available allow analysts "to test hundreds of ideas and look at hundreds of variables at one time. We can create models instead of testing one hypothesis at a time."[16]

So we have an opportunity to use social and enterprise social collaboration software to discover talent. We have large volumes of data that can now be analyzed to help us find and retain talent. We also have technologies, such as mobile and video, that can help us recruit and train talent. The next logical problem to review is how a business can use new methods to keep its employees (and customers) engaged with the company.

Engage Employees with Games

One of the biggest challenges facing companies today is limited employee engagement. Engagement is often limited in terms of bringing and driving new ideas within the company. It's limited in terms of helping the company acquire new talent. And, it's limited in terms of what applications and processes employees embrace. There are reasons why this is so, but the goal isn't to point a finger at either side. The goal is to understand how we fix the problem.

During the past five years, companies have spent millions of dollars on mobile applications, social software, document and collaboration management systems, human capital management, customer relationship management, and other technologies aimed at increasing customer loyalty and improving employee performance.

The problem is that employees, customers, and partners don't interact with these digital touch-points in the way companies intended. Despite our best efforts, many employees simply aren't engaged with the solutions we've spent millions of dollars building. As employees fail to make use of the powerful tools at their fingertips, the tools underperform and fall out of alignment with company goals. This may help account for the results in a Gallup Poll that found that more than 70 percent of employees are not engaged with their jobs.[17]

Inside enterprises, more than half of customer relationship management projects fail to meet expectations.[18] Social business software—hyped as the savior for antiquated business apps—is only employed by 12 percent of the workforce.[19] The challenge with delivering new software and transformative business process tools is getting people to use them. It's not having a tool for a tool's sake. For example, if you add microblogging (Twitter-like) functions to your apps, it needs to help a person accomplish a goal or make something easier. Employees, or consumers for that matter, will only embrace new tools if they add value to the process.

JJ Juan, global leader of enterprise innovation at Vodafone, described it to me as using collaboration tools to flatten the organization and make it so anyone can contribute to the dialogue. This is why you'd add new collaboration tools. But if you just blindly buy the tools without a clear sense of what you are trying to do, they are virtually worthless.[20]

I've discussed engagement strategies for your customers throughout the book. But here I discuss the emerging market of gamification as a way to improve both customer and employee engagement. The *Oxford Dictionaries* defines gamification as "The application of typical elements of game playing (e.g., point scoring, competition with others, rules of play) to other areas of activity, typically as an online marketing technique to encourage engagement with a product or service."[21]

The popularity of social networks and social gaming (think Facebook and Words With Friends) has demonstrated how behavioral psychology plays a role in a successful user experience. Those sites and games have proven that people crave personal progress in building social connections and in completing goals. Millions of people engage with these services without getting a dime directly in return.

Gamification is changing how people work and play. Game mechanics are being used to drive certain behaviors and engagement for a company's customers and its employees. These techniques drive certain desired behaviors by tapping into an individual's desire for status, achievement, competition, and self-expression. Businesses may use other terms that represent many of the same benefits, including engagement strategies, leader boards, loyalty programs, advocacy, and rewards. Gamification has risen in importance as it has become harder for companies to retain customers and engage employees.

Real-time feedback loops help create identity and reputation. These feedback loops recognize a person's attention and loyalty. Badgeville, a gamification platform company headquartered in Redwood City, California, describes the overall category as behavior life-cycle management (BLM). It's bigger than gamification because it incorporates all the methods a business can use to measure and influence behavior. Badgeville describes it as encompassing trends such as game mechanics, big data, identity, analytics, reputation, social, community, and collaboration. BLM is the process of measuring and influencing behavior to meet your business goals. A business must understand how and why gamification works and in what contexts it is most effective.

Inside companies, gamification has been applied to drive adoption and value of key enterprise systems and collaboration tools. Deloitte, the large consulting firm, had intense collaboration challenges among its 180,000-plus employees, who collaborated mostly over email, which left critical people excluded from knowledge or information that would help them do their job more efficiently. To address this challenge, Deloitte built a social intranet on Yammer, the enterprise social networking tool.

The challenge wasn't with implementing Yammer, however; it was motivating the behavior of consultants who had been used to working in email for more than 20 years. They weren't going to begin sharing documentation and engaging with business processes in this new environment overnight.

Working with Badgeville, Deloitte built upon a simple but powerful idea: Ask consultants to share who they met with, what they discussed, and where it took place. To do this, they built the Who-What-Where mobile app, which rewards consultants for checking in and sharing this information. Rewards are tied to expertise, so if a consultant checks into four green-tech companies, he or she could earn the "Green Tech Master" achievement, as an example.

Rewards earned in Who-What-Where are broadcasted into Deloitte's Yammer Activity Stream. There, colleagues and managers can praise the behavior—thus reinforcing it. People who resist using Yammer and other new tools will see that their colleagues are being rewarded for their engagement, making them more likely to start employing the new tools themselves.[22]

Gamification is also being employed in the B2C landscape. For example, media technology and digital marketing vendor Adobe Systems used gamification as a way to improve the number of trial users of its Photoshop product suite who purchased the product. Although the company offered a 30-day trial to on-board customers, people weren't signing up. Rajat Paharia, founder and chief product designer of Bunchball, who worked on Adobe to develop a gamification strategy, said part of the problem was the complexity of the product suite. Adobe wanted to increase revenue by converting more free trials into sales of Adobe Photoshop. The problem was that the free trial could be intimidating for new users and amateur photographers.

Paharia says that his firm worked with Adobe on ways to change the on-boarding process using gamification. "What we identified was that if you can get people to learn by doing and to gain fluency across 12 key areas with Photoshop, the likelihood of them buying will be much higher."[23]

Bunchball provided a plug-in called "Level up with Photoshop." This offered 12 missions (a.k.a. games), each exposing trial users to certain functions, such as removing red eye, removing objects, teeth whitening, and more. These were split across three levels of difficulty. Users earned points, unlocked badges, and could see a progress bar of their efforts. The software also had a number of links to tutorial content, which Adobe had always offered, in case users couldn't complete a specific mission.

"It flipped the typical learning model," says Paharia, "which is that ahead of time do the learning, read the manual, and then in future maybe you'll apply something you have learnt. Instead, this model was 'do and learn.' That learning is very directive; it's helping you accomplish a task and is that much stickier."[24] Bunchball's site states, "Adobe experienced a 4x increase from free trial to sales as new users learned the product and developed new skills. All users reported satisfaction and Adobe discovered how its customers like to learn and what they're doing with Photoshop."[25] Companies that want to engage their employees in training could also replicate Abode's example.

Samsung provides yet another example. Its website provides user-generated content tools next to its products and receives millions of users per month, but the corporation sometimes experienced challenges in getting visitors to return to the site and engage with those tools. To improve retention, Samsung, with Badgeville's help, launched an engagement program called Samsung Nation, which focuses on rewarding behaviors that require customer time and attention to create user-generated content, social sharing, and others, including a list of the following rewards:

Earn points to increase your community reputation complete any of the following:

500 pts	Register Samsung products
300 pts	Provide answers in Q&As
300 pts	Submit comments and reviews
200 pts	Watch videos
200 pts	Facebook "Likes"
100 pts	Share on Twitter
100 pts	Provide questions in Q&As

In this case, it's important to note that all behaviors are not created equal. While posting a question about a product is valuable (100 points), it's a lot easier to ask the question than it is to come up with an intelligent answer, which is why Samsung credits that behavior with 300 points.[26] Part of a gamification strategy is defining the ranking of certain behaviors and placing values on these behaviors. I've seen that through gamification, companies have dramatically increased user comments, time on a site, shopping clicks, social sales, employee engagement, and training compliance.

Gamification is broadly applicable across industries as well. Let's take a look at how it was applied in a health-care scenario. Unclean hands in hospitals are a cause of preventable infection, which kills nearly 100,000 Americans a year. Hospitals have installed antiseptic hand-wash dispensers, but doctors, nurses, and other staff are not using them as frequently as they should be. *The Economist* reports that compliance rate is below 40 percent in most hospitals. The DebMed Group Monitoring System (GMS), from Deb Worldwide Healthcare Inc., provides an example of how the Internet of Things and game mechanics can be used to encourage staff to wash their hands.

The DebMed GMS tracks information from a chip that is added to each antiseptic dispenser to monitor usage. The chip sends information to a remote server, where it's recorded, analyzed, and automatically made available either on the web or by email to hospital staff. The GMS records the number of times dispensers are used in different parts of a hospital and compares this with an estimated reasonable usage, customized to the circumstances of each hospital. The ratio of actual-to-target score gives the compliance rate for a particular unit or ward. Because this provides a rating for a group, it does not single out an individual. If compliance is low, the offenders can correct their behavior collectively, behind closed doors, without a confrontation. By making it about a score, the experience is more like a game than a compliance issue.

As *The Economist* notes, "It is the psychology behind it that is clever, because instead of being intrusive and allocating blame, it relies on peer pressure. What could be oppressive thus becomes a competition between groups, rather than a finger-wagging exercise within them."[27] It's a right-time experience, not because it happens in real time, but because it provides the insight hospital staff need to change behavior.

Engagement implies an ongoing dialogue. Games can help you understand what types of content users prefer, when and how they prefer to interact, and which marketing messages resonate the strongest. Right-time experiences are adaptable. Businesses that use employee gamification should also be thinking about adding game mechanics that are adaptable. These solutions should introduce new elements, refresh content, and publicize the change. It doesn't mean you can develop something, launch it, and move on to the next project. Game mechanics can be very effective if a program evolves with use.

My premise is that the term *gamification* doesn't accurately depict the benefits a business can achieve. It's a term that you need to explain, which normally stalls adoption. While executives may be interested in how they can use gamification for B2C engagement, most executives aren't thrilled at the prospect of creating Farmville for the enterprise. Many companies believe that once they've built an app or created a game mechanic environment, their work is done. Businesses believe adoption is the next big hurdle. To some extent, this is accurate. You can build a mobile application, a training program, or a new workflow, but it's useless if no one uses it.

However, it's just as bad when usage of a program, application, or service falls off a cliff after a few months of good engagement. In fact, this is the definition of engagement. It implies that you are listening and reacting to your customers', partners', and employees' experiences. But to date, not all the required back-end services have been available in a consumable on-demand model. How do you take advantage of this trend?

I recommend three tips for getting started. First, define what business goals could be enhanced by gamification and how you can drive user behavior to meet goals by using gamification techniques. Which goals should you start with? A company should select areas where it can measure outcomes (e.g., change in the number of employees that completed a certain training course, change in return visits, change in length of participation per visit).

Second, a company should embed experiences directly into its website and its business applications. Employees and customers are being asked to use enough tools. Instead of creating a gamification island, a business should create experiences that are inside its existing process, such as its collaboration suite or website.

Third, the experience should provide guidance and feedback to the user early and often. Gamification is about actively letting users know where they stand and guiding them to a desired behavior. This is one method of getting employees or customers engaged. Getting the technology team on board with a new direction is also a critical foundation element for success in any technology or business transformation.

Get IT on Board and Drive Change

Every company, regardless of size, is becoming a technology company. Line-of-business managers and the executive team recognize that a strong technology foundation is critical for a company's success. IT and business alignment must become more than an ideal or a vision. Likewise, the days of reactive IT have ended. The role of IT is changing as the organization begins to depend more heavily on technology to create a competitive advantage.

IT is constantly being challenged to find new ways that technology can help businesses do more with less. Today, delivering cost savings is table stakes. IT must find new ways to get business done faster and better—not just cheaper. IT must move beyond cost containment to becoming a strategic business partner through innovative uses of technology.

IT teams must overcome several challenges to help their companies make a successful transition into the new world. First, they must overcome the fear of cloud-based services replacing their jobs. Most cloud-based services focus on delivering commodity solutions more effectively or delivering functions that are critical, yet not strategic, from an IT design and management point of view. Cloud services only replace IT jobs if the technology team fails to grow and expand its skill set.

Martin Odgen, CIO at global oil and gas management company Expro Group, headquartered in Reading, England, said he faced resistance from his IT departments when choosing to roll out a cloud-based human capital management tool. IT was fearful that its role would be unnecessary if everything moved to the cloud. The decision to employ cloud computing, said Ogden, "has actually scared IT because they don't know what it means for their job—so I'm actually getting resistance from within the IT departments. But what it allows me to do is take those reasonably well paid, highly skilled members of staff and actually get them to do something useful for the organization."[28]

The second challenge is overcoming limited skill sets for new technologies, such as mobility and big data. While it may sound like a broken record, it's important for every group within the organization to have a training program. I discuss this in more detail in a moment.

The third challenge IT must surmount is collaborating across departments to develop new and interesting solutions.

At the end of 2013, *The Economist* magazine reported that the current environment is, in theory, "a fine opportunity for the IT department to place itself right at the center of corporate strategy. In practice, the rest of the company is not always sure that the IT guys are up to the job—and they are often prepared to buy their own IT from outsiders if need be."[29]

Gartner research fellow Dave Aron, citing preliminary data from a 2014 *CIO* survey, said that over the past few years, CIOs have moved from focusing more on "reactive effectiveness" (that is, making the systems run better and more efficiently) to "proactive value creation and innovation." While more than 70 percent of CIOs said their businesses are "satisfied" with IT, only about 19 percent of businesses think of IT as a "trusted ally."[30] If the IT department wants to move beyond cost containment to building strategic services, it needs a path to becoming a trusted ally. The decision to provide right-time experiences to employees, customers, and partners provides a path for IT to become the architect of business transformation.

Right-time experiences, if properly executed, help the organization save money or improve its value proposition or both. Mobile, cloud computing, and big data provide an opportunity for IT and the business to transform business processes. A successful technology strategy requires that the business units and the IT groups that support them work together. The information technology group has an essential role in understanding the best way to enable the organization's processes for mobility, big data, and analytics. Line-of-business managers can help define the business challenges that require mobile solutions and what data they need to provide actionable insights. The first step is to get business and IT leaders in the same room.

IT will provide strategic services by working with LOB managers to understand which tasks will improve overall efficiency and which will provide new revenue opportunities. But in my experience, the business and IT groups need to speak with each other more frequently. As mentioned earlier, right-time experiences will be designed as an iterative process with a constant feedback loop. Frequent communications are critical for creating right-time experiences and transforming business services. Senior management may have to change employee goals to encourage the business group and IT groups to get together and ensure that everyone works toward a common set of goals.

Be Open to Creating New Roles or Expanding Roles

We know that several tectonic shifts in technology are happening simultaneously. The pace of technology change only seems to accelerate. While IT and business units are aligning for a common cause, this may not be enough. Companies should also consider adding new roles and new teams to help guide the business over the initial hurdles of change. Let's discuss at least two of these opportunities.

Role of a Chief Digital or Technology Officer

One approach may be to appoint a chief digital officer (CDO) or chief technology officer (CTO). According to David Dumeresque of Tyzack Partners, an international executive search firm based in London, in many organizations the CIO continues to have the responsibility for managing the corporate digital footprint. As corporate digital technology rapidly evolves, however, to include "marketing, sales, public relations, and customer service channels, alongside recruitment, procurement and R&D, a different set of competencies and business-related expertise is now required." This is an opportunity for the CIO to expand his or her skill sets or work with a CDO/CTO to drive new technologies into the organization.

The CDO needs to be a highly practical and accomplished businessperson and a visionary, says Dumeresque. "He or she should have general business experience, functional expertise, and broad leadership and influencing skills. The CDO must be able not only to drive the business forward but also to enhance the experience of all who come into contact with the organization." This suggests someone with the skills to look at business workflows in new ways and interpret how new technologies (social, mobile, and big data) may be able to support these. Since this transcends any individual area within the organization, the CDO must focus on the company's overall business goals and have the personality to work closely with others.

Dumeresque says, "One of the most significant issues in recruiting a CDO is that demand is outstripping supply in all global markets. Those CEOs contemplating the need for a chief digital officer need to be thinking how quickly can they act to stay ahead of their competitors."[31]

Apigee, a San Jose–based a company that develops application programming interfaces and apps, cites its study showing that the need for a seasoned technology and business veteran to tie all things digital together is growing. "As mobile technology and data analytics completely reshape the business landscape, building a truly digital business DNA is an imperative for survival in today's competitive app economy. Many companies are seeking CDOs to lead this enterprise-wide transformation," says Bryan Kirschner, director of the Apigee Institute.[32]

The chief digital officer is not there to run the company's infrastructure. It's a transformative role used to break up the information and process silos within organizations. The CDO should analyze data and how it relates to the business and customer experience. "The way to best describe the CDO is that you need to be a silo-buster connecting different disciplines and departments," says Andy Gilman, president and CEO of CommCore Consulting Group.[33]

David Chivers is the chief digital officer of Jostens, the Bloomington, Minnesota, marketer of school and class rings. He says that his role at the business has three dimensions: "Enabling the world to interact with Jostens digitally. Digitizing as much of the organization from end-to-end as possible. And building a culture of evidence-based management based on as much meaningful, actionable data as we can collect, analyze and surface regularly to our customers and team members."

Chivers says he is "constantly looking for ways we can incorporate technology into our offerings to make the lives of our students and teachers easier—and better. For example, we at Jostens have just released a very cool iPad app for yearbook staffs called the Year-booker's Field Kit that allows advisors and staffs to make assignments, review layouts and collaborate on yearbooks. We use 3D printing (or rapid prototyping) to push the designs and speed through which we can create ring designs. We're driving new technologies to amplify the efforts of our physical sales force."[34]

Regardless of what you call the role, there needs to be a person or small team that's held accountable for helping the various groups within the company transition its business processes. It's not enough to say we want the teams to work together. We've said this before. There actually need to be goals for the company and measurable metrics associated with these goals. The mobile-enablement plan I discussed in Chapter 7 provides a good example of how these goals can be created and measured.

Aligning IT and the Business with a Mobile Center of Excellence

While I'm on the topic of mobile, it is also possible to set up what is known as a mobility center of excellence (MCoE) as one way to assist in this transition. Dan Rowinski, the mobile editor at ReadWrite.com, says that many of the world's biggest companies have only a couple of people in their entire IT department dedicated to mobile. "This skeleton crew is responsible for building and maintaining the company's mobile apps, devising strategies and solutions, handling employee issues around Bring Your Own Device policies, and distributing software (apps) that coworkers need to do their jobs."[35]

These poor souls are overworked because while senior management believes the company needs to "do mobile," it is not willing to invest more than the absolute minimum to squeak by. Truly going mobile means more than shrinking existing apps to fit on phones. It's the process of defining what a workflow or service will look like in the future. It's the process of IT and business units collaborating to design the workplace and the services of the future. It's exactly what some describe as the function of a CDO or CTO. So, an MCoE is another way of getting this done. Some firms I've spoken with say they are too small for an MCoE. I'd caution organizations not to get too hung up on terms. At the end of the day, what an organization needs is a group of people who are working on transitioning the company to take advantage of new technologies to improve business processes.

Research firm IDC describes a mobile center of excellence as a framework for businesses to organize, manage, and distribute their mobile enterprise solutions and initiatives. MCoEs provide guidance on getting started and best practices. Let's say a business needs a CRM app or an application accounting department. The group can ask the MCoE team for guidance. An MCoE would help define IT-related concerns such as security and BYOD issues, help implement infrastructure and cloud solutions for apps, and generally serve as the nerve center for everything mobile in the enterprise.

A mobility center of excellence centralizes governance, standards, and activities around a set of principles—organizational and architectural—so that the organization is able to use mobile technology effectively. As an SAP whitepaper points out, "By capturing experience, best practices, and reference architectures from mobility projects within the organization, the MCoE can accelerate deployment within the corporation." The center minimizes effort, as each business unit no longer has to reinvent and implement mobility policies on its own. An MCoE is able to deploy and manage personal and company-owned mobile devices seeking access to corporate data. Such a center facilitates success when it:

- Leverages existing IT processes (standards, governance) and people.

- Defines standards, vendor and technology selection, and security policies relevant to mobility.
- Acts as the trusted adviser to the line-of-business leaders.
- Reviews, evaluates, and approves mobility projects.
- Provides technology expertise to the business, authors best practices, and facilitates training and technical support during implementation.
- Offers thought leadership, consults on mobile technology, and provides metrics reporting and support after deployment.[36]

What the MCoE idea boils down to, says Rowinski, is that every big company needs a group of knowledgeable people who have the skills and resources to handle designing and implementing mobile solutions quickly and efficiently. "These people need to have power to make decisions, and well-defined jobs that give them autonomy they need to get things done. Enabling a group within your IT infrastructure to handle everything mobile could actually create competitive advantage for many companies."[37]

According to Appcelerator, an organization should ideally take five steps to establish a mobile center of excellence:

Step 1: Establish charter and acquire executive-level sponsorship. Gaining executive-level support is critical because the MCoE impact is company-wide, and certain managers may resist a mobility team's imposing standards. C-level executive buy-in gives the team the ability to enforce unwelcome policies. Step 1 includes setting the charter for the MCoE, which includes policy definitions, technology standards, and platform standards, as well as prioritizing business unit projects and applications. The charter guides the MCoE during its meetings and sets the tone for the first year of operation.

Step 2: Identify participating departments and individuals. The mobile center of excellence team identifies all affected departments and solicits representatives from them. Without executive-level support, of course, this task is virtually impossible. If business units already have mobile projects for which they are requesting funding or IT for assistance, these can be a motivation to join the MCoE, which must also include legal and HR because many policies go beyond technology enforcement and into personnel and employee activities, goals, and responsibilities. IT should take the leadership role in the MCoE because they manage and maintain the central infrastructure and technologies on which mobile relies.

Step 3: Define technical standards, policies, and the mobile reference architecture. This involves setting the technical standards for security, an appropriate use policy for bring your own device, and any additional standards that need to be enforced around brand management, graphics, colors, and so on. IT must identify the common data sources and services to all the business units for their mobile application projects. Successful central teams publish and share these visual diagrams and gain agreement among the units to ensure the center addresses their information needs. Additionally, any policies the center establishes should be enforced as part of the reference architecture and related mobile software infrastructure. In many cases, policies already exist concerning appropriate use, use of company equipment, and Internet and email policies, and those can be rewritten for mobile devices. Additional standards for security require new investments to enforce those standards on mobile devices (whether employee- or enterprise-owned).

Step 4: Prioritize development efforts. Establish a framework to evaluate and prioritize business unit application requests. It is critical to have a standard framework to weigh these requests when an enterprise deals with tens or hundreds of applications and when it can immediately fulfill only a fraction. We consistently see more mobile application ideas and requests than any organization can realize. Due to this inherent undercapacity, management must evaluate and prioritize regularly. Given the rate of innovation in mobile platforms, enhancements and new requests for applications will only grow.

Step 5: Implement software infrastructure to enable project delivery. This step integrates the technologies to plan, build, connect, test, deploy, and analyze mobile applications. Once the MCoE has set the policies and identified the technologies to enforce them, the center must provide the mobile software infrastructure and architecture. The team must make the technology investments and ready them for deployment to produce the applications and enforce the security standards and other agreed-upon policies. The best way to establish this is to pilot a first project with all participants engaged to ensure success before the MCoE is formally open for business and running full speed.[38]

Whether we establish a mobile center of excellence or just create a de facto subgroup within the organization that takes the lead in mobile practices isn't the point. The point is that enterprises can better manage their mobile priorities by assigning the task to a particular unit empowered to drive solutions for the entire company. Over time, the need for the MCoE will fade as mobility becomes well understood within the organization. The MCoE may become part of the company's overall center of excellence. However, the need for a chief technology lead of some kind will remain as technologies continue to evolve beyond today's concerns of mobility, cloud computing, big data, and analytics.

Summary

In summary, the opportunities that the new technology offers clearly stress traditional IT departments. The new technologies require not only new skills but an involvement with other functions in the organization. The possibility to give employees and customers the right experience at the right time means change. In some cases, this change upsets the status quo.

One approach to dealing with this challenge is to develop new roles, such as chief digital officer, marketing technology officer, or chief technology officer, that can help the company embrace technology and business transformation. Companies that have done so point out that a CDO does not replace the CIO but supplements the function. In some cases, progressive CIOs can play the role of CDO/CTO. Ideally, the CDO connects different disciplines and departments—including the IT department—within the enterprise. The CDO's function is to analyze data and relate it to the business and to the experience of employees, customers, prospects, partners, and other stakeholders.

Given the massive transition effects mobile has on companies, it makes sense for companies, regardless of size, to set up a dedicated team (if smaller) or a Mobile Center of Excellence (if a larger business).

Such a center leverages existing IT processes and people and defines standards and security policies relevant to mobility. It's a team that will review, evaluate, and approve mobility projects with the support of line-of-business managers. It also provides technology expertise and facilitates training and technical support during implementation. Finally, it provides metrics reporting and support after the organization has deployed an application.

As we've seen, the human resources department can now use big data, social, video, and mobile to improve recruiting and managing employees. Employees can use their own devices to learn company policies, procedures, and processes. Gamification is a way to engage employees and customers because the best app or service is useless if people do not use it. It means thinking like a user rather than like a supplier.

We've talked about aligning IT and evolving business realities for years. Building right-time experiences is a way to make this a reality. We can't design a right-time experience if we don't marry technology with business need. IT wants to be strategic, and creating right-time experiences is a growth path for IT. Instead of spending 80 percent of the department's time and budget to keep the lights on, IT can be building, and not just the foundation of new services; it can be leading the charge for business transformation.

This is also a great time for LOB managers, who can finally get what they need because (1) the technology is available, (2) IT and line of business are aligned to make it happen, and (3) business really requires it.

Good business strategies balance people, process, and technology. We often spend too much time on the technology and not enough on the people and processes. We need to engage people (employees and customers) with strategies such as gamification and better contextual experiences. The good news is that technology now enables new ways to create this engagement.

Notes

1. Scott Brinker, "*Harvard Business Review* publishes 'The Rise of the Chief Marketing Technologist'" June 25, 2014, www.chiefmartec.com/2014/06/harvard-business-review-publishes-rise-chief-marketing-technologist/.
2. http://www-03.ibm.com/press/us/en/pressrelease/39501.wss.
3. "More Employers Finding Reasons Not to Hire Candidates on Social Media, Finds CareerBuilder Survey," www.careerbuilder.com/share/aboutus/pressreleasesdetail .aspx?sd=6%2F26%2F2013&id=pr766&ed=12%2F31%2F2013.

4. www.simplyhired.com/press/archives/2012/11/simply_hired_fi.php.
5. iMomentous study on Corporate Mobile readiness, www.imomentous.com/corporate-mobile-readiness-v3/.
6. Rudy Karsan, "With Big Data, Companies Can Predict Your Success Before Your First Day on the Job," *Fast Company*, July 26, 2013, www.fastcompany.com.
7. Steve Lohr, "Big Data, Trying to Build Better Workers," *New York Times*, April 21, 2013, p. BU4.
8. Rudy Karsan, op. cit.
9. Rudy Karsan, op. cit.
10. www.evolv.net/success-stories/harte-hanks-case-study/.
11. www.businessweek.com/articles/2013-06-24/gigwalk-does-temp-worker-hiring-without-job-interviews.
12. "Reckitt Benckiser Takes Control of Holiday Sales with Gigwalk's Mobile Workforce," http://gigwalk.com/case_studies/Gigwalk_Reckitt_Sucess.pdf.
13. "Amid Anticipated Skills Shortages, Half of U.S. Businesses Plan to Increase Their Investment in Training in the Next Two Years, Accenture Research Finds," October 29, 2013, http://newsroom.accenture.com/news/amid-anticipated-skills-shortages-half-of-us-businesses-plan-to-increase-their-investment-in-training-in-the-next-two-years-accenture-research-finds.print.
14. Ibid.
15. "Amid Anticipated Skills Shortages, Half of U.S. Businesses Plan to Increase Their Investment in Training in the Next Two Years, Accenture Research Finds," October 29, 2013, http://newsroom.accenture.com.
16. Beth Ellen Rosenthal, "How Big Data Is Becoming Predictive, Helping Executives Make Better Decisions," *Outsourcing Center*, October 25, 2013, www.outsourcing-center.com.
17. "Majority of American Workers Not Engaged with Their Jobs," Gallup, October 28, 2011.
18. Michael Kriegsman, "Who's Accountable for Failure?" *ZDNet*, April 2012.
19. Dion Hinchecliffe, "Social Business and Enterprise Usage: The Lessons," *ZDNet*, April 2012.
20. Interview with JJ Juan, global leader of enterprise innovation at Vodafone Global Enterprise, in October 22, 2013.
21. http://www.oxforddictionaries.com/us/definition/american_english/gamification.
22. For more information, read "Gamification for Executive Training," http://badgeville.com/customer/case-study/deloitte.
23. Telephone meeting with Rajat Pahria on July 26, 2013.
24. Nadia Cameron, "Why Gamification and Big Data Go Hand-in-Hand," *CMO*, September 10, 2013, www.cmo.com.au.
25. Bunchball case study of Adobe, www.bunchball.com/customers/adobe.
26. "Five Key Engagement Imperatives," Badgeville whitepaper, 2012, www.badgeville.com.
27. "First, Wash Your Hands," *The Economist*, September 7, 2013, p. 8.
28. Derek du Preez, "Expro Group CIO Warns of IT's Fear of Job Loss with Cloud Computing," *Computerworld UK*, December 17, 2013, www.computerworlduk.com.
29. "Surfing a Digital Wave, or Drowning?" *The Economist*, December 7, 2013, p. 65.

30. Michael J. Miller, "Gartner: CIOs Need to Tame the Digital Dragon," PC magazine, October 7, 2013, http://forwardthinking.pcmag.com/show-reports/316626-gartner-cios-need-to-tame-the-digital-dragon.
31. David Dumeresque, "Chief Digital Officer—The New Superhero in the C-Suite," *International Business Times*, October 1, 2013, www.ibtimes.co.uk.
32. Apigee press release: "Research Reveals Seven Habits of Highly Effective Chief Digital Officers," http://apigee.com/about/pressrelease/research-reveals-seven-habits-highly-effective-chief-digital-officers.
33. Rich Hein, "Why the Chief Digital Officer Role Is on the Rise," *CIO* magazine, November 19, 2013, www.cio.com/article/743421.
34. "5 Questions With . . . David Chivers," *Chief Digital Officer*, September 30, 2013, http://chiefdigitalofficer.net.
35. Dan Rowinski, "Mobile Centers of Excellence: A Stupid Name for a Smart Enterprise IT Idea," April 26, 2013, http://readwrite.com.
36. "Best Practices for a Mobility Center of Excellence," SAP whitepaper, December 2012, www.sap.com/contactsap.
37. Dan Rowinski, op. cit.
38. "Adopting a Mobile Center of Excellence (MCoE) to Become a Mobile-First Enterprise," Appcelerator whitepaper, 2012, http://appcelerator.com.

CHAPTER 11

Closing Thoughts

We've seen how technology is changing possibilities for consumers, employees, and partners. In fact, we need to assume that there will continue to be rapid change. In 10 years, business will look different than it does today. What's happening right now is similar to the transition we went through with the development of the personal computer and again with the Internet. The only certainty is that it is impossible to know exactly the shape of business in the future. Some well-known organizations will be gone and others—either tiny or yet to be established—will be in their place.

If we look back 25 years, few companies have been able to maintain a ranking in the Fortune 500. In 1990, the 10 largest U.S. corporations were, in order, General Motors, Ford Motor, Exxon Mobil, IBM, General Electric, Mobil, Altria Group, Chrysler, DuPont, and Texaco. Three car companies and three oil companies took six of the top 10 spots.

In 2013, the top 10 were Walmart Stores, Exxon Mobil, Chevron, Phillips 66, Berkshire Hathaway, Apple, General Motors, General Electric, Vallero Energy, and Ford Motor. Two car companies, four oil companies, and Apple were bigger than GM, GE, and Ford. Of course, it's unfair to compare Walmart's rise to GM's bankruptcy and government bailout. Nevertheless, the handwriting on the wall should be clear. If companies don't respond rapidly and effectively to the constantly changing environment, they will be in serious trouble.

No one can predict the future. It is often simple to look back and point out management's mistakes, shortsightedness, or poor judgment. It is much more difficult to anticipate the right move, to skate where the puck will be rather than where you think it's going. Nevertheless, I believe that certain principles are always true. We seldom go wrong if we make our services, our processes, or our products more relevant and valuable to our customers, partners, and employees. A right-time experience is about trying to deliver that right information or service at the exact point of desire or need. It's about relevant, timely communications. It's not creepy because it's delivering value. It's not generic because it's based on analysis of a wide range of data. These experiences shouldn't be static. They must adapt as your users' needs and desires evolve. And, to be clear, users can be your customers, prospects, partners, and employees. Everyone deserves the opportunity to have a right-time experience.

Right-time experiences are contextual and adaptive, and eventually the best RTEs will be predictive. If you've done your job correctly, your users will define your experiences as something that "automagically" happens. These are the experiences that create "stickiness." Right-time experiences are synonymous with value and are the essence of creating a leading brand experience.

However, right-time experiences won't come without work. Our technology teams must add a new set of tools, such as enterprise mobile management, mobile app development platforms, big data, and analytics solutions. We need to embrace cloud computing and leverage new data sources, such as social streams and Internet of Things data. These tools will provide a foundation of flexibility that will help business leaders to at least partially adapt to "what comes next."

The world is filled with opportunity, but we have to grasp it. We do not live in a passive business world. Both consumers and companies are active participants in making this new world. At one time, business executives could model their enterprises on the command-and-control model. No more. Employees are now taking control of the technologies they use in the office and are demanding that the business respond with more flexible ways to work and better systems.

Products and services are now customer driven and cocreated with your employees, customers, and partners. In the past, teams received minimal, if any, input from customers. In the new generation of products, customers have a voice in building and refining a product. In some cases, like that of the Kickstarter campaigns, potential customers are funding and testing your prototypes. Employees, customers, and partners take part in creating and refining right-time experiences.

At one time, a manufacturer could put a product on the shelf and be fairly certain it would sell. No more. Thanks to the Internet, consumers can now easily compare features, benefits, and prices wherever they are. Not to mention that mobile, big data, and cloud computing now make it possible for a wide range of new competitors to enter the market.

The positive aspect of the technology is that we use it to become much more relevant to our customers. If we do so, they will stick with us longer and more enthusiastically. The better the relationship, the less important price tends to become—although of course the right price-to-value ratio is always important. Fortunately, many of these technologies have the opportunity to lower the cost of creating a personalized and contextual experience.

The easier it is to do business with us—everything else being equal—the more likely consumers will choose us from all the other possibilities. The more an enterprise can meet employees' needs beyond a weekly paycheck, the easier it is to retain them and help them grow and contribute as the organization grows.

In time, you will have a better handle on what might change. In doing so, you may be on an even playing field with disruptors because you already know what your clients are interested in. You're already talking to them and engaging them routinely. You're in their pocket all the time. They'll be brutally honest about what's working and what isn't. This is powerful. This is transformational.

We've never had this insight. We've never been able to ask and respond. We've never had such great tools for information gathering. We know what our employees are using and if they spend time engaging with our business systems or avoiding them at all costs. We can do business faster than ever before. It's a huge win for large companies that were previously in the dark. It's also a huge win for smaller businesses that can look larger because they have access to lower-cost, subscription-based software and hardware services. It's all-around amazing for everyone—if, and only if, we act now.

It's true that this isn't easy. As I remarked at the beginning of this book, many business transitions require a company to cannibalize an existing business to invest in an alternative that initially offers lower sales or profits or both. Wall Street expects public companies to grow, and smaller companies can be even more cautious when it comes to wholesale shifts in a business model. Any shift that deliberately leads to shrinking revenue or profits over the short term is a hard sell to the board of directors and stockholders, no matter what benefits the future promises. Yet the unanswerable argument remains: If we don't cannibalize ourselves, someone else will. If we don't invest in the technology and the systems, competitors who do will take our sales, our customers, and, eventually, our future. No business can approach the new market dynamics with old business practices.

I truly believe based on my experience that an organization can change, that employees can learn to use the new tools, and that with strategic vision a company can become stronger, more flexible, and more profitable. This is what's required to build right-time experiences. Success is within reach of any company willing to embrace this challenge.

About the Author

Maribel Lopez founded Lopez Research LLC in 2008 to research how technology trends such as mobile, big data, social, and cloud will transform business. She provides strategic market research and analysis of global markets. Her clients include start-ups through Fortune 500 companies. The company provides market research and strategy consulting to software vendors, networking vendors, and enterprise IT leaders as well as telecom providers.

Over the past two decades, she has observed, commented on, and engaged in the massive shifts in the data and telecommunications industries during her work with Motorola, International Data Corp., Shiva Corporation, and Forrester Research. Prior to founding Lopez Research, Maribel was a respected analyst for more than 10 years at Forrester Research, most recently as vice president of the tech industry strategies group. In this position at Forrester Research, Maribel provided analysis on multiple topics, including network and service strategies, enterprise communications, and consumer markets for voice, video, and data. She held positions in strategic marketing and product marketing at Shiva Corporation. Prior to joining Shiva, she worked for International Data Corporation as a data networking industry analyst. Maribel began her career at Motorola, holding positions in finance and global corporate development.

Maribel is frequently quoted by publications such as the *Wall Street Journal,* Dow Jones, the *Globe and Mail, BusinessWeek,* Reuters, and the Associated Press. She has also appeared on CNN, CNBC, and NPR. She is a much-sought-after public speaker. She has spoken at industry events, including All About Mobile, AppNation, Cloud Connect, Enterprise 2.0, Mobile Connect, Mobile World Congress, The Open Mobile Summit, and CTIA, as well as at corporate events. She's also the chairman of the M6 Mobility Xchange conference and a contributing columnist for Forbes. Maribel is a graduate of Babson College. She currently lives in San Francisco. You can follow her at http://blogs .forbes.com/maribellopez or on Twitter at @maribellopez.

Index